PRAY

for US

"*The* saint book for the rest of us who have failed more times than we care to admit."

Fr. Agustino Torres, C.F.R.
Founder of Corazon Puro

"What a diverse collection of captivating stories, so well told and so invigorating! These are not dull, saccharine accounts, stringing together bare facts and dates as most saint collections do. This book is like fiery magma, lively and flowing with verve. Meg Hunter-Kilmer's stories of relatively unknown saints will make your heart come alive, beating with new possibilities. Get this book for any person who thinks saints are boring and irrelevant."

Brandon Vogt
Senior content director at Word on Fire Catholic Ministries

"*Pray for Us* is a fresh take on holiness. Meg Hunter-Kilmer's vignettes reveal the humorous and relatable aspects of holy Catholics from all over the globe—lay people as well as clergy and religious."

Gloria Purvis
Catholic speaker, podcaster, and radio host

"With passion, captivating storytelling, and compelling insights, Hunter-Kilmer has provided a force of a resource to help tell the stories of the saints, the ones we know well and the ones we should take the time to meet."

Katie Prejean McGrady
SiriusXM Radio host and host of the *Ave Explores* podcast

PRAY *for* US

75 Saints Who Sinned, Suffered, and Struggled on Their Way to Holiness

MEG HUNTER-KILMER

AVE MARIA PRESS AVE Notre Dame, Indiana

To Natalie, John Paul, Hugo, Patrick, Thérèse, Teresa, Elijah, Peter, Patrick, Xavier, Marilyn, Hunter, Jenn, Joe, and Evie, with my fervent prayers that one day our whole godfamily will be surrounded by the men and women in this book, saints among the saints of God and held forever in his love.

Some of the stories in this book were first published at Aleteia.org and OSVnews.com. They have been revised and reprinted here with kind permission.

Scripture texts in this work are taken from the *New American Bible, revised edition* © 2010, 1991, 1986, 1970 Confraternity of Christian Doctrine, Washington, DC, and are used by permission of the copyright owner. All Rights Reserved. No part of the *New American Bible* may be reproduced in any form without permission in writing from the copyright owner.

Founded in 1865, Ave Maria Press is a ministry of the United States Province of Holy Cross.

www.avemariapress.com

Paperback: ISBN-13 978-1-64680-082-7

E-book: ISBN-13 978-1-64680-083-4

Saint illustrations on cover © 2021 Noah Gutierrez, https://www.deviantart.com/nowitzkitramonto.

Cover design by Christopher D. Tobin.

Text design by Kristen Hornyak Bonelli.

Printed and bound in the United States of America.

Library of Congress Cataloging-in-Publication Data is available.

Contents

Part 7: Saints Whose Ruined Plans Opened the Way to More Beautiful Things 135

Part 8: Saints Who Were Failures 157

Introduction

I never did love the Saints.

Because I never knew them.

Oh, I could tell you the patron Saint of athletes or musicians. But the Saints I knew were dull outlines of immaculate lives, saccharine plaster images gazing vapidly heavenward. And I tried to be holy like that; I really did. But God made me passionate and intense, and the more I tried to become sweet and mild, the more I felt I would never be anything but wrong.

Eventually I heard about St. Teresa of Avila, contented myself that there was at least one fiery female Saint, and moved on. I knew whom God was calling me to be, and if that didn't fit in a stained glass window, so be it.

But then I stumbled across a book that told the stories of the Saints—not just the dates, accomplishments, and implausible encounters with mythical beasts but also the sorrow, struggle, and idiosyncrasies. Suddenly I realized that these were real people, broken people made whole by grace, and that far from being the impossible standard I'd thought they represented, they offered nothing but hope.

There is, in so many lives, a hidden shame, a conviction that some aspect of your life makes you unloved and unlovable, even by God himself. Again and again I've seen the lives of the Saints speak the love of Jesus into that brokenness, showing the glory of a grace-filled life after abuse or abortion, amid disability or divorce. The Saints stand as witnesses to people who are certain they can't be holy if they have a mental illness, if their parents are unmarried, if prayer is always hard for them, if their lives are unremarkable, if they're too loud or too quiet, too smart or too slow. They stand beside us as people who've sinned, suffered, and struggled and come through to the other side, radiant with the glory of God.

The men, women, and children who've been raised to the altar have almost nothing in common with one another. They're princes and peasants, geniuses and fools. Some hardly sinned a day in their lives; others lived lives so vile even HBO might be tempted to censor them. There are explorers and housewives, theologians and farmers, people recognized as great even by a world that despises the Church, and others so ordinary that those closest to them hardly noticed anything special.

This is the legacy that's been handed to us: a Church filled with Saints so entirely different from one another that we who follow in their footsteps are free to pursue holiness in our own unique way. They stand before us as witnesses that holiness is possible, but they offer a challenge as well. Your addiction is no excuse, they tell us. Your broken home is no excuse. Your timidity, your inclination to rage, your disinclination to pray—there are no circumstances or characteristics that make holiness unattainable, which means every one of us is called to run after Jesus, however often we may stumble.

And Saints aren't just models. They're friends, older brothers and sisters who love us more than we've ever loved before. The stories in this book aren't just a quick shot in the arm to get you going on a tough day. They're an introduction to your family, to the heroes who've gone before who are alive in Christ and eager to pray for you, to walk with you, to cheer you on as you fight your way through this valley of tears.

This is why I love the Saints. Because while the Lord is never far from us, there are times when it seems impossible that he might be with us, suffering alongside us, handing his life over for us. In darkness, in shame, in wandering confusion, we may begin to feel that his perfect life has no connection to ours. We may feel overwhelmed by our addictions, our insurmountable circumstances, our suffering into which it seems God speaks no word of comfort.

But the Saints have suffered as we do. They have been tempted as we are. They lived with mental illness, chronic illness, and abusive families; with rage, shame, and fear; and with aspirations, brilliance, and wild success. They endured racism, torture, drudgery, disillusionment, and unfulfilled longings. They give us hope for what good might come and a witness of how to find peace if it doesn't. And the light they shed on our lives leads us back to the one who holds us in all our struggles and joys.

Every Saint I've loved has taught me to love Jesus better, and inspired me to embrace my cross once again and trust in this love that calls me ever onward. This is why I tell their stories. Because the more we know of them, the more we know of him. The more we see how he loved them in their brokenness, the more we believe in his love for us. The more we witness their faithfulness in suffering, the more we believe that God can bring good through the ugliness that threatens to overwhelm us. Praise God for this Church of ours that spans the great divide and calls us to join them around the throne of the one who loves us every bit as much as he loves them. Through their intercession, may every one of us become a saint.

How to Use This Book

This is a book of stories, not an encyclopedia. Feel free to start at page 1 and keep reading to the end, skim the table of contents for stories that jump out at you, or turn to the back, where you'll find the indices. Then again, maybe just say a little prayer and flip and point to see if the Holy Spirit has a new Saintly friend to offer you.

In this book, I'll use the term "Saint" to refer to anyone who is an official Saint in the Catholic Church or is on the path to canonization: Servants of God, Venerables, and Blesseds. Though the official title Saint refers only to those who have been put forward by the Church for universal veneration, my use of the term here isn't intended to preemptively canonize anyone or to make assertions about the eternal fate of those men and women on whose sanctity the Church hasn't yet officially spoken. Instead, it's a shorthand intended to group all those who have been presented as models of Christian living, whether or not they have yet been canonized.

As you read this book, you'll notice these different titles being used. It may be helpful to know what each term signifies. A Saint, of course, is a person who has been declared to be in heaven, and is offered by the Church for universal veneration. For nearly a thousand years, this declaration has come through an official canonization from Rome, usually at the end of a long process. For many centuries, though, holy men and women were declared Saints by their local bishops, generally as a response to popular acclaim. St. Peter, for example, was never canonized in a formal ceremony, but his status as a Saint is not in question.

Today, when a cause for canonization is officially opened, the person in question is given the title **Servant of God**. This title serves to indicate that there is an open cause for canonization but is not a judgment as to the person's holiness. At this point, research is still being done to make the person's case.

Once the Congregation for the Causes of Saints has read and reviewed the materials submitted on behalf of the Servant of God, they determine whether her life demonstrated heroic virtue. If so, a decree of heroic virtue is issued and the person is given the title Venerable Servant of God and usually referred to as **Venerable**. At this point, there has been no assertion as to the Venerable's presence in heaven. She still has no feast day, and permission has not been granted to build churches in her honor, but the faithful are permitted to seek miracles through her intercession.

Usually, the cause of a Venerable is advanced by the verification of a miracle. This miracle must have taken place through the Venerable's intercession after his death and must be unexplainable by science. However, the requirement of this first miracle can be waived if the Venerable has been officially declared a martyr. At the beatification, it is declared to be "worthy of belief" that the **Blessed** (also referred to as a beatus/beata) is in heaven. He is given a feast day and, with special permission, a parish may be named in his honor. Still, the Blessed is put forward for limited public veneration; though any individual may revere him, he is celebrated in the liturgy only in certain dioceses (generally where he lived) or religious communities.

Finally, a verified miracle is required for canonization. Once this miracle has been approved, a canonization Mass is scheduled, after which the newly minted **Saint** is held up as a model for the universal Church, to be honored throughout the world. Occasionally this last step is bypassed by the Holy Father, who may choose to perform an equivalent or equipollent canonization for a long-revered Blessed.

In this book, I will use the term "Saint" loosely, to refer to all men and women who are at any step in this process. Where the word "saint" appears, it refers to anybody in heaven, whether or not they are known to any on earth. Few who read this book will ever become Saints, but it is my fervent hope that every single person who reads it will one day be a saint, surrounded by the Saints who fill these pages. All you holy men and women, pray for us!

Part 1
Saints Who Defied Expectations

I was always quite sure that there was one way to be a Saint. One had to be meek and pious, speaking only in a cheerful whisper, with no inclination to shout or rage or laugh with glee. Unfortunately for me, I thought, fitting into that mold would take a lifetime of cramming my enormous, intense, emotional self into the confines of holiness. I felt absolutely smothered by the saccharine stories of quiet, pleasant Saints.

But then I heard a little bit about St. Teresa of Avila, and I realized that maybe a handful of the Saints were rather more like me than the Snow White image of sanctity I'd built up in my head. Then, as I began to study the Saints, I realized that many of them were decidedly unsaintly, at least by the qualifications I'd imagined. Some of them were even wild, intense, emotional, and unrestrained—just like me.

I found out years later that I wasn't the only person with this misconception but that others had entirely different misunderstandings of holiness. My brilliant friends looked at the simpleminded Saints and thought the academically minded didn't belong in their ranks. My less intellectual friends were sure that if they couldn't be St. Thomas Aquinas, they might as well give up. The quiet ones thought they had to shout the name of Jesus from the rooftops. The excitable ones thought only mellow people could be Saints.

Yet the Saints stood in mute defiance of every box we tried to put them in. Because there is no one way to be holy, nor even a thousand ways to be holy. There are as many ways to be holy as there are souls ever created. This section is filled with Saints who will surprise you—a tough-as-nails poet, a brilliant scientist, a chain-smoking journalist, and a mischievous smuggler. There may not be anyone in this book who speaks to the particular aspect of your personality that you worry disqualifies you for holiness, but there's someone in heaven with that attribute. I can almost guarantee it.

BL. CATHERINE JARRIGE

A Mischievous Woman
Who Smuggled Priests to Safety

(1754–1836) ✳ Country: France
Feast Day: July 4

How does a high-spirited, mischievous, prank-pulling little girl become a Saint? By growing into a high-spirited, mischievous, prank-pulling adult—particularly if the pranks are pulled on the persecutors of the Church.

Bl. Catherine Jarrige was the youngest of seven children born to a poor French farmer. She was a sweet child—called "the little nun" by those who knew her—but was fond of practical jokes and innocent naughtiness. At age nine she began work as a servant, and trained as a lace maker at age thirteen. Despite the hard work that filled her days, Catherine always had time to dance, particularly the traditional bourrée.

Catinon, as she was called, was a woman full of life and joy, but she was more than just a girl who loved to dance. When Catherine got off work, she would walk the streets begging alms for the poor. Gradually her love of the Lord and the poor led her to imitate St. Catherine of Siena, her patron Saint, and take vows as a lay Dominican. "Catinon Menette" (Cathy the little nun) stopped dancing, feeling it improper for a consecrated woman. But it wasn't easy; in fact, years later she said, "The greatest sacrifice that I made in my life is that of dancing."[1] Still, her mischievous spirit remained and would serve her well during the difficult years to come.

In 1789, the French Revolution began. By the end of 1791, priests who refused to pledge their allegiance to the anti-Catholic government ("non-juring" priests) were imprisoned. Within two years, the sentence became immediate death for all non-juring priests and anyone found helping them.

Catherine's hour had come. This was a time not for pious church ladies (though their prayers must surely have helped) but rather for loud, powerful, brazen women. Catherine had been born for this; she set to work saving the lives of every priest she could, creating an underground system to hide priests and smuggle them where they were needed. She provided them with vestments and with bread and wine to celebrate Mass, hidden in the hermetically sealed copper pockets she tied around her waist after fabric pockets proved inadequate for her needs. She brought them babies to baptize, led them to families in need of sacraments, and hid them in the forest. She dressed like a revolutionary, sang revolutionary songs to pass unquestioned by sentries, and begged food from revolutionaries themselves—food that she then gave to starving priests.

It wasn't always easy, of course. Some nights Catherine would sneak through the forest under cover of darkness, wading through mud up to her ankles to bring supplies to needy priests, only to turn around immediately on arriving and return to town to continue her work. Other times, she slept in the forest. Sometimes the priests would move undetected under cover of darkness, aided by Catherine's network of informers among the revolutionaries. Other times, they came face-to-face with soldiers. Once, Catherine was guiding two priests through the streets when she and the woman aiding her saw a revolutionary ahead. Thinking quickly, Catherine told the priests to pretend to be drunk, while she and her companion nagged and shrieked at them as though they were beleaguered wives dragging their husbands home from a bar. Seeing this spectacle, their enemy taunted the men, insisting that if *his* wife spoke to him thus he'd throw her off a bridge. At this, Catherine turned on him and began to hurl abuse at him. Finally, she threatened to knock him out, at which the man took his leave (while the two priests and their guides tried desperately not to erupt in laughter).[2]

Though at first Catherine told "white lies" to protect the priests, she found that these untruths tormented her conscience. So she looked for ways to speak only the truth, though often in a sarcastic tone of voice. When carrying a chalice (covered in straw) in her apron, she was stopped and asked what she was carrying. "A chalice!" cunning Catherine spat. "Would you like to see it?" When she opened her apron to reveal the straw, the soldiers took her truthful response for sarcasm and let her pass.[3] Another time, she was stopped on her way home from taking food to hidden priests. When asked where she'd come from, she said, "Over there!" "But where over there?" she was asked. "Over there!" she repeated, until the exasperated soldiers let her go.[4]

For nine years Catherine worked to protect the priests of her region and is credited with saving the lives of hundreds of priests and making the sacraments available to thousands of the faithful. She was most proud of the fact that over a stretch of two years there was not one person in her town who went unbaptized or died without the sacraments. In a time when being a priest was a capital crime, this was nothing short of miraculous. Only once did a priest she was protecting get caught, and the fearless little Dominican walked boldly to his death with him. After he died, Catherine took the blood of this priest, Ven. François Filiol, and applied it to the eyes of a blind child whose sight was immediately restored.

Catherine was arrested more than once. In court, when she couldn't answer a question truthfully without incriminating anyone, she would just make the Sign of the Cross and remain silent. After watching this several times, the court dismissed her, thinking her insane. One time she was imprisoned, but she was so popular that she was released for fear of what the people would do if she were killed.

After ten years, the persecution of the Church ended and Catherine looked to serve where the need was greatest: begging for the poor. By this time, her reputation was so great that she had no trouble obtaining what she needed. Her work as spy and smuggler over, Catherine had no real need to be fierce and fiery anymore, so she tempered herself once again—except on one occasion, when she encountered a miser who could only be broken with harsh words. Then the little beggar (who usually supplied the poor well by gentleness and patience in seeking alms) would shout and threaten, reminding her soon-to-be benefactor of the fate that awaits those who ignore the poor. Because of her decades of service, Catherine was respected by laity and clerics alike; one bishop visiting her town even insisted on receiving her blessing—the blessing of a laywoman—before he would consent to give her his.

To the day of her death at eighty-one, Catherine remained humble, despite the honors the world attempted to bestow on her. She only wanted to serve the Lord and his people, and she did that without conforming to anyone's expectations, even those of her pious neighbors. God had made Catherine strong and spirited, and she served him best by being exactly who she was. Through her intercession, may we all rejoice in whom God made us to be and not attempt to fit into some other mold. Bl. Catherine Jarrige, pray for us!

BL. NICOLAS STENO

The Father of Geology, a Proto-Paleontologist, a Convert, and a Bishop

———— ≈ ————

(1638–1686) ✳ Country: Denmark, Germany
Feast Day: December 5

For all the modern world's inclination to pit science and faith against each other, the dichotomy fails under scrutiny. Any number of scientific discoveries have been made by men and women of faith, and a good number of scientists have even been raised to the altar. Bl. Nicolas Steno's work was so important to the development of various sciences that NASA's website features a 3,700-word biography of the man.[5] He is recognized as the father of geology whose work led to the fields of paleontology and crystallography and contributed significantly to the study of anatomy.

Born to a Lutheran family in Denmark in 1638, Steno had a rather tumultuous childhood. His father died when Steno was only six, and his mother, unable to care for him on her own, sent the little boy to be raised by relatives. When he was sixteen, a plague hit Copenhagen, killing a third of its population, including 240 students at Steno's school.

Perhaps this is what drew the multilingual polymath to his interest in medical science. Steno started university intending to study medicine, but he was unable to contain his curiosity. This multiplicity of interests frustrated the young scholar, who would have preferred to focus all his attention on one discipline. He even prayed to be freed from interest in other subjects, writing,

"I pray, thee, O God, take this plague from me and free my soul of all distraction, to work on one thing alone, and to make myself familiar with the tables of medicine alone."[6]

Mercifully, that prayer went unanswered. Steno went on to do important work in anatomy; he discovered how the circulatory system works, how muscles contract, where saliva comes from (the eponymous Stensen duct), and that the heart is a muscle, among many, many other discoveries. But Steno didn't limit himself to physiological research. He also studied fossils, famously realizing that the tooth-shaped stones then believed to fall from the sky on moonless nights were, in fact, the fossilized teeth of prehistoric animals. This led to Steno's most significant contributions to science: the basic laws of stratigraphy (still in use today) that ultimately made it possible for scientists to understand which dinosaurs came from which eras and to determine the approximate age of the earth. This research earned him the moniker "the father of geology" and led ultimately to the entire field of paleontology.

All Steno's studies led him to a deeper love of God. He said of anatomy, "This is the true purpose of anatomy: to lead the audience by the wonderful artwork of the human body to the dignity of the soul and by the admirable structure of both to the knowledge and love of God."[7]

But his travels through a post-Reformation Europe led Steno to question which was the true Church. He read the Church Fathers and found them a compelling argument for Catholicism, but it wasn't enough. It took an encounter with his eucharistic Lord for Nicolas Steno to be converted. Standing in an Italian town one day, he witnessed a eucharistic procession and saw the way the people fell on their knees before the Lord. As he watched, he knew that logically they were either bewitched by a lie from hell itself, or they were right. And if they were right, he had no choice but to worship alongside them. Having read John

6 and studied the writings of the Church Fathers, Steno knew which side he had to take. He became Catholic.

Steno continued working as a scientist for seven years after his conversion, making his crucial observations about the earth's strata in this period. But soon he felt the call to become a priest and was ordained in 1675. Brilliant Danish Catholics being in short supply at the time, he was asked to serve as bishop only two years later and was sent to northern Europe to work for the conversion of Danish, Norwegian, and German Protestants. Though still inclined to take time for research (studying the brain while serving as bishop), Bishop Steno left behind the accolades he had earned, honors afforded to him at every court in Europe, and lived a life of humility and poverty instead.

His time as bishop was marked not by wealth and leisure but by fasting and poverty, his episcopal ring sold so that he might feed the poor. He had no more stability than he'd had as a scientist, moving from one town to another attempting to witness to Protestants and serve Catholics in hostile areas. When he took sick, he was too far from any other clergy to receive the sacraments before he died at forty-eight, worn out from living radically for others.

Nicolas Steno was a genius who was unconcerned with accomplishments or renown. He sought truth in the lab, in the field, and in the Word of God. Through his intercession, may those who struggle with doubts be granted faith, shored up by reason. Bl. Nicolas Steno, pray for us!

BL. SARA SALKAHÁZI

A Chain-Smoking Socialist Who Became a Misfit Sister

———— ≈ ————

(1899–1944) ✳ Country: Hungary
Feast Day: December 27

Bl. Sara Salkaházi was all wrong: a chain-smoking socialist journalist. She was loud and brazen and drew far too much attention
to herself. She didn't fit in—not in society and certainly not with
the Sisters of Social Service. Fortunately for them, Sara Salkaházi
was no quitter.

Born to an upper-class Hungarian family, Sara was something of a wild thing—a strong-willed tomboy who trained as a
teacher not for love of the work but because it was one of the few
jobs available to women who were intellectuals. Sara had always
loved writing, and her time in the classroom gave her plenty of
fodder as she was exposed to the plight of the working class. She
became their champion, writing newspaper articles about their
struggles and ultimately joining their ranks when she became a
bookbinder and later worked in a milliner's shop. Sara wanted
to live in solidarity with the poor; this desire to fight for the
underprivileged soon led her to the Socialist Party. By this time,
Sara was earning most of her wages as a journalist, supplemented
by the publication of novels and short stories. She relished the
freedom of the bohemian life she had chosen: cigarettes, coarse
language, coffeehouses, and all the friends who came with life
as a Socialist journalist.

Sara wasn't looking for a religious vocation; she had only
recently broken off an engagement. And while she was searching

Pray for Us

for something more, she did not expect to find herself in a habit. A friend asked Sara to join her at a meeting led by the Sisters of Social Service, and when she heard one of the sisters speak, Sara was overcome by a sense of calling. Before long, she applied to the order—and was summarily rejected because she was a fast-talking, brash chain-smoker. Sara wasn't interested in changing her personality, but she was willing to give up smoking. It took her a year to quit, but she was eventually admitted to the young order.

Still, Sr. Sara didn't quite fit. She was too loud, too big, too much. The sisters thought she was trying to draw attention to herself by her work, her speech, her gestures. She wasn't permitted to make vows with the rest of her group and was even told not to wear the habit for a year. The sisters did not want to be associated with her. Around this time, Sr. Sara wrote,

> I am short-tempered, vehement, nervous, and passion-
> ate, but still I love you!
> I am disobedient, stubborn, and defiant, but I love you!
> I am restless, hasty, and confused, but I love you!
> I am dark, envious, and making comparison, but I love
> you![8]

Sr. Sara persisted. Ultimately she was permitted to make vows, and she became a powerful worker in the vineyard; she published a Catholic women's periodical, established a working-class women's college, and ran a Catholic bookstore, in addition to all her charitable works. She continued to write articles, short stories, and even plays, usually focusing on the rights of women, children, and workers. As the Nazis came to power in Germany, Sr. Sara wrote articles attacking their ideology. She changed her name from Schalkház to the more Hungarian-sounding Salkaházi to needle the Nazis, and she began to work to hide Jewish people and smuggle them to safety, disguising some Jewish women as sisters to save their lives, hiding some elsewhere in Budapest, and arranging papers and transport for others. She even influenced her order (which was at first so reluctant to appreciate Sr. Sara's particular gifts) to do the same. Sr. Sara is credited with single-handedly saving at least one hundred Jewish lives during World War II and helping her order to save another nine hundred.

In 1944, Sr. Sara was returning to the home where she was hiding Jews and saw Nazi soldiers. Rather than save herself, she chose to die with those she loved. She approached, announced herself as head of the house, and was arrested on the spot, alongside the handful of Jewish people whose forged papers hadn't been enough to clear them.

Upon being arrested, Sr. Sara smiled and said, "Yes, let me go in here for a minute." She entered the chapel and genuflected, staying in that position until a soldier grabber her. She then rose and turned, radiant, ready to go to her death. Sr. Sara was stripped naked and made to stand on the banks of the Danube. She knelt instead and made the Sign of the Cross before being shot, her body thrown into the river. For her work to save Jews—at the cost of her life—Sr. Sara was posthumously declared Righteous Among the Nations by the nation of Israel, a title currently held by only one Saint and five other Blesseds.

Sara Salkaházi, a misfit and a martyr, didn't match anyone's idea of holiness but refused to deny her nature to fit the mold. In being fully herself, she became fully Christ's. Through her intercession, may the misfits among us do the same. Bl. Sara Salkaházi, pray for us!

ST. MARTHA WANG LUO MANDE

A Quiet Homemaker with the Courage of a Warrior

---≈---

(1802–1861) ✳ Country: China
Feast Day: July 29

For those who feel too big and too loud, the stories of Saints always seem to show them praying silently and piously acceding to all the demands of their superiors. Those who are less inclined to take center stage, on the other hand, often find themselves convinced that all the Saints were eloquent and extroverted, predisposed to standing on street corners and shouting about the Good News. But Saints come in every style—even quiet, unflappable housekeepers.

St. Martha Wang Luo Mande wasn't the kind of woman you expect to make history. Born to a non-Christian family in China, she married a non-Christian man. When they were unable to have children, they adopted their two nephews and raised them on their farm. Unfortunately, their sons became accustomed to wild living, spending their parents' money even after their father's death left their mother alone. Realizing that she had done all she could for them, Mande moved to a small inn outside of town, which she ran to support herself. She made sandals and cleaned and cooked (especially steamed buns, for which she was famous among her acquaintances) and contented herself with a life of hard work and friendly neighbors.

It wasn't until she was nearly fifty years old that the industrious widow heard the Gospel preached for the first time. She was deeply moved by the thought that a man would give up everything to travel all the way from Europe just so that she might be saved. Mande was so honored that she invited fifty friends over and hosted a feast in honor of the missionary priest. As he spoke to her of Jesus, she became desperate to know more. She devoured the teaching of the Church and was soon baptized, taking the name Martha in honor of the New Testament Saint who had worked as hard as her Chinese namesake.

From that moment, Mande's life was not her own. She gave herself over to the Gospel and before long realized that she needed to live in a town with more Christians, where she would be able to attend Mass daily. When she was preparing for her journey, some friends expressed concern over her safety on the road. The quiet woman shrugged and gestured at a spear. "As long as there are only two or three bandits," she said nonchalantly, "I'll run them through like soybean paste." When she arrived in Guiyang, she served in a convent as cook and laundress and then rejoiced to be assigned to an orphanage where she loved the children as her own. Later she managed the kitchen at the local seminary until persecutions required them to close.

But Mande had a servant's heart and wouldn't stop taking care of the seminarians just because some of them were in prison. Instead, she calmly took up a basket and carried food to the prisoners, took their laundry away to wash it, and smuggled letters into and out of the prison.

The quiet old woman kept her head down. She attracted no attention. But when her seminarians were being taken to the place of their execution, they passed Mande scrubbing clothes in the river. Realizing that her friends were being taken to their deaths, Mande began to follow. The guards decided to have a little fun with her, shouting at her and threatening her. If Mande had kept her mouth shut (as she always had before), she would have been fine. But her inclination to be quiet had nothing to do with weakness or cowardice. When the soldiers threatened to kill her, Mande stood up and nodded. "Ah, well, that's fine," she said, as simply as always. "If they can die, so can I." So she did.

A simple widowed housewife, Mande was beheaded alongside seminarians St. Joseph Zhang Wenlan and St. Paul Chen Changping and local farmer St. John Baptist Luo Tingyin. It was the feast of St. Martha—and later, the feast of St. Martha Wang Luo Mande.

Martha Wang Luo Mande wasn't brilliant. She wasn't a miracle worker. She didn't stand up in a pulpit to proclaim the message of Jesus. She was a quiet, hardworking, ordinary woman whose faithfulness in ordinary things gave her the strength to be faithful unto death. Through her intercession, may the quiet, unnoticed men and women among us be strengthened to become saints. St. Martha Wang Luo Mande, pray for us!

ST. HYACINTHA MARISCOTTI

A Self-Obsessed Mean Girl Who Learned to Love God

(1585–1640) ✳ Country: Italy
Feast Day: January 30

St. Hyacintha Mariscotti was a stereotypical teenager before such a thing existed. Baptized Clarice, she had been rather pious as a child, but as an adolescent she became a Renaissance version of a Mean Girl. She believed in Christ and his Church, as most everyone did in seventeenth-century Italy, but she didn't have much use for the faith beyond that. Her life was miraculously preserved from a near-fatal accident when she was seventeen, but still Clarice was uninterested in anything but her plans for a romantic marriage and a wealthy lifestyle of self-indulgence.

And then, for the first time it seems, her will was thwarted. The dreamy young nobleman she'd set her sights on married someone else. Worse, the someone else was Clarice's younger sister. Clarice, having a penchant for the dramatic and a very petulant approach to life, was not about to let that slide. She sulked and raged and generally made life so miserable for her poor family that they packed her up and sent her off to a Franciscan convent. She escaped once but was escorted back under guard to live out her days in sullen despair—or so she thought.

Generally speaking, being forced to enter a convent because you're too miserable to live with doesn't end well. For some time it seemed that Clarice (now called Sr. Hyacintha) would be no exception to that rule. She declared to her father that she would live as a nun but *would not* live beneath her station. A noblewoman she was and a noblewoman she would remain, and vow of poverty be hanged.

For some fifteen years, Sr. Hyacintha did just that. She wore habits of the finest materials, had delicacies brought in to supplement the simple meals provided, and spent her days entertaining guests in her private rooms. Though she submitted to the life of prayer required by the community and to the vow of chastity, her vows of poverty and obedience were meaningless. Scandal or no scandal, Sr. Hyacintha would live as she wanted.

In bed with a minor illness some years after her entrance, Sr. Hyacintha received a visit from her confessor who was so shocked at the luxury of her rooms that he declared the only reason she was in the convent was to give entry to the devil. Sr. Hyacintha was stunned by his words and resolved to amend her life.

And then she didn't.

It's no great surprise, this. The longer you're ruled by self-will, the harder it is to repent and submit. Fortunately for Sr. Hyacintha (and for all of us), God is patient and merciful. Again Sr. Hyacintha fell ill, this time with a much more serious illness, and finally she repented, realizing just how her vanity and willfulness had hurt Christ. She made a public confession of her sins before the community and resolved to live according to the rule set out for her.

That she did, and more. From that point on, Sr. Hyacintha lived a life of extreme penance. She gave generously to the poor, excelled in contemplative prayer, and became so united to Christ that he gave her the ability to prophesy and work miracles, including discerning the hidden thoughts of others when necessary for their souls. Having been so frivolous and indulgent in the past, Sr. Hyacintha developed a horror of luxuries and a commitment to the poor so powerful that she gave away her own dinner when someone came knocking. Her love for the poor inspired her to found two confraternities to aid them, particularly those in prison. By the time she died, the ill-tempered, self-indulgent girl's reputation for holiness was so strong that they had to replace her habit three times during her wake as the faithful kept cutting off pieces of it to be kept as relics. God's abundant mercy had transformed her from a Mean Girl into a great Saint.

Hyacintha Mariscotti didn't fade into a sweet, pious silent type, repressing her wild spirit and passionate heart. Instead, she eventually channeled that passion, learning to love the Lord and his poor even more intensely than she had ever loved herself. There is something so encouraging about an ordinary sinner (and a backslider to boot) who was finally able to oust herself as the center of her life and live for Christ alone. Through her intercession, may all that is worldly and selfish in us be transformed by God's grace and may all who follow Christ halfheartedly be drawn to deep conversion. St. Hyacintha Mariscotti, pray for us!

ST. ROBERT SOUTHWELL

*A Poet of Legendary Good Looks
Who Was Unbreakable under Torture*

---≈---

(1561–1595) ✳ Country: England
Feast Day: February 21

St. Robert Southwell—a poet, a priest, and a martyr—defies expectations on every front. Though his family was Catholic in Protestant England, their fortune came from a monastery seized by Henry VIII, and Robert's father and grandfather both wavered between Catholicism and Protestantism. Still, Robert was sent to Europe for a Catholic education when he was fifteen, and not long after he petitioned the Jesuits to accept him. When he was denied, the gentle and artistic Southwell walked to Rome to ask more forcefully. His determination paid off and his request was approved.

Ordained at twenty-three, Fr. Southwell asked his superiors to send him to England, a country already running red with the blood of priests. In the footsteps of the martyr St. Edmund Campion, he set off for England as his superior shook his head, murmuring, "Lambs sent to the slaughter." For the next three years, Fr. Southwell moved from house to house reconciling sinners and celebrating Mass. He then took up residence at the home of St. Philip Howard, who was in prison for his faith and would later be martyred. Fr. Southwell became the chaplain to Howard's wife, the countess of Arundel, while frequently leaving the relative safety of her house to bring the sacraments all over England.

Like every hidden priest in England, Fr. Southwell knew that his primary duty was to offer the sacraments to the faithful. But he had a particular gift the Church needed desperately. The purpose of the priests in England wasn't just to minister to the souls who were still there but to maintain a Catholic Church in England. The hope was that one day the persecutions would subside, and the Catholic Church could emerge as something authentically English, not something foreign reintroduced from without. For the Church to survive, she needed not only sacraments but an intellectual life and a culture. These Fr. Southwell could give. Set up with a printing press, the man some believe was a cousin of William Shakespeare began to write and publish both poetry and prose. His work flew to the farthest reaches of the kingdom, giving hope and joy to recusant Catholics (those who had refused to abandon their faith) who had been approaching despair.

Contemporary Catholic culture often seems to have forgotten the power of art, the power of literature. We settle for trite films and banal novels, not realizing that a people starved for beauty will truly starve. Fr. Southwell understood this, and in his poetic genius (a genius still recognized by secular scholars today) he sustained his people.

But he was a priest before he was a poet, and Fr. Southwell spent the six years of his ministry in England celebrating sacraments, traveling under cover of darkness, and hiding beneath floorboards as did many others. Finally, he was betrayed and brought before the sadistic Richard Topcliffe to be broken.

His whole life, Fr. Southwell had been a remarkably handsome man, described as almost feminine in his beauty. Faced with a delicately beautiful poet, his captors were not expecting to find steel beneath his soft exterior. But Topcliffe, Elizabeth I's expert torturer, interrogated him at least thirteen times and each time was met only with the information that he was a Jesuit priest who had come to England to preach the Catholic faith and was willing to die for it. Not a word more. Fr. Southwell then spent two and a half years in solitary confinement in the Tower of London, after which he was finally given a trial of sorts and sentenced to be hanged, drawn, and quartered.

Robert Southwell was a sensitive man of strength, a Christian genius, a poet whose art strengthened the persecuted. But with all the gifts nature could offer, he longed for only one thing: Jesus Christ and him crucified. He yearned to pour out his blood for the glory of God, and his request was granted. In death he gained not only the crown of martyrdom but also an enduring legacy as the poet who reminded English Catholics of their heritage and strengthened them to endure. Through his intercession, may Christian men flourish in an authentic masculinity, one that values beauty, wisdom, and sensitivity as well as courage and strength. St. Robert Southwell, pray for us.

Part 2

Saints Who Never Gave Up

The life of holiness is not, fundamentally, a matter of a single conversion, as though one act of repentance could leave people glowing with the joy of the Spirit and untroubled for the rest of their lives. Often it's not conversion that's the hardest but perseverance. Perseverance not just through persecution and torture but through boredom, red tape, uncertainty and disillusionment, and loneliness and rejection.

The times when the Christian life seems too hard are not, generally, moments when we stand before the scaffold. They're small challenges to our purity, our charity, and our piety, moments that seem unimportant in the grand scheme of things. But one leads to another and then to another, and soon a return to faithfulness requires an enormous change of life. In times when we're tempted to give ourselves a little break from the pursuit of holiness, it helps to look to Saints who endured far worse than we do, for far longer.

The stories that follow tell of people who resisted temptation for years, who traveled to the other side of the world in pursuit of Christ, whose intellectual labor ultimately brought thousands to Jesus. Some of them persevered through impossible circumstances, such as solitary confinement, terrorist attacks, or predatory monarchs; others endured all-too-familiar racism and slander. But they lived with hearts so fixed on Jesus that the things of this world couldn't pull them away. With them as our companions, our own trials don't seem quite so daunting.

BL. PETER KASUI KIBE

The Most Determined Man on the Face of the Planet

<hr>

(1587–1639) ✳ Country: Japan
Feast Day: July 1

Born of Japanese Christian parents in 1587, Bl. Peter Kasui Kibe was raised in a country already hostile to the faith. Even his family's noble (samurai) status didn't protect them. Despite persecutions, Peter entered a Jesuit minor seminary with hopes of being ordained one day. After graduating, he asked to enter the Society of Jesus but was denied; the superior was concerned that he wasn't determined enough to persevere in his vocation.

Rather than accept this response, Kibe made a private vow that he would continue to pursue a Jesuit vocation. He spent eight years working alongside the Jesuit missionaries. When all foreign missionaries were exiled by the anti-Christian Japanese government in 1614, Kibe went with them to Portuguese Macao (China), where he was refused ordination because authorities claimed the time wasn't right for native Japanese priests.

Undaunted, Kibe looked elsewhere. He sailed to Goa in India, to a seminary founded by St. Francis Xavier for the purpose of forming native clergy. When he found the doors closed there as well—this time not just to the Japanese but to all non-Europeans—Kibe might have turned his back on a Church so rife with racism. Instead, he set off for Rome. On foot. Kibe walked all the way from India to the Holy Land along the Silk Road, spending time in Baghdad and occasionally traveling with caravans through the desert.

In all, he walked about 3,700 miles.

Kibe became the first Japanese person ever to visit Jerusalem. He then made his way to Rome, convinced the ecclesial authorities of his qualifications, and was ordained a priest six months after arriving. Asked to make a two-year novitiate with the Jesuits before returning to Japan, Fr. Kibe managed to convince his superior that there was no time to waste, that the Japanese people needed him immediately.

This being the seventeenth century, though, nothing was ever immediate. It took him fourteen months just to get to India. When he finally made it to Macao, he was told that the government would allow no Christians to sail on their ships to Japan. Fr. Kibe journeyed to Siam (today's Thailand), where he found the same difficulty. For two years he tried to sail from Siam, and then he headed to Manila. Still unable to find a ship that would take him to Japan, he built one.

Termites attacked the boat. Fr. Kibe plugged the holes and set off. Eight years after leaving Europe, he finally had Japan in his sights—and was overcome by a typhoon that smashed his boat to bits.

When the victims of the shipwreck pulled themselves together, they found that they were in Kagoshima, the same spot from which St. Francis Xavier had launched his mission to Japan some eighty years earlier. With the zeal of Xavier (whose canonization he had attended in Rome), Fr. Kibe arrived in Japan at last. He had spent twenty-four years trying to become a priest in Japan before he finally returned to Japan a priest of Jesus Christ, all the time knowing that he was headed for torture and certain death.

Fr. Kibe managed to minister for nine years under constant threat of death. When he was betrayed by one of his flock, he was brought before Fr. Ferreira (the notorious apostate priest of *Silence* fame). Rather than succumb to Ferreira's entreaties that he apostatize, Fr. Kibe implored Ferreira to return to the faith. "Let us go to die together," he begged an astonished Ferreira.

Ferreira refused, sending in a master torturer in his place. But Fr. Kibe (perhaps the most determined man on the face of the planet) wouldn't budge. His iron will unbent by Ferreira's arguments, Fr. Kibe was tortured beyond all reason. As he hung in the pit, Fr. Kibe encouraged those suffering with him until he himself was removed for fear he'd prevent all the others from breaking. Inoue, the most infamous torturer in all of Japan, called him "the man who would not say *I give in*."[1] He built a fire on Fr. Kibe's stomach and pulled out his insides.

Many of us are unwilling to drive half an hour for Mass when we're on vacation; Peter Kasui Kibe walked 3,700 miles. We give up on God's will when an obstacle or two present themselves; Kibe traveled halfway around the world. We run from suffering; Kibe ran toward it. Through his intercession, may we begin to live radically for Christ, refusing to give in to sin or despair but fighting to become all God has called us to be. Bl. Peter Kasui Kibe, pray for us!

VEN. MATT TALBOT

An Alcoholic Who Didn't Have a Drink for Forty Years

———— ≋ ————

(1856–1925) ❊ Country: Ireland

Ven. Matt Talbot was a drunk. His father was a drunk. Nearly every one of his brothers was a drunk. He was uneducated and unskilled and died in obscurity. And someday soon, God willing, Ven. Matt Talbot will be canonized a Saint.

Matt was the second of twelve children born to a working-class Dublin family at a time when work and food were scarce and hope scarcer still. Matt's home life was unstable and his schooling inconsistent. After a few years of sporadic attendance, Matt quit school entirely and entered the workforce.

His first job at age twelve was for a wine seller, and the occasional taste he took of the merchandise soon turned him into a full-fledged alcoholic. By the time he was thirteen, Matt's life was driven by his need to drink. He spent all his wages on alcohol, even pawning his boots when he didn't have enough for a pint. Matt's father beat him and made him change jobs, but it was too late. The alcohol had taken hold of him and, as his father well knew, it wouldn't let go without a fight.

But Matt didn't want to fight. He wanted to drink. And only to drink. His friends later said that he "only wanted one thing—the drink; he wouldn't go with us to a dance or a party or a school function. But for the drink he'd do anything."[2] For fifteen years, Matt begged, borrowed, and stole whatever he needed to feed his addiction, once stealing the fiddle from a blind beggar to sell it for a drink.

Pray for Us

Matt Talbot was the life of the party, but one day, when he was twenty-eight, he suddenly saw how false his happiness was, how false his friendships. He had been out of work for a few days and had drunk all his wages, so he stood outside a pub waiting for one of his many drinking buddies to offer to buy him a drink. But as one old friend after another passed him by, Matt began to realize the emptiness of his life.

Disgusted with his friends and himself, he went home to a mother very surprised to find her son sober and home so early in the day. After dinner, he announced his intention to "take the pledge," to vow that he would abstain from all alcohol. His mother, whose pessimism was not unfounded, urged him not to make such a vow unless he intended to keep it.

But Matt's heart had been seized, first by misery, then by remorse, and soon by love. He made his first confession in years and returned to the sacraments. He promised sobriety for three months, then six, then for all his life. He worked even harder at his blue-collar jobs and gave the money he would have spent on beer to the poor. He went to Mass daily, lived simply, and performed powerful acts of penance and asceticism. He became a Third Order Franciscan and taught himself to read so that he could study the Bible and the lives of the Saints. And he never touched a drop of alcohol again.

But he never stopped being an alcoholic; the temptation to drink remained with him. Early into his abstinence he decided never to carry money with him as it was too tempting to go into a pub and buy a pint of beer. After work, as his friends went off to the pub, Matt went to church; if he didn't fill his time with something, he knew he would relapse.

On Trinity Sunday, at age sixty-nine, Matt Talbot was making his way slowly through the streets of Dublin on his way to Mass. His body weakened by decades of hard labor, he collapsed of heart failure and was discovered later, an unidentified elderly man found dead in the street. He died as he had lived, in simple obscurity. But he was born that day into glory.

Matt Talbot is proof that being a follower of Christ doesn't make virtue easy; it just makes it possible. Jesus fell three times under his Cross to show us what it looks like to persevere in weakness, and Matt Talbot does the same, a model of living with an addiction without being ruled by it. Through his intercession, may all those suffering from addiction be given the courage to choose sobriety and persevere on the hard road of recovery. Ven. Matt Talbot, pray for us!

VEN. TERESA CHIKABA

A Ghanaian Princess (and Miracle Worker) Despised for Her Race

(1676–1748) ✳ Country: Ghana, Spain

We're accustomed to stories of Saints who are persecuted by pagans, Communists, or even Protestants, and we're comfortable with those images of our heroes rising up against The Other. But when Saints are persecuted by "good" Catholics, we become uneasy, wondering whether we ought to identify with the protagonists or their oppressors—wondering whether *we* are the protagonists or the aggressors. This is particularly the case with Ven. Teresa Chikaba, whose suffering came at the hands of racist Catholics, even racist nuns.

Chikaba was born to a chieftain (or perhaps a king) of the Ewe people of the Gold Coast of West Africa, in modern Ghana. From childhood she was drawn to heavenly things, always wondering who the maker was of the beauty she saw around her. When her older brother told her the morning star had made all creation, Chikaba was unconvinced. "Whoever put it there in the sky put the rest in the same place," she insisted. "That is the one I look for, the one I desire, the one I want you to make me know."[3]

Rather than bridle at the child's impudence, her people wondered at her wisdom, revering her as a little philosopher and looking forward to the time when she might rule over them. Meanwhile, little Chikaba kept searching for the author of the beauty she saw. One day, when standing by a spring and pondering who its creator might be, she saw a vision of a white woman carrying a little boy. After that, Chikaba told her brother that she was going to marry that white child. It sounds like a pious legend, the idea that a girl with no exposure to Christianity could have such a vision, but the story is told by her biographer only four years after her death, in the midst of assertions that he is only writing history, not embellishing it with piety.

Chikaba continued to wander and wonder; that's what she was doing when, at nine, she was kidnapped and sold into slavery. She was baptized en route to Spain and given the name Teresa. When they reached Spain, Teresa was presented to the king, who gifted her to the marchioness of Mancera. The little girl was then trained to work in the house, but it seems she was treated with more dignity than most enslaved people. She was given an education and allowed to eat with the family. Though the pain of separation from her family remained, Teresa was spared many of the worst horrors of slavery, treated always as a human being and not merely as property—by the mistress of the house, at least. The white servants in the household saw how the marchioness doted on Teresa and responded with cruelty and contempt. They ridiculed her for her piety as well as her race and even tried to kill her on more than one occasion. However kind her owners may have been, Teresa was still a captive. She still suffered the dehumanizing effects of slavery at the hands of free servants who reviled and physically attacked her. Even the governess who was assigned to educate her treated her not as a student but as a slave, once beating her so badly that Teresa lived with chronic pain as a result. Despite all this, Teresa continued to grow spiritually, spending long hours before the Blessed Sacrament and eventually serving as spiritual director to her mistress, who valued the young woman's wisdom (though not enough to free her).

Teresa was first offered her freedom when her uncle arrived at the marquis's home. He passed along the joyful news that her family in Africa had been baptized and the sorrowful news that they had all since died. Teresa was overwhelmed at all this, and even more thrown by her uncle's marriage proposal. The marquis and his wife encouraged her to accept him, offering her freedom and a chance to return to her home. But Teresa had long since determined that she was called to belong to Christ alone, something she'd known even longer than she'd known the name of Jesus. She refused to marry, even when her uncle insisted that they could rule together and bring their people to Christ. Teresa had found a more worthy bridegroom, and nothing could convince her to forsake him, not even the promise of a return to her homeland, a restoration of her royal dignity, and evangelical influence over her people.

It's a mercy that Teresa had the strength to resist the entreaties of her uncle, whose true character was proven when he attempted to abduct her and take her back to Africa by force. His plot was foiled, and those who had insisted on the marriage realized that such a man was unworthy of her. After the marchioness's death a few years later, Teresa was given her freedom, an inheritance, and the marquis's help in finding her a religious home.

But even the influence and wealth of her benefactor couldn't open the many doors slammed in her face because of her race. She was denied entrance to several convents that preferred to alienate a wealthy patron rather than accept a Black sister. When the Dominican nuns in Salamanca consented to allow Teresa entrance, they remained unwilling to accept her on equal footing with the other educated women of means. Teresa could join them, but as a maid rather than a sister. She would be allowed to profess vows as a Third Order Dominican, but that made her a decidedly second-class sister. She was made to sit at the back of the chapel, in a separate section reserved for the laity. She ate separately from the others, slept outside the cloister, and wasn't even given a bed.

Still Sr. Teresa knew herself to be a princess—by birth, yes, but (more importantly) by her baptism. She refused to allow the mistreatment of racist nuns to destroy the peace she had been given by Jesus her bridegroom, and focused instead on pursuing Jesus. So powerful were Sr. Teresa's prayers that her reputation grew as a wonder worker. Petitioners grateful for prayers answered returned to the convent to offer gifts to their intercessor, which Sr. Teresa used to help impoverished women who wanted to enter the convent but didn't have the customary dowry. She levitated, had mystical visions, cast out demons, fasted, and wrote poetry—the first African woman known to have written in a modern European language. But regardless of her accomplishments she remained despised and was made to perform the most degrading tasks.

Over the years, though, Sr. Teresa's holiness became so evident that the same sisters who despised her for her race began to revere her as a Saint. Even before Sr. Teresa's death, Fr. Juan Carlos Miguel de Paniagua (a Theatine priest) began preparing her vita in anticipation of a cause for canonization (though that didn't keep her sisters from complaining when she wasn't buried in a separate part of the cemetery from the white sisters). Had her cause progressed, she would have been the first modern African woman to be canonized. Instead, it would take another 250 years for that honor to be bestowed on St. Josephine Bakhita, another enslaved African woman who became a sister in Europe.

Though esteemed by many for her holiness, Teresa Chikaba lived and died reviled for her race, never allowed to become a choir nun despite her wisdom and virtue. But her legacy is not defined by the racist treatment she endured. She became holy not through submitting to harsh treatment but through pursuing Christ regardless of what his representatives did and said. Through her intercession, may all who suffer racism, especially at the hands of Catholics, find the strength to resist, and may we discover and root out the prejudices we hold. Ven. Teresa Chikaba, pray for us!

IO

SERVANT OF GOD RAGHEED AZIZ GANNI

A Popular Young Priest Killed by Terrorists

———— ≋ ————

(1972–2007) ✳ Country: Iraq

Servant of God Ragheed Aziz Ganni was one of those impassioned young priests every parish delights in. He was newly returned from seminary in Rome, where he'd played soccer for his seminary and made many visits to Ireland with his classmates. Once ordained, he was popular with the youth in his parish and gave talks at local youth rallies. With a bachelor's degree in civil engineering and some military service before entering the seminary, he was eminently relatable.

He was killed by terrorists at age thirty-five.

It came as no great surprise. Fr. Ragheed was Iraqi, a Chaldean Catholic priest serving in Mosul. Returning home shortly after the US invasion of Iraq in 2003, he knew the kind of danger he would be in. When asked why he had returned, he admitted his fear: "I am afraid. But I have always prayed that God's will be done. Here in Mosul is my diocese. I had to return because people need spiritual fathers."[4]

With the heart of a father, the young priest returned to his people, though he was in danger from the first. There were frequent terrorist attacks on Christians in Mosul, which was considered the second-most dangerous city in Iraq. In the four years Fr. Ragheed spent as a parish priest, his sister was wounded when a grenade was thrown into a church, a car bomb after Mass killed two Christians, and the bishop's residence was bombed. Fr. Ragheed's parish was attacked at least ten times, but the people continued to return. After one Saturday bombing, Fr. Ragheed expected the church to be empty the following day; instead, there were five hundred people at the Divine Liturgy.

It was clear to him why: "Without the Eucharist," Fr. Ragheed explained, "the Christians in Iraq cannot survive."[5] At an Italian Eucharistic Congress, Fr. Ragheed spoke with great honesty. "Sometimes I myself feel frail and full of fear," he told the faithful. "When, holding the Eucharist, I say 'Behold the Lamb of God who takes away the sins of the world,' I feel his strength in me. I hold in my hand the host, but in reality it is he who keeps me and all of us, defying the terrorists and keeping us united in his boundless love."[6]

The constant threat of terrorist attack wasn't enough to thwart the young priest's pastoral efforts. He taught his people theology, got involved in youth ministry, and served the poor and the sick. While he mourned the loss of friends and relatives, he taught his people to unite their sufferings with Christ's, to be sanctified by their pain. And whatever the threats, whatever the destruction, the faith of the Chaldean Catholics could not be shaken. Children walked through bombed-out streets and braved checkpoints to attend catechism classes in preparation for their first Holy Communion. And there were always, always people at Mass.

For Fr. Ragheed, as for the rest of the Chaldean Catholics, the Eucharist was nonnegotiable. "We will not stop celebrating Mass," he said when attending Mass became increasingly dangerous in Mosul. "We will do it underground, where we are safer."[7] On another occasion, he spoke from the heart of his people: "Mosul Christians are not theologians; some are even illiterate. And yet inside of us for many generations one truth has become embedded: without the Sunday Eucharist we cannot live."[8]

It was in the Eucharist that Fr. Ragheed found the strength to resist and to hope. And it was for the Eucharist that he died. The terrorists had demanded that he close the church. He refused. And so one Sunday, he and three subdeacons (his cousin, Basman Yousef Daud, and friends Wahid Hanna Isho and Gassan Isam Bidawed, all now Servants of God) were returning from Mass with Isho's wife when they were stopped by a group of armed men. Ordering them out of the car, one of their captors began screaming at Fr. Ragheed: "How many times did we tell you to close the church? How many times did we tell you not to pray in the church?"

Fr. Ragheed responded quite simply, "How can I close the house of God?"

It was too much. The armed men demanded that the group of Catholics convert to Islam. When they refused, the terrorists killed the four Christian men. Isho's wife escaped, bringing to her people a tale of horror and heroism, of the priest who had so often spoken to them of the Eucharist and had died for love of Jesus.

Ragheed Aziz Ganni was a passionate and compassionate young priest whose heart was centered on the Eucharist, whatever the cost. Through his intercession, may we orient our lives around the Eucharist as radically as he did and run after Christ, fueled by the strength we receive in his Body and his Blood. Servant of God Ragheed Aziz Ganni, pray for us!

ST. CHARLES LWANGA AND COMPANIONS

Royal Attendants Who Preferred Death to Sin

(1860–1886) ✳ Country: Uganda
Feast Day: June 3

King Mutesa of Uganda was open to missionaries of various sects, Christian and non-Christian, because it helped him play foreign powers against each other. His son Mwanga might have taken the same approach when he took the throne in October of 1884, but he found that the Christian converts among his subjects made his life less pleasurable.

Though barely into adulthood himself, Mwanga was in the habit of compelling the pages—teenage boys who were sent to the palace to serve the king—to satisfy his carnal urges. Mwanga's Christian pages were generally eager to obey their king (*kabaka* in the local tongue), but this was one area where they felt compelled to resist. Unlike many who are abused by people in positions of power, these young men had known going into this situation what they would face. They had been prepared by other Christians and encouraged to refuse the kabaka's advances.

Most importantly, they were protected by older men who themselves exercised a certain amount of power. The Catholic head of the pages, St. Joseph Mukasa Balikuddembe (who had secretly baptized the previous king on his deathbed) was initially able to thwart Mwanga's predatory intentions with some success, encouraging the young Christian pages to avoid and rebuff the king. When Mwanga called for a page under suspicious circumstances, Mukasa would send the page away from the palace and tell the king that the page was unavailable. It seems that Mukasa even reproached Mwanga for his abuse of the young pages, but to no avail.

This dance continued until November 1885. Mwanga had decided to have the Anglican bishop and several missionaries killed, ostensibly out of concern over colonialist tendencies, though his desire not to have his behavior corrected likely played into it. Mukasa begged the king to reverse his order, fearing both divine justice and temporal repercussions.

Finally fed up with being rebuked by Mukasa, Mwanga ordered him beheaded and burned to ashes. The Catholic pro-tomartyr of Uganda died with words of forgiveness for the king on his lips but also a challenge: "Let him repent, for if he does not, I shall be his accuser before the judgment seat of God."[9] Mukasa spoke these words of judgment not because he refused to forgive but because he was worried about the fate of the king's attendants and the fate of the king's soul.

Mwanga repented of his decision to have Mukasa killed, but too late. Mukasa's body had turned to ash by the time messengers arrived with a stay of execution. Unfortunately Mwanga's repentance didn't extend to his rapacious behavior, and the Christian pages who refused his advances were in even greater danger in Mukasa's absence. St. Charles Lwanga, a catechumen who was struck by Mukasa's courage and dignity, was baptized the very night of Mukasa's martyrdom and took over his position as head of the court pages. Lwanga continued Mukasa's work of catechizing and protecting the pages in his care.

For six months, Mwanga and the Christians in his service were in a standoff. Though serving him well in all other areas, they refused to submit to his predations. But in May 1886, the king killed sixteen-year-old St. Denis Ssebuggwawo for teaching catechism lessons to the pages who were interested. He had all the Christian pages (Catholic and Anglican) thrown in prison. Some had not yet been baptized, so Lwanga administered the sacrament in their prison cell. St. Kizito had been begging for baptism for months, but the missionaries had been unsure of his resolve. As he awaited execution, there could be no doubt. Lwanga baptized him with the other catechumens.

St. Mukasa Kiriwawanvu had been imprisoned a short while earlier for fighting with St. Gyavira (who had teased him with the nickname Long Legs); held in a separate prison cell, Kiriwawanvu was unable to receive baptism of water and was baptized with his blood instead. St. Bruno Sserunkuuma's faith was unknown to the king, but when the Christians were assembled to begin their death march, he silently left his place with the other pages and joined the condemned men. St. Mbaaga Tuzinde's family begged him to apostatize. His adoptive father, the executioner, asked him again and again to let his family hide him. Mbaaga refused. He went gladly to his death.

St. Gonzaga Gonza was no stranger to the king's prison; he had a friend who had been imprisoned for an alleged flirtation with one of the king's wives. Rather than allow this young catechumen to miss catechism classes, Gonza had made a deal with the jailer: Gonza would take his place in the prison during classes so that his friend could attend. Gonza spent his sojourns in the prison being tortured by a jailer who despised him for his generosity. But this torture had strengthened him. During his death march, bound by chains that had caused his flesh to swell around them, he made no complaint, not even a groan of pain, such that even his murderers looked on him as a hero.

The men were led from one village to another for nearly thirty miles, leaving a martyr's corpse at every major crossroads. Those who were still living at the end were burned alive. Over the course of this fourteen-month period, twenty-two Catholic men were martyred, along with twenty-three Anglicans. Among them were converts from paganism and Islam, unmarried men who had made a vow of chastity, men who left behind many wives to be faithful to the Church's vision of marriage, former slaves and members of the royal family, herdsmen, and the chief drummer to the king. They were all men who persisted even to death.

Though the records don't seem to indicate that Mwanga was successful in his attempts to prey on any of these Saints, those who were pages in his court were certainly subject to harassment and repeated attempts at abuse. St. Kizito, the youngest of the martyrs, and St. Mugagga Lubowa, who endured some of the most persistent attempts at assault, are particularly powerful intercessors for the many survivors of sexual violence. Through the prayers of the Ugandan martyrs, may all who have suffered sexual abuse find healing.

Through the intercession of Joseph Mukasa Balikuddembe and Charles Lwanga in particular, may God strengthen those who are responsible for the protection of youth and vulnerable adults, giving them the courage and wisdom to fight corruption and abuse and to risk their lives and reputations in defense of those entrusted to their care. St. Charles Lwanga and companions, pray for us!

SERVANT OF GOD JOHN BAPTIST YI BYEOK

The Teenage Pagan Who Introduced the Gospel to Korea

———— ≈ ————

(1754–1785) ✳ Country: South Korea

The history of the Church is driven by missionaries, brave men and women who left family and homeland behind to engage alien cultures, risking their lives to introduce strangers to the love of Jesus. Every country has its founders: St. Francis Xavier in sixteenth-century Japan, St. Augustine of Canterbury in sixth-century England, and St. Thomas in first-century India.

In Korea, the story is different.

Korea wasn't introduced to the Gospel by a charismatic priest or a company of selfless friars. Korea is the only country to have evangelized itself. More than two centuries after Xavier brought the Gospel to Japan and more than a millennium after Nestorians first preached Christ in China, there had still been no mission to Korea. The occasional Christian had entered the peninsula, of course, mostly for trade or military expeditions, but nobody had yet preached Jesus to the people.

A handful of Christian books had come to Korea, studied by Buddhist sages and others who were intrigued by Christianity as a foreign philosophy, not a religion. Among those who encountered Christianity this way was Servant of God John Baptist Yi Byeok, a young non-Christian man who began in 1770 to study a Catholic book by Servant of God Matteo Ricci, written in Chinese. Though tall and strong, Byeok had refused to join the military like the other men in his family. He preferred to study. At only sixteen, Byeok was so intrigued by what he read that he devoted himself to the study of the faith. After about seven years of study, he began gathering other men around him at Chon Jin Am, known now as the birthplace of Catholicism in Korea.

For another seven years, these men wrestled with the deepest questions of human existence, guided only by a handful of books smuggled in from China. They left behind parents, wives, and children for the pursuit of truth. Gradually they became convinced that Catholicism was true and began to practice it. Every seven days they would celebrate a sort of Sabbath, though without any way of knowing which day was actually Sunday. They studied, debated, and worshipped together, always led by Byeok who was known throughout the region for his wisdom and learning.

Finally, in 1784, Byeok learned that one of their number, Yi Seung-Hun, had plans to travel to China. Known as "The Hermit Kingdom," Korea was entirely closed to the outside world except for this annual embassy to China, and Byeok jumped at the opportunity to have contact with Christians. Seung-Hun was sent with instructions to learn all he could, to obtain books and sacred articles, and to seek Baptism. Baptized Peter, Seung-Hun returned to Korea to confer Baptism on the others, notably Byeok, the forerunner, whom he baptized with the name John the Baptist.

The companions then began to evangelize, moving their meetings to Seoul so that the increasing numbers of Christians would be able to attend. In just over a year, records indicate, there were already more than a thousand Christians in Korea. But the Korean government, extremely xenophobic after having seen the effects of Western imperialism on other Asian nations, was suspicious of this new faith. In 1785, Christianity was outlawed, though there seems to have been very little torture or outright

Pray for Us

martyrdom until 1791, when Korea went through a cycle of persecution and then relative tolerance for nearly a century.

While most Christians were safe in those early years, Byeok was the exception. The center of the movement and clear leader of the new Church, Byeok drew powerful criticism from the government and from his influential family. His father demanded that Byeok stop preaching, even putting a noose around his own neck, threatening to hang himself if his son didn't stop disgracing the family. Byeok felt trapped—how could he act in a way that would bring about his father's death? How could anyone in his family be led to Jesus with such a memory? He submitted.

Some later commentators considered this concession to be apostasy, but when Byeok was asked to deny his faith outright, he refused. His family knew that nothing more could be done. Byeok was not, in fact, his birth name, but a nickname referring to his stubbornness. Having made his stand, he would never back down. Still they hoped they could break him, so they locked him in his room, refusing him all visitors until he recanted his confession of Christianity. Byeok was never seen by his friends and followers again. After a few months under house arrest, he died. Some sources say he was starved to death, others that his fasting overcame him and he died of exhaustion, but certainly Byeok died as he had lived: completely given over to the Gospel.

After Byeok's death, Christianity continued to spread. Despite there being no priests at all in the country for the next ten years, the lay Christians went out as missionaries, even attempting to celebrate Mass and hear confessions before discovering that this was impossible for laymen. Though there was only one priest in all of Korea for fifty years after the Korean Church's foundation (and that one, Bl. James Zhou Wen-mo, only for six years before he was martyred), the faith continued to spread. Through persecution after persecution, the Church endured. Today, 11 percent of South Koreans are Catholic and hundreds are Saints, Blesseds, or Servants of God, including John Baptist Yi Byeok and his 132 companions.

John Baptist Yi Byeok was a man who sought truth, wherever it might be found, however long it took, and whatever the cost. Through his intercession, may God bless all who are seeking truth, especially those who rely on their intellect, that they would be led to a relationship with Jesus. Servant of God John Baptist Yi Byeok, pray for us!

SERVANT OF GOD MARY ELIZABETH LANGE

The Haitian Immigrant at the Heart of Black Catholic Baltimore

(1784/1794–1882) ✳ Country: Cuba, United States

Servant of God Mary Elizabeth Lange was a fighter. Elizabeth was born to a well-to-do Haitian family. Her family having fled Haiti just before the coming revolution, Elizabeth spent her childhood in the Haitian community in Cuba. Around 1813, she and her mother left Cuba for the United States. While Mrs. Lange soon returned to Cuba, Elizabeth settled in Baltimore, in the slave state of Maryland. There, no amount of inheritance could buy a Black woman a place in society. Elizabeth's light skin afforded her none of the privilege it had in Cuba, priests and even sisters owned enslaved people, and Elizabeth's beautiful

Pray for Us

French and Spanish would get her nowhere if her English didn't improve. Unconcerned with the prejudice she knew she would face, Elizabeth settled into the Haitian expatriate community and began to serve.

Well educated and of independent means, Elizabeth started a school for free Black children in her Baltimore home. Though it wasn't an illegal venture, Maryland in the 1820s was certainly not a place where educating Black children was encouraged. Indeed, the first public schools serving Black children wouldn't open until after the Civil War. But Elizabeth and her friend Marie Magdalene Balas knew that these children needed an education, so they set about to provide one. They succeeded for some years, but a lack of funding forced them to close the school in 1827.

As discouraging as this turn of events must have been, Elizabeth was soon to see the hand of Providence in it. She approached Fr. James Hector Joubert, a French Sulpician priest, with her concerns about the needs of the community. As it turned out, Fr. Joubert had himself become frustrated in his attempts to catechize his illiterate parishioners. Here was the solution! Fr. Joubert would arrange funding for Elizabeth, and Elizabeth would provide the school.

But Elizabeth longed for more than just work. She wanted the unattainable: she wanted to be a religious sister. It was impossible, not just in the South but in the whole country. There were no orders for women of African descent, and discrimination even within the Church made the idea of joining a white order laughable. But with Fr. Joubert's support, Elizabeth founded the Oblate Sisters of Providence, the first successful order for African American women in the Church. The order was devoted to the service of Black people, especially through education. Elizabeth took the simple name Mother Mary.

The sisters founded a school for girls of color, nearly forty years before the Emancipation Proclamation, and started a program to train teachers, both acts of defiance in a culture that found the education of Black people threatening. Soon they offered night school for adults and vocational training, opened an orphanage and a home for widows, offered spiritual direction, cared for the sick and the elderly, and taught catechism. More than anything, they taught a people degraded by slavery and prejudice how to hope, how to believe in their dignity again.

When the cholera epidemic of 1832 began, the sisters set to work alongside many of the white sisters of Baltimore. The white sisters were publicly commended for their service; the Oblates received no such recognition. Over the years, they endured scorn and contempt from the white community, even from white Catholics who resented the sight of a Black woman in a habit. They were ridiculed, physically threatened, and regularly forced to walk in the street rather than share the sidewalk with white people. They endured prejudice from racist Catholics on one side and from anti-Catholics on the other, but they persisted in their dedication to the Lord and their work in the service of his people.

All this became even more difficult in 1843, when the sisters' patron Fr. Joubert died. Mother Mary had exhausted her inheritance, and as Fr. Joubert's funds dried up, the sisters found themselves in great financial difficulty. Their unsupportive bishop insisted that they disband. But Mother Mary hadn't come so far just to be forced out of religious life. She refused to allow the bishop to dissolve her order. Instead, she and the sisters began taking in laundry, working as maids and cooks—whatever it took to pay the bills and stay together. They made it through that financial crisis, through the era of the Know-Nothing Party and their anti-Catholic violence, through the Civil War, and through its aftermath.

Mother Mary's motto was "Our sole wish is to do the will of God."[10] Once she had discerned that something was God's will, nothing could stop Mother Mary and the Oblate Sisters of Providence. She has been described as strict, even severe in her leadership of the fledgling congregation. How else was she to shepherd these souls entrusted to her when wolves loomed on every side? But shepherd she did, and none of them were lost.

In fact, the order continued to grow. By 1860, the Oblate Sisters were running all the Catholic schools for children of color in Baltimore. They spread throughout the United States and even to other countries. By the time of Mother Mary's death in 1882, there were fifty sisters in her order, freeborn women and women who had been born into slavery, all of them daughters of a woman of unfailing determination.

Mary Elizabeth Lange is a witness not just to those communities experiencing prejudice but to all who need encouragement to persevere. Through her intercession, may we fight unceasingly to do the will of God. Servant of God Mary Elizabeth Lange, pray for us!

14

VEN. FRANCIS XAVIER NGUYỄN VĂN THUẬN

An Archbishop Who Embraced Life in Solitary Confinement in a Communist Prison

———≋———

(1928–2002) ✳ Country: Vietnam

Ven. Francis Xavier Nguyễn Văn Thuận took as his episcopal motto the phrase *Gaudium et Spes*—"Joy and Hope." These were the two hallmarks of his life: in a communist work camp, in solitary confinement, and in exile.

The first surviving of eight children, Văn Thuận was ordained a priest at twenty-five and became a bishop at thirty-nine. Eight years later he was appointed coadjutor archbishop of Saigon, the most prestigious see in the country. Archbishop Văn Thuận understood that, given the political situation at the time, the appointment could well be a death sentence—his own parents had recently fled the country. But he accepted for love of his people. A week after his consecration, Saigon fell to the North Vietnamese forces. The Communists had won the war. A few months later the young archbishop was taken away.

As his imprisonment began, Archbishop Văn Thuận remembered Bishop John Walsh who, after twelve years in prison in Communist China, said, "I have spent half my life waiting."[11] Archbishop Văn Thuận decided in that moment that he would not waste his imprisonment waiting and longing for freedom. Instead, he would live each moment with joy and hope.

Archbishop Văn Thuận's greatest suffering came from his separation from his people at the time when they needed him the most. Like St. Paul, he decided to write to them from prison— but by stealth. He wrote on a calendar, tearing off a page each day to smuggle out with a boy who visited him. Those pages became his first book: *A Road of Hope*. There in a communist prison, Archbishop Văn Thuận became, in the words Pope Benedict XVI later wrote of him, "a witness to hope—to that great hope which does not wane even in the nights of solitude."[12]

Archbishop Văn Thuận learned to let go of his plans and desires, trusting that God could comfort his people and that they could form seminarians, build schools, and evangelize non-Christians without him. His job was to be faithful in the present moment, to love and serve God where he was. He said to himself, as he sat in prison, "Here is my cathedral, here are the people God has given me to care for, here is my mission: to ensure the presence of God among these, my despairing,

Pray for Us

miserable brothers. It is God's will that I am here. I accept his will."[13] This attitude made all the difference.

In the thirteen years he spent in prison, prayer didn't always come easily to Archbishop Văn Thuận. Solitary confinement made prayer particularly difficult, as the days ran together, and it became hard even to form coherent thoughts. But whenever possible, the faithful smuggled in hosts and wine to their pastor, the wine disguised as medicine for his ailing stomach. Archbishop Văn Thuận would celebrate the Mass from memory with no chalice but his hand, holding three drops of wine and one of water. During the years he was among other prisoners, the Catholic prisoners would kneel as the archbishop celebrated a silent Mass after lights out. He would distribute Communion to the men who were there and hide the Blessed Sacrament in packages made from cigarette paper to be given to other Catholics at the weekly indoctrination sessions, Communist anti-liturgies that Archbishop Văn Thuận made vessels of grace.

Through Archbishop Văn Thuận's prison ministry, many lapsed Catholics were brought back to the faith and many non-Catholics were converted—even many of his Communist captors. So that they could understand each other better, the archbishop told his guards, he needed to write out a glossary of sorts for them. He then used that book as a religion textbook for Communists, leading them to understand the goodness of God. Other guards wanted to learn new languages, so Archbishop Văn Thuận taught them, but in those lessons he also taught them about the beauty of the Gospel.

Ultimately it wasn't his explanation that made the difference. Archbishop Văn Thuận had determined to love these men with the love of Jesus. He smiled at them, told them stories, and became their friend. They were baffled by his love—and transformed. Only then was he able to speak of the one who had made such love possible.

After thirteen fruitful years, Archbishop Văn Thuận was released, not to serve his people but to live under house arrest until, three years later, he was sent to Australia and refused reentry to Vietnam. In exile, the archbishop moved to Rome, where he was made president of the Pontifical Council for Justice and Peace and became a world traveler, a cardinal, and a diplomat. Rather than raging against his former captors and the injustices they were continuing to perpetrate, Archbishop Văn Thuận worked with Vietnamese officials, spending the last decade of his life gently chipping away at the restrictions Catholics labored under in his homeland.

In 2002, Cardinal Văn Thuận's health began to decline. Some months before his death, as he prepared for a major surgery, he was asked if he was afraid. He spoke, as always, with joy and hope: "No, since there are three possibilities. I can die, and this would be a good time since I am ready. I could also continue living but suffer forever. Or I will be able to work again. All three possibilities are equally good!"[14] He died of cancer at seventy-four, never once lamenting the lot he had been given.

Francis Xavier Nguyễn Văn Thuận isn't just an intercessor for those unjustly imprisoned. He is a model for all who are inclined to lament their circumstances, waiting to serve the Lord until they can serve as they had planned. Cardinal Văn Thuận shows us instead how to become saints in the mess of the present moment, not waiting for the right time to be holy but embracing what we're given as though from the hand of God himself. Through his intercession, may we all persevere in our pursuit of holiness, learning to seek God in the reality of our lives rather than waiting for some idealized version to arrive. Ven. Francis Xavier Nguyễn Văn Thuận, pray for us!

Part 3
Saints Who Had Great Adventures

A glance at the stained glass windows in most churches might lead one to suspect that the Christian life is generally a rather insipid one, involving hours spent gazing at a cross, with breaks to write on a chalkboard or bathe a leper. But the lives of most Saints are anything but dull. The annals of hagiography are filled with perilous journeys, harrowing escapes, and battles in which both the Saint and his enemy landed more than a few blows.

There is, unfortunately, a pious inclination to gloss over the most exciting parts of the stories, accentuating the Saints' reverence or listing all their significant writings while ignoring the wild adventures. But when Pope John Paul II said, "Life with Christ is a wonderful adventure,"[1] he didn't just mean for those who stay placidly in their pew. Sometimes handing your life over to Jesus leads to more excitement and wonder than you could ever have imagined.

I have spoken to many people who are on the fence about Christianity (young people in particular) for the simple reason that it sounds boring. They imagine that they'll have to give up wild concerts for the gentle rattle of rosary beads, leave behind whirlwind travels for suburban domesticity. And some people do. But holiness doesn't require tedium—if anything, those who follow Christ often find themselves in the most outrageous of circumstances. Many of the stories in this book can be retold as powerful tools for evangelization, showing the way God can work in broken, complicated, and mundane situations. The stories in this section speak in a particular way to those who are reluctant to let go of their exciting lives for the apparent monotony of holiness. As we'll see, there is no greater adventure than following Jesus.

BL. MARIA TRONCATTI

A War Nurse Jungle Surgeon Evangelist Sister

(1883–1969) ✳ Country: Italy, Ecuador
Feast Day: August 25

Born in northern Italy in 1883, Bl. Maria Troncatti grew up in a large, happy family. As a young girl, Maria was fascinated with the newsletter of the Salesian sisters and the stories of those missionaries. Her heart was captured, and in her twenties she entered the Salesian order. Though her father was heartbroken at her departure, and Sr. Maria herself was devastatingly homesick for some time after she entered, she was determined to serve as God had called her.

Much though Sr. Maria wanted to go straight to the lepers, the advent of World War I derailed her plans. She trained as a Red Cross nurse, then worked in a military hospital, experiencing the primitive techniques and horrific conditions of hospitals during the Great War. When the war was finally over, the sister who had dreamed of the missions since childhood boarded a boat for Ecuador at the age of thirty-nine. She had been sent to evangelize the Shuar people, a tribe of warriors who passionately resisted colonization and are best known for their shamanic practice of shrinking the heads of their slain enemies. Undeterred by ominous warnings whispered by those who were concerned for her safety, Sr. Maria set off into the jungle with her companions.

The missionaries (sisters and priests) were greeted with spears at the first village they reached. The chief's daughter had been shot, and the wound had become infected. With weapons held at the ready, dozens of warriors stood by as the chief told the missionaries they must heal the girl or die themselves. So Sr. Maria, trembling, sterilized her pocketknife and removed the bullet, praying under her breath throughout the impromptu jungle surgery. Afterward she would tell the villagers that Mary had held her hand the whole time. "She is everything to me," she used to say.

After that successful surgery, Sr. Maria and her companions were assured of safe conduct throughout the region. Drums beat out the news that she had arrived, and with her the healing power of God. For the next forty-five years, Sr. Maria Troncatti moved through the Amazon rain forest on foot or on horseback, and eventually by plane, through a country whose mountains put Colorado's to shame. She braved vipers, jaguars, and tarantulas; waded through fast-moving rivers; and crossed rickety bridges suspended thousands of feet above the ground. And after that first run-in with the chief, where her life was threatened and she showed no fear, the people loved her. *Mamacita,* or "little mother," they called her, and she was. Mother, doctor, dentist, preacher, and teacher—she healed their physical ills as well as the spiritual.

Sr. Maria's work for the Shuar women brought liberation they had never known, most notably in the innovation of marriage freely chosen rather than demanded by the families, and monogamous marriage at that. She built hospitals to deal with the regular epidemics of measles and smallpox and trained the Shuar women as nurses. She founded homes for disabled and illegitimate babies who would otherwise have been killed according to custom. She established schools and worked for integration between Indigenous and white people, no matter how they had been taught to hate each other.

When arson destroyed the mission, the missionaries were quick to forgive, but the villagers came out armed for war. Sr.

Maria interceded with them, begging them to forgive, and finally she pleaded, "If you truly love me, lay your weapons at my feet." And the most feared warriors of the rain forest did just that.

In her decades of hard work under impossible conditions, Sr. Maria found strength in the Blessed Mother and above all in the sacrifice of Christ: "A look at the crucifix gives me life and the courage to work," she said.[2] She continued to evangelize the jungles until she was eighty-six years old, when she was killed in a plane crash.

Maria Troncatti lived in faithfulness to God with no regard for the limitations the world wanted to impose on her. Through her intercession, may God bring peace to the hearts of women, that they may strive after authentic femininity defined not by stereotypes but by faithfulness to the call of God. Bl. Maria Troncatti, pray for us!

16

BL. NATALIA TULASIEWICZ

*A Polish Intellectual Who Fought
the Nazis by Preaching the Gospel*

———— ≈ ————

(1906–1945) ✳ Country: Poland
Feast Day: March 31

Bl. Natalia Tulasiewicz wasn't exactly the woman you'd expect to be a member of the Polish resistance during World War II. She was a poet, a violinist, and a middle-aged high school teacher with tuberculosis and dreams of a PhD. She was intelligent and courageous, but not spy material.

But the Resistance didn't just need spies. Fighting the Nazis wasn't only about political power but also about reminding downtrodden people how to hope. And Natalia was just the person for that.

Born to Polish intellectuals, Natalia was an active child despite chronic tuberculosis that often left her weak. Though she dreamed of being a professional violinist, a neck surgery left her unable to play as well as she had before. So she continued the family tradition of academic excellence, studying musicology, philosophy, psychology, and Polish language and literature.

But Natalia's life wasn't all study and ambition. She was a delight to be around, an energetic girl who liked skiing and loved her friends, but who sometimes snuck away to write poetry. And soon she was a woman in love. Her fiancé, Janek, was a brilliant man, but also an atheist and a Communist. Natalia wouldn't marry an unbeliever, and so for eight years the two wrestled with this division. She finally broke off their tumultuous engagement when she was twenty-seven, but her letters and diaries indicate that she never stopped loving Janek. Though she knew she couldn't have married him and had no regrets about ending their relationship, Natalia mourned the loss of that love.

Suddenly single again, Natalia knew she wasn't called to religious life, nor (after losing Janek) to marriage. Instead, she would belong to Christ in the world. At first this manifested itself in her love for the students she had recently begun teaching, her friendships in the community, and her poetry, novels, and newspaper articles.

Natalia loved her vocation as a teacher (though she referred to grading as "a nail in the coffin"). But this life of education and the arts couldn't last. When the Germans invaded Poland, the Tulasiewicz family was unceremoniously ejected from their home in the middle of the night. In the scramble to collect what belongings they could take with them, Natalia paused to write a note to the Germans who would live in their home: Would they please water the plants?

These were the things Natalia thought of, even in the darkness of war: the beauty of music, the power of poetry, and the witness of hope that even a small potted plant can bring. In the weeks that her family was forced to live in a transit camp, Natalia's joy reminded them of what they were staying alive for: for truth, goodness, and beauty. For God himself.

After the family relocated to Krakow, Natalia worked publicly as a librarian and surreptitiously as a teacher, subversively ensuring that Polish culture wouldn't be lost despite the Nazis' best efforts to suppress the art, music, and literature of Poland. Through all this, Natalia wrote of hungering for holiness and beauty, and she knew that the women corralled into forced labor had the same hunger. So the young intellectual left behind musical instruments and secret poetry readings and the consolation of family, and snuck into a group of Polish women being deported to Germany to work in a factory.

There, Natalia organized prayer circles. She taught religion, Polish, and German. She set up a tiny image of Jesus on a makeshift altar and organized the women in her barracks to sing and pray together, to listen as she gave talks about the deep love of Jesus, about hope and joy and beauty. She organized a choir, ran a Lenten retreat, and even found priests who could bring the women sacraments. Through the work of this apostle to the barracks, countless women came to know Jesus, or to remember that he was with them even in the misery of Nazi Germany.

But the Nazis eventually caught wind of Natalia's work, considered treasonous because it was pro-Polish. She was tortured; when she didn't betray anyone, she was sent to Ravensbrück, the same concentration camp in which Corrie ten Boom (a Dutch Protestant member of the Resistance) was then living. Natalia continued her work there, preaching, singing, and praying with the women around her. On Palm Sunday, she led the women in worship, then preached one last time on Good Friday. Later that day, she was selected for the gas chamber and executed on Holy Saturday.

Natalia Tulasiewicz could have wasted her life wishing to be the kind of woman who could nurse the wounded or smuggle Jews out of Poland. She could have filled her life with music and culture so as to ignore the horrors surrounding her. Instead, she trusted in who she was and who God was in her. She allowed God to do amazing things through her. She gave her life (as only she could) for love of God and neighbor. Through her intercession, may all who feel useless trust that they are fearfully and wonderfully made, that they are a gift to this world, made exactly as God wanted them. Bl. Natalia Tulasiewicz, pray for us!

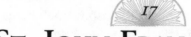

St. John Francis Regis

The Mountain-Climbing, Prostitute-Rescuing Priest Who Was a Role Model to St. John Vianney

────── ≋ ──────

(1597–1640) ✳ Country: France
Feast Day: December 31

In 1806, a struggling seminarian made a pilgrimage to a remote village in the French Alps. He longed to be a priest, but all the desire in the world couldn't make him a good enough student. Kneeling at the tomb of St. John Francis Regis, the young man put his vocation into the hands of this great priest. More than

Pray for Us

half a century later, as he lay dying, St. John Vianney testified to the witness and the intercession of St. John Francis Regis: "Everything good that I have done, I owe to him."[3]

Born in France in 1597, Regis was remarkably holy from childhood. He was uninterested in children's games, preferring instead to contemplate the things of God. Sensitive and devout as he was, he managed not to be insufferable and was still well liked by his peers. At nineteen, he entered the Jesuit order and began to prepare for a priestly ministry that would save thousands of souls.

Though he longed for the mission fields of North America, to give his life in service with the likes of St. Isaac Jogues, Fr. Regis was sent instead to the mission fields of France. In the years since the Protestant Reformation, many French Catholics had become Protestant. Others were so disillusioned by the wars of religion that they had abandoned Christianity entirely. Poverty had forced countless women into prostitution, and many towns were entirely without priests—often because the townspeople had killed or driven them out and burned down the church. Many of the priests who remained were woefully ill educated, ordained hurriedly to replace their martyred predecessors.

It seemed a hopeless situation, but Fr. Regis knew that God had done great things with poorer instruments, so off he went. He began by feeding the poor and caring for the sick, and soon they were turning out in crowds to listen to his simple but powerful sermons. As he preached, the crowds multiplied. In one parish mission in Sommières, a town that was almost entirely Protestant, nearly every inhabitant returned to the Catholic faith. This happened again and again, in dozens of towns filled with hardened souls that loathed the very sight of a priest—until they met Fr. Regis, that is. He was no great orator, but he was a man who knew Jesus, spoke simply and compellingly, and radiated holiness.

Every summer, Fr. Regis worked in town, preaching, hearing confessions, tending the sick, and serving the poor. Like St. Vitalis of Gaza,[4] he had a particular ministry to prostitutes, pounding on brothel doors and demanding that new "recruits" be given into his custody so that he could take them somewhere safe. Sometimes, he would see a woman being dragged off by an attacker and would throw himself upon the man, pulling the woman from the grasp of her assailant and allowing himself to be beaten instead.

This work to rescue victims of human trafficking didn't earn Fr. Regis many friends. He received frequent death threats, many of which resulted in actual attacks. Each time, his life was saved, whether by God's providence or by outright miracle. On one occasion, three men were determined to kill him. Though the murder of a priest wasn't enough to trouble their consciences, apparently they were reluctant to defile a sanctuary, so one of their number ran into the church to call out Fr. Regis, alleging that there was a man dying in the street. Fr. Regis looked at him and warned him coldly of the consequences of murdering a priest. Then his voice softened. "Listen to me. Confess your sins and return to God immediately. He is waiting to pardon you. Here, enter the confessional. It will be easy and I promise you peace of soul."[5] The shocked criminal did just that, then went out to his companions and convinced them to do the same. Another time a man was about to plunge a knife in the priest's chest when Fr. Regis calmly asked if he could have a moment to make an act of contrition before he died. The would-be murderer was so stunned by the peace with which Fr. Regis spoke that he was converted right there.

When he wasn't evading assassination attempts, Fr. Regis established a refuge for rescued women, obtained training in lacemaking for them so that they could support themselves, founded a group of charitable women, and miraculously multiplied grain to feed the poor. But mostly he preached and heard confessions for hours on end, loving nothing more than to reconcile a sinner to God. And when his penitents went home, Fr. Regis remained in the church praying, rarely sleeping for more than three or four hours a night.

Fr. Regis's mission wasn't only to towns; the young man who had longed to evangelize the frozen wilds of Canada had snow aplenty in the French Alps. While he spent summers in town, in winters he hiked. Leaving in the wee hours of the morning, he climbed mountains, pushed through waist-deep snow, and arrived in each village with no thought for food or rest. Instead, he went straight to the church to hear confessions. On one particularly treacherous journey, Fr. Regis slipped and broke his leg. Leaning on his companion, he managed to make it to town, where he refused the doctor's help in favor of spending a few hours in the confessional. Fr. Regis knew that in confession a priest is the hands of Christ hauling sinners back from the brink of damnation, and nothing could keep him from that sacred duty. When he emerged several hours later, his badly broken leg had been healed.

In the country as well as in the city, Fr. Regis had great success in preaching. The people saw all that he endured in his snowy treks and were convinced that this priest must have something worthwhile to offer them if he was willing to go to such trouble. So they came, they listened, and they confessed. Fr. Regis slept little and ate less, glad to sit in the confessional for many hours each day.

It was this commitment that ultimately killed him. Trapped in a snowstorm, Fr. Regis had caught a bad chill, but he refused to rest when souls were on the line. Instead, he continued to preach and hear confessions hour after hour until finally he collapsed in the confessional. When he came to, he insisted on hearing more confessions until he lost consciousness again two hours later. This time, he did not recover, dying as he had lived: entirely poured out for souls. He had sought the adventure of life as a missionary to Native Americans; obedience had led him to an entirely different people but an adventure just as grand.

John Francis Regis was a model for St. John Vianney, and he's a model for all priests. Through his intercession, may God give our priests a deep love of the sacraments, zeal for souls, and the courage to pour themselves out in love. St. John Francis Regis, pray for us!

18

St. Luigi Versiglia

A Missionary Bishop Who Fought
Communist Pirates to Save His People

———————≈———————

(1873–1930) ❋ Country: Italy, China
Feast Day: February 25

The history of the Church in China is a long and complicated one, with mission after mission lasting only a short time before being driven out by persecution. In the nineteenth century, St. John Bosco (who influenced so many Saints it sometimes seems everything he touched turned to a halo) had a dream about the future of the Church in China: a chalice filled with sweat and another filled with the blood of Salesians.

St. Luigi Versiglia had no idea that this dream was a prophecy of his life—and death. A faithful altar server as a child in Italy, the young Luigi had no intention of becoming a priest; his goal was to be a veterinarian. Desire for a good education led him to John Bosco's Oratory in Turin, where his hard work earned him the Saint's attention and his open heart led him to a Salesian vocation and a dream of serving in the missions.

Received into the order by Bl. Michael Rua, Luigi was ordained at twenty-two and settled into a life that was far from the missionary vocation he desired. For nearly a decade, he worked on the formation of young Salesians, but he frequently reminded those around him of his longing to be a missionary. "My trunk can be packed at a minute's notice,"[6] he would say, ever willing to pour out both his sweat and blood as the then-famous dream of John Bosco had foretold.

In God's time, Fr. Versiglia's wish was granted: he was sent to China where, with five other Salesians, he opened an orphanage and a school. Fr. Versiglia was gentle and loving, willing to do whatever it took to serve his people. He was a true father to them, and as the political situation of China became more unstable and the position of Christians more precarious, Fr. Versiglia refused to abandon his post. Whatever his people suffered, he would suffer with them.

With this attitude in his heart and the dream of John Bosco on his mind, Fr. Versiglia was offered a gift by his superiors: a chalice. As he received this chalice, he submitted: "Don Bosco saw the Chinese missions flourish when a chalice would be filled with the blood of his sons. This chalice was sent to me, and I will have to fill it."[7] Fr. Versiglia accepted the chalice of suffering for his Chinese children.

When Fr. Versiglia heard that the area in which he served was going to become a vicariate, he immediately wrote to his superiors asking not to be made a bishop; he preferred to stay with his people. To his chagrin (but no one's surprise), he was ordained a bishop not long after. But he refused to allow the dignity of his office to keep him at a distance from his people, and he spent much of his time traveling to visit every corner of the diocese. Bishop Versiglia anchored his life in the Eucharist, before which he prayed every morning and night, while spending the rest of his time in direct service to his people.

It was this desire to know his people personally that led him to accept the chalice of martyrdom. He was traveling with one of his priests, St. Callisto Caravario, to Fr. Caravario's parish when the group was attacked by Communist pirates. When the Saints realized that the pirates were after the three young women in their party, they tried to reason with them and ultimately tried to fight them off physically, putting themselves between the women and danger. Bishop Versiglia and Fr. Caravario were beaten with sticks and rifle butts until the bishop collapsed, still weakly begging that the pirates leave them.

As the two clerics were dragged off into the wilderness, one of their captors asked why they begged only for the lives of the laypeople with them: "Do you not fear death?" Bishop Versiglia responded calmly, "We are priests; why should we fear death?"[8] As they watched the pirates rummage through their luggage, the two Saints heard each other's confessions. The other captives were then released. Fr. Caravario and Bishop Versiglia were shot dead.

The image never left these women: as they cowered in the bottom of the boat, their spiritual fathers fought for them tooth and nail, were beaten for them, and finally died for them. These were no foreign imperialists, no bachelor priests seeking glory in a successful career; these were true fathers, fathers who had laid down their lives for their daughters.

With his companion, Luigi Versiglia had filled the chalice with his blood, never once hesitating to give his life for his children. Through his intercession, may all priests be strengthened to live as fathers to their people, defending them from all abuse and laying down their lives that others might live. St. Luigi Versiglia, pray for us.

Part 4

Saints Who Lived Ordinary Lives

There was, in nineteenth-century France, a young nun so ordinary that as she lay dying, she heard one of the other Carmelites speaking outside her window. "What are we going to put in her obituary?" the nun wondered. "She entered young and died early. That's it."

You may be familiar with this nun—St. Thérèse of Lisieux, called "the greatest Saint of modern times" by Pope Pius X. Yet it was in her very ordinariness that God called her to be a great Saint. Some of us are called to be world-wandering missionaries, others to rebuild God's Church, but most of us are called to be ordinary.

It can be discouraging, this daily slog through unremarkable occurrences—even when we're able to remember God's perspective: that marriage, family, ministry, and faithfulness are beautiful even when they're unremarkable. The lives of the Saints seem so much more exciting, while ours seem like the mediocre lives of mediocre people.

Some Saints certainly lived wild and exotic lives, but many others found holiness through ordinary circumstances, ordinary relationships, and ordinary lives. This section focuses on people the world could so easily have forgotten, people who didn't found an order, convert a nation, levitate, or raise the dead. Instead, they lived ordinary lives so beautifully that everyone who met them was drawn deeper into the heart of Jesus because of those encounters. These Saints may never have known the impact they had—we may never know the impact we have—but they did everything for love of God.

19

VEN. JAN TYRANOWSKI

A Working-Class Bachelor Whose
"Unsuccessful" Life Changed the World

———≈———

(1901–1947) ✳ Country: Poland

Maybe it's too much of a stretch to say that an unmarried tailor who lived with his mother is the reason Communism fell in the West. Then again, maybe it's not.

Ven. Jan Tyranowski was, in many respects, an ordinary working-class bachelor. After studying accounting, he began work in an office, but a chronic stomach ailment forced him to leave accounting and join his father as a tailor. He found that he was much happier there, working with family, with time left over for gardening, photography, and long walks.

But when he was thirty-five, a homily changed his life. "It is not difficult to become a saint," the priest said, and Tyranowski believed him. Tyranowski began reading the Carmelite mystics and praying up to four hours a day. In the freedom of his family's tailor shop, he was able to schedule his life around prayer and focus his heart on the things of God even as he worked. Content with hidden holiness masked by the trappings of an ordinary life, he made a private vow of chastity and embarked on a life that was monastic—even eremitical.

But Poland in the 1940s was no place for ordinary men. There were thirteen priests serving at the Salesian parish Tyranowski attended: eleven were arrested by the Nazis and sent to their deaths. Overwhelmed, one of the two elderly priests left behind asked Tyranowski to become more involved in youth ministry. It doesn't sound like much to ask, if one forgets the circumstances. There was the danger of being arrested by the Nazis, of course, for attempting to form young minds in anything but National Socialism. Then there was the cultural expectation that only priests would take on such a role. Not to mention the reclusive Tyranowski's complete disinclination toward social settings and his apparent lack of qualification, never having studied theology.

But Poland's priests were, by and large, awaiting execution, and Tyranowski had (like all of us) been called to be a saint. So the awkward tailor said yes, and he began meeting with small groups of young men, teaching them about contemplative prayer. He offered them the wisdom he'd gained in four years of devouring St. Teresa of Avila and St. John of the Cross. More importantly, he offered them the fruit of hundreds of hours of prayer: the witness of his life, showing his young directees that it is possible to know God.

Into his youth group walked a twenty-year-old quarry work-er who had become unsure about the wisdom of putting so much emphasis on the Blessed Mother. Tyranowski became the young man's spiritual director, a surrogate father to him. He taught him about the life of prayer and pointed him to the work of St. Louis de Montfort, which led the young man to renew his devotion to Mary.

With Tyranowski's help, the quarry worker discerned a voca-tion to the priesthood (as did ten others from the group) and took as his motto *Totus tuus, Maria*, "I am completely yours, Mary." It remained his motto as a priest, a bishop, and eventually as pope: St. John Paul II owed his vocation and love of Mary to his youth minister.

Ven. Jan Tyranowski died of tuberculosis only a few months after Fr. Karol Wojtyła was ordained. He didn't live to see his young friend consecrated bishop or elected pope. He didn't see the work of the Polish pope break the stranglehold of Commu-nism on Poland and its neighbors. He saw very little fruit from his life, and the world saw even less: a chronically ill, unmarried tailor who died young. But what would our world be today if Jan Tyranowski hadn't fought for holiness? With no Theology of the Body, no Luminous Mysteries, no JPII generation? Perhaps young Karol Wojtyła would have turned out much the same. But he kept a picture of his youth minister on his desk throughout his papacy; clearly he knew that he owed much to a man the world overlooked.

You may never do anything spectacular. The world may never know your name. And maybe your efforts won't bear fruit in this world at all.

But maybe they will.

You may never see the good the Lord is doing through your earnest failures, through futility and frustration. But he is working. And it's quite possible that the entire world will be changed forever because of your daily small yes to God.

Jan Tyranowski was made a Saint in the ordinary suffering of his life. It wasn't martyrdom, theological acumen, or moments of heroism that made him holy, but a decision. He decided that he would live fully for Christ, and so he did. He made time for prayer and for service. And because he gave his life over to God and neighbor, he became a man whose life gave glory to God— and changed the course of human history forever. Through his intercession, may all who live ordinary lives, fearing failure and obscurity, learn to trust that God's providence is at work even when they can't see it. Ven. Jan Tyranowski, pray for us!

20

BLS. LUIGI AND MARIA BELTRAME QUATTROCCHI

An Ordinary Marriage Shot Through with Glory

---❦---

(1880–1951) and (1884–1965) ✳ Country: Italy
Feast Days: November 9 and August 26

Bls. Luigi and Maria Beltrame Quattrocchi weren't foreign missionaries or martyrs; they didn't raise popes or bishops; they didn't start a world-changing movement. They were just a holy married couple raising four holy kids—the most extraordinary of ordinary callings.

Luigi was adopted at age eleven by a childless uncle and aunt. He studied law and embarked on a career in law and finance, working for various banks and government organizations. Though he was a good man, marked by kindness and integrity, he wasn't a particularly faithful Catholic in his youth. Maria, on the other hand, was remarkably pious, despite her parents' tempers. She was a cultured Florentine, a well-educated woman poised to embark on a life of academic and social success.

Luigi and Maria met as young adults and became fast friends, but only friends until Luigi fell ill and Maria realized her love for him. She sent him an image of Our Lady of Pompeii, begging Mary's intercession, and later wrote, "I prayed and cried so hard for your recovery." Not long after, the couple's courtship began in earnest and they were married on November 25, 1905. As with many couples who are madly in love, babies followed—and fast. On their fourth anniversary, Maria was two days away from giving birth to their third child. The oldest had just turned three.

Luigi and Maria were open to life, but that openness didn't mean that discovering they were expecting another child always brought feelings of unadulterated joy. For Maria in particular, each pregnancy was filled with mixed emotions. Her first child sparked fear in her, the second despair. "Who will give me the strength to think of two children?" she wrote to her husband. "To endure the physical and physiological exhaustion of pregnancy and the rest? Believe me, I am truly in despair."[1]

"I'd prefer anything to another pregnancy," she wrote in another letter. "How can I take care of both children in the state I'm in?"[2] There's something terribly comforting in realizing that emotions aren't sins and that even the Saints may have taken some time to warm up to the idea of an unexpected pregnancy.

Overwhelmed as Maria may have been each time she conceived, God was doing beautiful things in her and in Luigi through their marriage and parenthood. While Luigi had previously been apathetic about his faith, his relationship with Maria had inspired him to strive after holiness. The couple began each day in silence until after morning Mass. They prayed the Rosary as a family. They were also noisy and active, enjoying hiking and trips to the beach.

It was a beautiful way to live—until Maria's fourth pregnancy. In 1913, she was diagnosed with placenta previa, a condition that was nearly always fatal at the time. The doctors gave mother and child a 5 percent chance of survival if she attempted to carry to term and urged the young mother to abort her child. For the Quattrocchis, such a step was out of the question. They laid the lives of mother and child in the hands of their loving Savior, despite the doctor's pleas that Luigi was sentencing himself to life as a widower with three orphaned children. In her eighth month, a very weak Maria was induced and, by God's grace, little Enrichetta Beltrame Quattrocchi (who has now been declared a Servant of God) was born healthy.

After that scare, ordinary life continued. Though they were always eager to outdo each other in charity, the couple occasionally fought (notably over Luigi's cigarette habit). While Luigi earned most of the money, Maria handled the finances. She also served as a volunteer nurse for the Red Cross, worked extensively with Catholic Action, and wrote at least two books while her children were still young (on motherhood and education) and edited two others; later she would write ten more. She spoke to women's groups as well, encouraged by her admiring husband, with whom she raised four holy children.

They may, for a time, have been dismayed at how holy. Both sons became priests and their oldest daughter a nun. One would expect two Saints to be delighted at such a turn of events, but the Quattrocchis were human. As much as they wanted their children to follow God's will—and supported them in doing so—it still hurt to feel that they were losing their children. Many years later, their daughter Enrichetta described it: "My sister's departure made a violent tear in Papa's heart. I can still see, more than seventy years later, the silent, discrete tears of my father on his knees, while on the other side of the grille, the ceremony of his daughter's taking of the habit took place."[3]

Over the forty-six years of their marriage, Luigi and Maria worked with various different lay Catholic groups and took theology courses at the Pontifical Gregorian University, but there was nothing showy about their faith, nothing that demanded attention. Perhaps the most unusual element of the Quattrocchis' life was the vow of abstinence they took after twenty years of marriage, but even that was simply a flourishing of their desire to sacrifice everything for love of their Lord. At Luigi's funeral, a friend of his who had long been an atheist and a freemason said to Luigi and Maria's sons, "You see, during all the years that we worked together, your father never pestered me with sermons. But I want to tell you; it's through his life that I discovered God and that I love the Gospel. Pray for me!"[4]

This is the message of Luigi and Maria Beltrame Quattrocchi's life: a life so filled with small moments of beauty, love, and sacrifice that in the end it all blurs together into what seems like an ordinary life, but an ordinary life shot through with glory, one that leaves the world forever changed. Through their intercession, may the lives and homes of all married couples be radically surrendered to Christ. Bls. Luigi and Maria Beltrame Quattrocchi, pray for us!

VEN. ANTONIETTA MEO

A Sweet Little Girl Who Knew How to Suffer Well

———— ≋ ————

(1930–1937) ✳ Country: Italy

Until 2017, St. Dominic Savio was the youngest non-martyr ever canonized, at only fourteen. In 2017, Sts. Francisco and Jacinta Marto edged him out. At ten and nine respectively, the Fatima visionaries stand as the youngest non-martyrs raised to the altar to date. But as far as models of holiness go, imitating two children who saw the Blessed Mother and were persecuted by atheistic socialists for it might be a bit of a stretch for most children.

Nennolina, on the other hand, offers an absolutely attainable model of holiness. Ven. Antonietta Meo (nicknamed Nennolina) was a perfectly ordinary little girl. Born to a well-to-do Roman family, she was a charming and mischievous child who would often stop by the tabernacle to invite Jesus to come play with her. At five, she was diagnosed with bone cancer and it became clear that doctors would have to amputate her leg. When her mother broke the news, Nennolina said, "Mamma, if Jesus wants my leg, he can have it!"

This simplicity and generosity were the hallmarks of young Nennolina's spirituality. Not long after her amputation, Nennolina began dictating letters to Jesus, asking her mother to write them out and put them under a statue of Jesus for him to read while Nennolina was sleeping. In her first letter, the little girl who hungered for the Eucharist said, "I'm going for a walk to the nuns and I'll tell them that I would like to make my first Communion this Christmas. Jesus, come into my heart soon so I can hug you very tightly and kiss you. O Jesus, I want you to stay in my heart always!"[5] For months, Nennolina's letters counted down the days until Christmas—not because she was looking forward to presents and parties but because Christmas was the day that had been set for her first Holy Communion.

Throughout her letters, Nennolina makes mention of *fioretti*, or "little flowers"; this was what she called sacrifices offered to Jesus. When her prosthetic leg hurt her or her parents disciplined her, Nennolina offered her suffering to the Lord, a sweet little bouquet given to the God she loved. Still, Nennolina was clearly no holy card but a true flesh-and-blood-and-concupiscence child. Often in her letters she apologizes to Jesus for the tantrums she'd thrown that day, or admits, "Truthfully, I was a little bad last night."[6] Other times, she asks for help to avoid future tantrums. For all her childlike sweetness and piety, holiness for Nennolina involved rather a lot of repenting of her willfulness.

The faith and love that are evident in Nennolina's letters speak to the hearts of adults as well as children, inviting us to love the Lord as tenderly and intimately as sweet Nennolina, who wrote sometimes to "Baby Jesus" and other times to "Big Jesus," as well as to the Father, the Spirit, and the Blessed Mother. She wrote effusively of her love, saying, "I love you very, very—no!—*super* very much!"[7] In one particularly charming letter, she had her mother write, "Dear Jesus, today I learned to write an *O*, so soon I'm going to write to you myself."[8]

Though Nennolina accepted her amputation in peace (and even threw a party on the anniversary of her surgery to celebrate having been able to give so much to Jesus), she wasn't always placid about the sacrifice. She once wrote to baby Jesus, "Give me back my little leg, if you want to. If you don't want to, thy will be done."[9] Even when she asked for this miracle—with no doubt in her mind that God could, indeed, give her back her little leg—she was resigned to God's will.

In the end, the amputation did not save her. The cancer continued to spread. Nennolina suffered terribly, though always with joy. She was allowed to make her first Communion early and died six months later. The last words she wrote to Jesus were, "Your little girl sends you a lot of kisses."[10]

Antonietta Meo is a breath of fresh air in the life of Christians who have become bogged down by attempts at poetic piety or suffocated by bitterness at their suffering. Through her intercession, may we learn to suffer well, to love God with childlike sincerity, and to surrender to God's will, whatever it may be. Ven. Antonietta Meo, pray for us!

22

BL. LUCIEN BOTOVASOA

A Man Whose Wife Was Resentful of His Piety

(1908–1947) ✴ Country: Madagascar
Feast Day: April 14

There's something encouraging in seeing a saintly marriage that was filled with ordinary strife, neither the (apparent) perfect harmony of Bls. Luigi and Maria Beltrame Quattrocchi[11] nor the infidelity and ridicule of Servants of God Cyprien and Daphrose Rugamba.[12] Bl. Lucien Botovasoa's marriage, like most of ours, was hard in all the ordinary ways.

Born into a non-Christian family, Lucien was baptized in his early teens and studied to be a teacher. He was a talented singer and athlete, the director of the church choir, a skilled harmonium player, and a polyglot, speaking five languages in addition to his native Malagasy. At twenty-two, he married a young woman, Suzanne, and they began a family. Lucien was a generous husband and a loving father to his eight children (three of whom died young), but Suzanne was concerned. Her husband would get up in the middle of the night to pray. He would leave the house at 6 a.m. to make a holy hour before work. He was always visiting the sick and caring for other people's children, not to mention the hours he spent after school telling Saint stories to his students.

Suzanne was a Catholic and a good woman, but she was overworked at home and saw less of her husband than she wanted. If he would just leave his time-consuming teaching job and use his intellect for something more lucrative, she thought,

Pray for Us

things would be easier. And then if he would tone down his vigils and fasting, act more like the other men, spend a little less time in prayer—why, then things would be just fine.

Suzanne wasn't trying to undermine her husband's pursuit of holiness, but she couldn't understand the love that drove him to live in such an illogical way. And what she didn't understand frightened her. Underneath all her practical concerns was a deep fear that Lucien really wanted to be a priest, that he would leave her and the children to enter seminary.

When Lucien finally got to the bottom of Suzanne's relentless complaints, he was so startled that he laughed. Of course he wouldn't leave them, he reassured his wife. He had no desire to become a priest. Even if he had, it would be a grave sin for a married man to abandon his family.

Suzanne was comforted by his response, but she continued to be irked by the way her unflappably pleasant husband lived. Indeed, his gentle smile and incessant acts of piety led many to wonder if he should have been a priest. But Lucien hadn't stumbled into his vocation. He had felt called to marriage, and he had no regrets. When a religious sister lamented that such a holy man as Lucien was unable to be a priest, Lucien interrupted her to point out that he could witness to people who would ignore her. He lived in and among everyday people; his life was accessible to them, an invitation to holiness that the pagan majority could hear from a layman, but not from a cleric.

Still, Lucien wanted something more. He read about Saints who had consecrated their lives to God and longed to offer his life in a more concrete way, knowing that holiness had to be lived through daily sacrifice before martyrdom was possible. It was then that he discovered Third Order Franciscans, a group of men and women who lived a type of consecration in the midst of their lay vocations. Lucien was delighted! Here was the opportunity to offer himself even more fully to Jesus while continuing to love and serve his family. He gathered a few people to join him and then left behind his teacher's wardrobe to dress all in khaki with a rope as a belt, an approximation of the Franciscan habit.

Suzanne was not thrilled. While she couldn't deny that Lucien was a loving and kind husband, she would much have preferred a man who earned more and prayed less. One day, in frustration, she gestured at an image of St. Francis hanging on their wall and shouted, "He's the one who makes you crazy!"[13] Lucien just chuckled and tried once again to support his wife without turning his back on God's call.

But Madagascar was in the midst of a civil war and Catholics were suspected of siding with the French colonial powers. Lucien could see the writing on the wall, especially after Holy Week, when Christians were massacred and eighteen churches were burned down. The churches were closed for Easter, but Lucien led a prayer service in the forest, where Catholics, Protestants, and Muslims prayed together.

After that, he had clearly marked himself as a Christian leader. He warned Suzanne that he was likely to be killed. When she protested, insisting that he could hide in the forest, Lucien refused. He knew that if they couldn't find him, they would hurt his family. "I'm not afraid of death," he told her. "What I'm sorry about is abandoning you, but I'll be close to you."[14] Lucien spent his remaining hours with his family before soldiers arrived to take him to his death.

It may seem strange to beatify a man who was the source of strife in his marriage. Perhaps Lucien ought to have taken his wife's concerns more seriously, toning down his prayer life and caring a bit more about financial security. Maybe if he had lived he would eventually have found a better balance. Maybe Suzanne would have been more deeply converted. There's no telling what might have become of their marriage given more time. But regardless of what might have been, Lucien was genuinely seeking holiness, longing to give himself completely to God while loving his wife and family. He listened to his wife; likely he curtailed his spiritual life, just not as much as she would have liked. He tried to serve both God and man.

For men and women who feel misunderstood by their spouses, who find themselves having the same arguments again and again (knowing that neither party is going to budge), who experience tension in their marriage over matters of faith, Lucien Botovasoa stands as witness and intercessor. It is possible to become holy through the ordinary struggles of marriage and to love your spouse well when one of you is more devout than the other. Through his intercession, may we become saints in the ordinary difficulties of our lives. Bl. Lucien Botovasoa, pray for us!

VEN. TERESITA QUEVEDO

The Captain of the Basketball Team
Who Was Voted Best Dressed in Her Class

———— ≋ ————

(1930–1950) ✳ Country: Spain

Ven. Teresita Quevedo was a difficult child. The youngest of three children in a wealthy Spanish family, she was quite spoiled. "Teresita is a bundle of happiness. Everyone loves her," her mother wrote. "Pretty as a picture but terribly self-willed."[15] Her self-will led to tantrums, often in response to being served food she didn't like. She was such a little terror that she was given the nickname Venenito, which means "little poison."

Teresita's parents were overwhelmed by her temper and desperate for relief; but finicky, volatile Teresita was destined for more, and it was her first Holy Communion that spurred her on. As she received her Lord for the first time, little Teresita made a sort of consecration to Mary, promising to offer all her little sacrifices, especially of taste and temper, as gifts to the Blessed Mother. From that moment, she was a changed girl. A few years later, ten-year-old Teresita was on a school retreat when she wrote out her life's resolution: "I have decided to become a saint."[16]

But for all her devotion to our Lady and her desire for holiness, Teresita remained a high-spirited child and often got into trouble at home and school. She wrote notes to her friends during study hall, chatted when the girls were supposed to be quiet, and sometimes played tricks on the sisters.

In short, Teresita was fun. She was beautiful, popular, and a bit mischievous. Her desire for holiness and love of the Lord—even her motto, "Mother, may those who see me, see you"[17]—didn't make her awkward or dull, like some plaster image of a saccharine Saint.

Teresita understood well that holiness is being fully alive, fully yourself, for the glory of God. Though not much of a student, she was a talented artist and athlete. She was elected best dressed in her class, became captain of the basketball team, and loved to watch bullfights. She drove a car—a little too fast for her father's tastes—loved dancing, was excellent at tennis, and once pierced her friend's ears. She was well loved by all. But for Teresita, it was love of the Lord and his mother that mattered most.

Teresita was passionately devoted to the Virgin Mary. "I love our Lord with all my heart," she explained. "But he wants me to love our Lady in a special way and to go to him with my hand in Mary's."[18] She loved the Blessed Mother so much that when she heard of St. Louis de Montfort's Total Consecration to Mary and asked a priest about it, he explained to her that she had already been living this consecration. Rather than preparing her for a month to offer herself to the Lord through Mary's hands, the priest invited her to do so the very next morning.

As Teresita approached her senior year of high school, she became aware that Mary was drawing her to belong to Jesus in a profound way. And so, at just seventeen, Teresita Quevedo left behind home and family, pretty clothes and tennis rackets, and dance cards and bullfights to become a bride of Christ. She threw herself into the life of the convent as she had thrown herself into her life in the world, writing to a missionary priest, "The thought of being a mediocre religious terrifies me."[19] Though the extroverted little nun struggled mightily with the silence and long hours of prayer expected of her, she offered all her successes and failures to Mary each day, to be purified and given to Christ. On the day Teresita received the Carmelite habit, she made a vow never to commit a deliberate venial sin.

Only two years after entering the convent, Teresita received a premonition that she would die soon. Rather than being afraid, she was overjoyed at the prospect of going home to heaven. Not long after, Teresita contracted tuberculosis meningitis. She suffered terribly, refusing painkillers even for spinal taps so that she could unite her sufferings to Christ's. Finally, on Holy Saturday 1950, Teresita's eyes cleared, her face lit up, and she called out her last words, "How beautiful! O Mary, how beautiful you are!"[20]

Teresita Quevedo stands as a witness to God's power to transform the most ill tempered and to capture the hearts of the most popular and beautiful among us as well as the lost and the broken. Through her intercession, may God grant courage and perseverance to young people who are hesitant to give their hearts to Christ because of what they fear they might lose. Ven. Teresita Quevedo, pray for us!

SERVANT OF GOD ANTONIO CUIPA

A Husband and Father Whose Skill as a Musician Made Him a Star Evangelist

———— ≋ ————

(d. 1704) ✳ Country: United States (Apalachee People)

From 1549 to 1761, hundreds of European and Indigenous Catholics were martyred in the land stretching from Florida to Virginia. Known as the Martyrs of La Florida (or Servant of God Antonio Cuipa and Companions), the cause for canonization of these eighty-six individuals is now open, centered on an Apalachee leader who was a husband and father, a musician, a carpenter, an evangelist, and a martyr.

Antonio Cuipa was born to a Christian Apalachee family in present-day Tallahassee, Florida, and grew up in San Luis de Talimali, the largest Spanish mission in the region. The son of a *cacique* (chief), Antonio was educated by the same Franciscan friars who had converted his parents. When he reached adulthood, Antonio, too, became a leader in his village, married a Christian woman, and had two children, named Francisco and Clara in honor of the Franciscan Saints. He was *inija* (second in command) over the thousands of people associated with the mission.

Antonio also accompanied the Franciscans on their missions to non-Christian tribes and villages, to interpret for the Spaniards and to preach himself. The missionaries quickly realized that Antonio was a true evangelist, a man who could speak to the hearts of the Native Americans and proclaim the Gospel in a way they could understand.

Nor was Antonio limited to the work he could do alongside the European missionaries. A talented flutist, Antonio would take a group of Native American friends out into the forest in search of people who hadn't yet heard the Gospel. When they encountered such a group, he would impress them with his musical abilities. Only when they were suitably awed would he put down the flute he had so carefully carved, give out hand-carved flutes and maize cakes that he'd brought as gifts, and begin to speak of the love of God.

Antonio spoke gently of Jesus, telling the Native Americans that the creator God they already worshipped had a Son who had become a man and died to save them. His success in leading people to Jesus was astonishing to the missionaries. Though Antonio chalked it all up to patience and perseverance, Lieutenant Governor Manuel de Solano spoke of the joy of the young evangelist in a 1701 letter: "All of this happiness and joy which this Don Antonio exudes in everything he does and accomplishes derives from his great faith and love for the things of the Church and the Catholic teaching."[21] Surely such joy must have drawn the hearts of men and women who wanted to experience it for themselves.

Antonio had a deep devotion to St. Joseph, whom he imitated as he sought to unite his people into one family. He played guitar, taught Latin, repaired buildings, and preached the Gospel. His was a simple life marked by ordinary heroism, until the extraordinary was asked of him.

In 1704, British colonists attacked the mission of La Concepción de Ayubale (some twenty-five miles from Antonio's home). Antonio set out with a crew of Spanish soldiers and Native American archers to defend their brethren, but they were routed and Antonio was among the many captured in the fighting. The Creek people who fought alongside the British had a deep animosity for Christian Native Americans; they tied

Antonio and some forty other captives to crosses to be tortured for their refusal to abandon their faith. Fires were built beneath the prisoners' feet, slowly burning them to death as they were mocked and brutalized.

In the hours of their agony, Antonio remained the leader he had always been. He proclaimed from the cross that he wasn't afraid to die, begged God to forgive his torturers, and encouraged those dying along with him to remain steadfast. Finally, he looked into the sky, his face radiant, and spoke of the Blessed Mother whom he saw before him. "Our Lady is near," he said to his companions. "Be strong; be strong. Our Lady is here with us."[22] It's the first known Marian apparition in what would become the United States, a moment of divine encouragement offered to a man whose entire life had been a gift to God and his people.

Antonio Cuipa was every inch a man of St. Joseph: a leader who found direction in prayer, a father who taught with love, and an evangelist whose greatest testimony was the joy he found in knowing Jesus. Through his intercession, may all husbands and fathers be strengthened to live in imitation of good St. Joseph. May all of us use our gifts to draw hearts to the Lord. Servant of God Antonio Cuipa, pray for us!

VEN. MARGARET SINCLAIR

*A Factory Worker from the Slums Who
Became a Poor Clare Nun*

(1900–1925) ✳ Country: Scotland

Ven. Margaret Sinclair is often compared to St. Thérèse of Lisieux, a young nun who lived an ordinary life and attained great holiness. But if Thérèse Martin was ordinary, Margaret was simply beneath notice. Though a rough sketch of her life explains her nickname, the Little Flower of Scotland, Margaret's upbringing was far from genteel and her family, unlike the Martins, was not made up of Saints. No, Margaret was a little flower of the tenements, but it's in her lowly origins and everyday holiness that the life of Margaret Sinclair can call us to greatness.

One of nine children, Margaret was brought up in a two-room basement apartment in Edinburgh. Her father was a garbage collector and her mother frequently ill, so Margaret worked from a young age at various odd jobs. When Margaret was fourteen, her father and brother went off to fight in World War I and Margaret left school for good, taking work in a cabinet factory.

As a factory worker, Margaret was not only a union member but also a union representative, protesting when the workers' wages were docked unjustly. She had a standing feud with her supervisor over a picture of the Blessed Mother that Margaret hung over her workstation. Each evening, he took it down; each morning, Margaret quietly hung it back up. Her persistence showed in everything she did, most especially with her mother who was often overcome by the difficulties of her circumstances.

Each time her mother felt she couldn't go on, Margaret would look her in the eyes and say the same thing: "*Dinnae* give in." Do not give in.

After the war ended, the Depression that followed left Margaret unemployed and urgently seeking work. Eventually she found a job in a cookie factory. Though she worked a demanding schedule, Margaret loved spending time in prayer and went to daily Mass whenever she could. On one family holiday, Margaret and her sister Bella were able to go to Mass every day and receive Communion daily, an uncommon practice at the time. When Bella expressed concern that they weren't holy enough to receive so frequently, Margaret countered with utter common sense, "We're not going because we *are* good but because we *want* to be good."[23]

Working still left her plenty of energy for dancing, and her spirit (and love of pretty clothes) made Margaret much admired, particularly by Patrick Lynch. Lynch had fallen away from the sacraments, and when Margaret spent some time encouraging him to return to the faith, he fell quite in love with her. He presented her with an engagement ring and threatened suicide if she refused him. Her parents were pleased by the match, but Margaret was distraught, especially when prayer and the wise counsel of a priest helped her to see that her vocation lay elsewhere. "I thought it was the will of God, and that I might grow to like him,"[24] she confessed, but her heart was fixed on the cloister.

So Margaret bade her family (and her erstwhile fiancé) farewell and entered the Poor Clares in London, where her accent and lack of education set her apart in a community where many of the nuns were aristocrats by birth. Though she had hoped to be a choir sister, one who sings the Divine Office for eight hours a day, she seemed better suited to be an ordinary extern sister, one who has much more contact with the outside world and goes out begging several times a year.

This begging, it seems, was the death of her. Only two years after she entered religious life, Sr. Mary Francis of the Five Wounds (as Margaret was known in religion) contracted tuberculosis, likely from sitting by an obviously ill woman on a bus. Eight painful months later, she died at the age of twenty-five.

There were in Margaret Sinclair no heroics except those of an ordinary life: smiling rather than raging, working when one would rather not, and accepting God's will no matter how hard it may be. She understood that (in the words of St. Josemaría Escrivá) "great holiness consists in carrying out the little duties of each moment."[25] Through her intercession, may workers and the unemployed find the strength to live their ordinary lives in extraordinary ways. Ven. Margaret Sinclair, pray for us!

26
BL. CARLOS MANUEL RODRÍGUEZ SANTIAGO

A Chronically Ill College Dropout Who Taught His People to Love the Mass

―――――≈―――――

(1918–1963) ✳ Country: Puerto Rico
Feast Day: July 13

A chronically ill college dropout seems an unlikely candidate to be the first Puerto Rican Saint, but Bl. Carlos Manuel Rodríguez Santiago was never terribly concerned about other people's expectations.

Born to a faithful Catholic family in 1918, Carlos learned a deep love for the Eucharist from his mother, and until his health failed, he had hopes of becoming a priest. Diagnosed with ulcerative colitis, a violent digestive ailment, Carlos had to leave high school for a time and didn't earn his diploma until he was twenty-one. He worked as an office clerk for seven more years before attempting to continue his studies. Again his illness made this impossible, and despite excellent grades, Carlos was forced to withdraw from the university.

Though ulcerative colitis complicated his life, it didn't control it. Carlos read incessantly, loved to hike, and learned enough from a year of piano lessons to play the organ at Mass. But despite his love of books and music, Carlos was unattached to the things of this world—so much so that in his entire adult life he only ever owned one pair of shoes.

This man of poverty and simplicity was also a man of great learning. He studied science, philosophy, and the arts, but the great love of Bl. Carlos's life was the liturgy. During a time when the Mass was celebrated in Latin, he longed for the faithful to understand the liturgy more fully. He translated the prayers of the Mass into Spanish and, with his modest income, published a newsletter making the prayers available to the laity, along with articles explaining the liturgy. He organized groups to study and learn about the liturgy, spoke before crowds on its beauty, led retreats for young adults, and taught high school catechism classes. Eventually he quit his job as an office clerk to teach liturgy classes full time at the University of Puerto Rico's Catholic student center.

Above all, Carlos loved the Easter Vigil. "We live for this night,"[26] he would say, reminding all those he met that the heart of the Christian life is the Paschal Mystery: the truth that the God of the universe, died for love of you and rose again, conquering sin and death. Despite constant pain, Bl. Carlos lived in hope and called all those he knew to do the same.

For centuries, the Easter Vigil had been celebrated on the morning of Holy Saturday and mostly in monasteries. Carlos prayed and advocated for its return to its proper place at night so that modern Christians could join in the ancient tradition of watching the light of Christ defeat the darkness. In 1952, Pope Pius XII restored the Easter Vigil to the night of Holy Saturday, and Carlos rejoiced.

Much of the work Carlos did seemed almost prophetic. While remaining entirely faithful to the Church, he advocated for use of the vernacular and for increased lay participation, reforms that would come shortly after his death. His belief in the universal call to holiness was infectious, drawing hundreds of people into a deeper relationship with Christ.

But he wouldn't live to see all his hopes realized. His health had slowly declined, though his spirits never did, and Carlos died of a painful rectal cancer at forty-four, one year into the Second Vatican Council. During his last months, Carlos felt himself abandoned by God, living the darkness of Good Friday and Holy Saturday. But before he died, the light of Easter came back into his life and with it the joy of being loved by God. As Carlos breathed his last, surrounded by family, his brother sang Carlos's favorite hymn: the Easter *Exultet*. And when he died, he was welcomed by choirs of angels rejoicing in the heavenly liturgy that Carlos had loved and served so well.

After his death, Carlos's family had no idea how they would pay off the enormous medical debt he'd accumulated. But his doctors refused any payment, insisting that Carlos had done far more for the hospital's staff than they'd ever done for him.

By many measures, the life of this chronically ill dropout may have seemed a failure, but Carlos Manuel Rodríguez Santiago was an enormous gift to his people, drawing them to love God more in the Mass. Through his intercession, may those who live with chronic illness be blessed in the knowledge that their lives have great value, regardless of what they are able to produce or contribute. Bl. Carlos Manuel Rodríguez Santiago, pray for us!

BL. CEFERINO GIMÉNEZ MALLA

A Grandpa Killed for Being Armed with a Rosary

———————≋———————

(1861–1936) ✳ Country: Spain (of the Kalo Romani people)
Feast Day: August 2

Toward the end of his life, Bl. Ceferino Giménez Malla probably looked like a thousand other old men praying the Rosary after daily Mass. His path to holiness wasn't typical, nor was his pursuit of virtue, but when he was shot for praying the Rosary, nobody who knew him was surprised to hear that he had given his life for God.

The very fact that Ceferino's holiness was taken for granted is remarkable given his ethnicity; Ceferino was Romani (a people often pejoratively referred to as Gypsies) and grew up in a world that looked down on him for his origin and lifestyle. Rather than become embittered or abandon his people, Ceferino embraced the Roma way of life and acted as a peacemaker between Kalos (his tribe) and Spaniards.

After his father abandoned the family, Ceferino was raised by a single mother in a poor family of wandering basket weavers.

He was baptized as an infant, but accounts of Ceferino's youth tell us little about his faith life. The fact that he prayed in Catalan indicates that he likely learned his prayers when living in Catalonia as a child, but his marriage outside the Church at eighteen could indicate that his religious formation wasn't terribly strong.

He may not have known his faith, but Ceferino strove for goodness. He was a horse trader, a profession known for its dishonesty, but he refused to deceive. Despite having no formal schooling and being entirely illiterate, his natural virtue made him a good businessman and his generosity and willingness to risk himself for others made him many friends. Once, his former mayor began coughing up blood in the public square. Fearful of tuberculosis, those around him fled, but Ceferino, known as El Pelé ("the strong one" or "the brave one"), helped the man home. His grateful family gave El Pelé a large sum of money, which he used to make quite a fortune as a horse trader.

As the years went by, Ceferino went from good to holy. Thirty-two years after his traditional Roma marriage to Teresa, the couple finally celebrated the Sacrament of Marriage in the Church. Soon El Pelé was a daily communicant, with a devotion to the Rosary. Though he and his wife were unable to have children, they adopted Teresa's niece Pepita, and Ceferino was a marvelous father and later a grandfather who delighted in his grandchildren.

Ceferino was once accused of selling stolen mules but was able to present documents clearing his name. When he was acquitted, his lawyer proclaimed, "El Pelé is not a thief, he is St. Ceferino, patron of Gypsies."[27] Ceferino walked on his knees to the cathedral to give thanks, but there were no jeers or rolled eyes; people knew that El Pelé was someone special.

After Ceferino's wife died in 1922, he became a Third Order Franciscan and a member of the Society of St. Vincent de Paul. He was so generous that despite his great fortune he became quite poor later in life, "ruined" by his refusal to allow others, particularly poor Roma, to go without. Though he was illiterate, he knew the faith well and became a catechist, captivating children with stories of Jesus before giving them chocolate and sending them on their way. He wore elegant clothes and loved dancing, village fairs, and Roma feasts. All in all, he was a kind and generous old man, much like many kind and generous old men who can be found in every parish in the world.

But Ceferino was also a Catholic living in Spain during the Spanish Civil War. One day he saw a priest being arrested and called for the soldiers to stop. They turned on him, asking if he had a weapon. "Only this," El Pelé answered, holding up his rosary. He was beaten for it and dragged to jail.

In prison he prayed the Rosary faithfully, antagonizing his anti-Catholic captors. An anarchist advised him that if he stopped praying so obviously, his life might be saved. His daughter visited, begging him to give up his rosary. But El Pelé felt that to do so would be to deny his faith. And so the dignified grandfather was executed and thrown in a mass grave. Sixty years later, he became the first of the Romani ever to be beatified.

Ceferino Giménez Malla was an ordinary man whose life was sustained by the very same practices that many of us enjoy. He became a martyr only because of the grace of God and the strength he built through years of saying yes to God in small things. Through his intercession, may we live lives of quiet faithfulness that strengthen us to be heroes when necessary. Bl. Ceferino Giménez Malla, pray for us!

28

Bl. Carlo Acutis

A Teenage Boy with a PlayStation and a Website

---~≈~---

(1991–2006) ✳ Country: Italy
Feast Day: October 12

He had a PlayStation. He made awkward videos with his friends. His favorite cartoon was Pokémon. And he's well on his way to being canonized.

Bl. Carlo Acutis's mother, Antonia, doesn't know how Carlo came to love Jesus. He'd been baptized as a baby, but the family didn't practice the faith. Perhaps, she says, it was their Polish nanny who told Carlo about Jesus. Regardless of the source, Carlo had a deep love for Jesus even as a preschooler, asking his mother if they could stop in to see Jesus when they walked past churches in their Milanese neighborhood and even insisting on taking flowers to place at the feet of the Blessed Mother.

Antonia wasn't sure what to do with her young son's piety, and she wasn't prepared to answer his many questions. But as he asked, she began to wonder as well. His curiosity eventually prompted her to take theology classes, return to Mass, and dive into her faith. "He was like a little savior for me,"[28] she said of the child who pointed her to her true Savior.

Carlo's longing for the Eucharist drove him to ask permission to make his first Holy Communion earlier than was customary. After that, he became a daily communicant. His parents sometimes went with him, but Carlo often went alone. Even when they traveled, Carlo's first order of business was to find a church and figure out Mass times.

And they traveled quite a bit. Carlo's deep love of Mary (whom he called "the only woman in my life"[29]) led the family to Marian apparition sites all over Europe. But their pilgrimages became more intentional when Carlo was eleven and got an idea.

After receiving his first Holy Communion, Carlo had begun to notice that people would stand in line for hours to go to a concert or a soccer game but wouldn't stay even a moment before the tabernacle. Eager to do something to draw souls to Jesus, young Carlo began to research eucharistic miracles, convinced that people would attend Mass if they knew about the miracles of Lanciano, Poznan, and the dozens of others recognized by the Church. He dragged his parents from one shrine to another to pray and to take pictures for the website he was building.

Carlo was something of a prodigy when it came to technology. At eight or nine years old, he used a university-level computer science textbook to teach himself C++ before progressing to Java, Adobe, and Photoshop. From there, he moved into animation and video editing, making videos with his friends and dubbing voiceovers onto videos of his dogs. Carlo's tech savvy resulted in a website documenting nearly 150 miracles, which was eventually developed into an exhibit that has traveled the world.

But Carlo was no computer geek closeted in a back bedroom. For all his technological skill, Carlo was a friendly, outgoing kid. He was so friendly, his family was reluctant to go on walks with him; Carlo couldn't help but stop to talk to every person he passed. He had a sensitive heart and was always looking out for those who were suffering: classmates whose parents were going through a divorce, kids who were being bullied. Carlo's approach was always friendship. And through that friendship, people were drawn to Jesus. As pure and pious as Carlo was, nobody felt judged by him. Being with Carlo filled your heart with a joy that left people seeking and wondering, as Carlo's mother had years before. A young Hindu man who worked for

Carlo's family was baptized as a direct result of his friendship with Carlo, while many others returned to the faith.

Carlo was particularly close to the homeless people in his neighborhood, packing up food most days to take out to his friends on the street. Though his family was wealthy, Carlo had no patience for excess. He saved up his pocket money to buy a sleeping bag for a homeless friend, and when his mother suggested they buy Carlo such "luxuries" as a second pair of shoes, he revolted. Technology, though, wasn't a luxury. It was an important part of his apostolate, and Carlo had no qualms about using three computers when building his website.

Through all this, every day: Mass, the Rosary, and silent time before the tabernacle. Carlo insisted that holiness was impossible otherwise. "The Eucharist is my highway to heaven,"[30] he would say, and nothing could get between him and his daily appointment with the Lord. "The more we receive the Eucharist, the more we will become like Jesus,"[31] Carlo said.

How did he have the time? In between teaching himself to code, playing soccer and basketball, riding his bike around Milan to visit the poor, learning karate, walking his dogs, teaching himself the saxophone, patiently explaining technology to his older relatives, going skiing or canoeing, and making movies? According to his mother, Carlo didn't waste time on useless things. He limited himself to an hour a week of video games (because, he said, he didn't want to become a slave to them) and focused the rest of his time on things that were valuable. But that didn't exclude silly animations or videos of his dogs— Carlo knew that something doesn't need to be catechetical to be valuable, and he enjoyed leisure all the more because its greatest value was in being fun.

Carlo hungered for heaven. "We have always been awaited in heaven,"[32] he said, and throughout his life his eyes were fixed on eternity. So when, at fifteen, he went to the hospital with the flu and was diagnosed instead with acute and untreatable leukemia,

Carlo wasn't upset. He was ready to go home. "I can die happy," he told his mother, "because I haven't wasted even a minute on things that aren't pleasing to God."[33] Within three days, Carlo Acutis was dead.

He was a remarkable young man, but he was also fairly ordinary. He had no visions, worked no miracles. He didn't levitate when he prayed. He just lived like heaven was real. He was completely himself (video games and computer programming and all) but entirely Christ's. On his website, Carlo listed instructions for becoming holy, encouraging people to go to Mass daily and Confession weekly. But his very first rule for becoming holy was this: "You have to want it with all your heart."[34]

This is the legacy of Carlo Acutis: an ordinary, modern kid who watched cartoons, used the internet, and wanted holiness with all his heart. The world loves him because he shows us that holiness is possible—for every one of us, even if you have an Instagram account or you're a gamer. Through his intercession, may we begin to live as though we want holiness with all our hearts. Bl. Carlo Acutis, pray for us!

Part 5
Saints with Difficult Families

When we read about St. Thérèse's family, St. Basil the Great's family, or St. Clare of Assisi's family, it's easy to become discouraged. Holiness begets holiness, we think, and lament our prospects as we tally the instances of abuse, addiction, and adultery in our own family histories. But Saints don't all come from idyllic families, surrounded by loving siblings with doting parents leading them all merrily to heaven. Many were raised in families just as broken as ours, and some found holiness not in spite of their philandering siblings and incompetent parents but because of them.

It's important to note that some Saints are to be admired but not imitated. The Church honors our need to be physically and emotionally safe, and these stories mustn't suggest that people enduring abuse should just stay where they are and learn to offer it up. Like Servant of God Rose Hawthorne Lathrop,[1] we have the right to remove ourselves from abusive situations. But the Saints aren't given to us as models of perfectly prudent choices; we can learn from them (and feel loved by them) even while wondering if some of their decisions were ill advised.

Most of our family difficulties are less extreme than those that follow. Or perhaps the extreme suffering we've endured is something in the past. Regardless, it is a great gift to have a heavenly friend who understands the struggle of life in a dysfunctional family. In this section, you'll find Saints whose difficult families were their paths to holiness or whose wounds were transformed into glory. When we read their stories, we begin to find hope that our frustrating marriages, manipulative siblings, or codependent parents might be not merely a burden but an opportunity for radical holiness. With St. Josemaría Escrivá, may we learn to say, "That person sanctifies me."

29

St. Marguerite Bays

A Saint Who Loved Her Dysfunctional Family

$\approx$

(1815–1879) ✳ Country: Switzerland
Feast Day: June 27

St. Marguerite Bays was a mystic and a stigmatist whose cancer was miraculously healed at the very moment that Bl. Pope Pius IX declared Mary's Immaculate Conception to be a dogma of the Church. When she was young, she made a 250-mile pilgrimage on foot—eleven times. Later, she lived on the Eucharist alone, once receiving it from an angel when no priest was available.

That's all lovely. But what the world needs from Marguerite isn't so much her beautiful piety as her messy family—or rather the fact that the former was possible in the midst of the latter.

The second of seven children in a poor Swiss family, Marguerite was a working-class seamstress who lived at home until her death at sixty-three. The rest of the family was in and out of the same house: her sister who left to get married but came home again after the marriage failed; her younger brother, who had a violent temper and ended up in prison; her nephew, born out of wedlock and entrusted to his Aunt Marguerite to raise.

Marguerite's older brother was the head of the household after their parents died. His wife, Josette, the mistress of the house, hated Marguerite. Josette had been the housemaid before her marriage and may have felt the need to defend her new-found status. That, combined with watching Marguerite dote on her nephew (the illegitimate child of Josette's husband), led this embittered sister-in-law to scorn and slight Marguerite for years. She particularly lashed out at Marguerite for the time she "wasted" in going to Mass daily and retreating to her room to pray. But Marguerite never raised her voice, never criticized Josette. She loved her unlovable sister-in-law, and by that love she chipped away at Josette's stony heart. Eventually Marguerite became so dear to the mistress of the house that when Josette lay dying she would allow none but Marguerite to nurse her. And Marguerite, who would have had every right to refuse to offer such generosity to a woman who had treated her so badly, delighted in staying by her side until the end.

None of this was the result of chance. Marguerite wasn't trapped in her family situation. A woman like her could easily have found a convent to accept her, even without the money for a dowry. But Marguerite felt called to stay home. Perhaps she saw that her family needed her. Perhaps she saw that she needed them, needed to learn generosity and patience in the crucible of a dysfunctional family. Perhaps she really enjoyed them—conflict, drama, and brawling brothers notwithstanding. Whatever the reason, Marguerite spent all her sixty-three years dealing with her family, with snippy remarks from a sister-in-law who resented her presence and her "wasted time" in prayer; with tears from a sister whose life had fallen apart; with gossip from neighbors who delighted in the shame of the illegitimate child or the prison sentence or the arguments between the brother who was a mayor and the brother who was a convict. Through it all, Marguerite stayed.

Marguerite was a godmother and a catechist, an aunt and a foster mother. She was a lover of the poor (whom she called "God's favorites") and tended them in sickness and death. She was a spiritual mother to the town's children, with whom she both played and prayed. She was a constant call to holiness, happy to ignore sarcastic remarks made at her expense but quick to put a stop to criticism of anyone else. She was a mystic and a stigmatist, a Third Order Franciscan who lived with chronic pain.

But what's most inspiring about Marguerite Bays is that she had a hard family to love and she loved them anyway. There was drama and intrigue, and she loved them anyway. They were faithless and ungrateful, and she loved them anyway. Her sister-in-law detested her, and she loved her anyway. Her brother was a criminal, and she loved him anyway. She knew that their sin, their suffering, their anger and disdain didn't define her, so she loved them anyway. If that's not the kind of Saint we need for family life, I don't know what is. Through her intercession, may God give us all the patience and selflessness to love our families well. St. Marguerite Bays, pray for us!

30

SERVANT OF GOD ROSE HAWTHORNE LATHROP

A Frivolous Socialite Who Left Her Alcoholic Husband

(1851–1926) ✳ Country: United States

Servant of God Rose Hawthorne Lathrop might have ended life as a footnote on the biography of her father, famed American author Nathaniel Hawthorne. Instead, her followers hope this descendant of Puritans will soon be canonized.

The youngest of Hawthorne's three children, Rose was raised in Massachusetts but spent much of her childhood in Europe, where she was first exposed to Catholicism. She was an impetuous and moody young woman, prone to rash judgment and passionate repentance. Though her beloved father had taught her to love the poor, Rose was disinclined to get her hands dirty in the process. She was disgusted by dirt and disease. When her older sister Una remarked that she would like to help unwashed children in the slums, Rose replied, shuddering, "Let other people do it."

As a teenager, Rose fell in love with the poet and author George Parson Lathrop. When he proposed to the twenty-year-old Rose, Una insisted that George was hers and had jilted her. Una raged against the treacherous Rose (who was baffled by the whole affair) and became so unstable that she had to be committed to an asylum so the young couple could make their escape—a debacle Rose's brother later used as inspiration for a novel featuring a love triangle. From this point, relations between Rose and her siblings were often disagreeable, and occasionally publicly hostile as they battled through various disagreements in the press.

It was an inauspicious beginning to a tumultuous marriage, one Rose's brother immediately declared, "an error, not to be repaired." Though the couple struggled financially, they found their footing in the New York social scene as published authors and popular party guests. Rose illustrated children's books as well as writing poetry and the occasional book, though her father had loathed the idea of female writers.

When Rose was twenty-five, she gave birth to a son, Francis. Drawn to Catholicism from her youth, she had the baby baptized a Catholic, though she and George remained unaffiliated to any particular denomination. After Francis's birth, Rose suffered from postpartum depression and psychosis to the point that the baby was taken from her and she was sent to an asylum for a time. Once she had recovered, Rose and George entered into the only peaceful time in their marriage. Both were inclined to wax poetic over their married bliss; George once wrote of Rose and Francis, "They do tempt one to write poems; but I never feel I can quite do them justice, so I just go on loving them in prose." But when five-year-old Francis died of diphtheria, things began to unravel.

Always a social drinker, George began to drink heavily, while Rose immersed herself in her writing. They traveled from one country to another, often separately, and tried to ignore their grief. Their search for healing and meaning took them to the Catholic Church, which they entered ten years after Francis's death, shocking their Protestant friends and family, most of whom had imbibed the anti-Catholic spirit of the age.

But conversion doesn't necessarily heal addiction, and George's drinking had spiraled out of control, leaving Rose concerned for her safety. Though she loved her husband, she knew that love wasn't enough to heal him. Four years after their conversion, Rose appealed to diocesan authorities for an ecclesiastical separation of spouses and it was granted. In the eyes of the Church, Rose was a married woman who (by necessity) lived apart from her husband; in the eyes of society, she was a Papist convert and a divorcée.

Rose had no real idea of what she was going to do when she left George, but she had been disturbed by the death of her friend Emma Lazarus (who wrote the poem inscribed on the base of the Statue of Liberty). Having seen how her rich friend Emma died, Rose wondered what indignities the poor suffered in their last months. So the stylish society matron took a three-month nursing course, where she surprised her instructors when she didn't flee in disgust on the first morning. But Rose knew she must overcome her deep aversion to ugliness and filth if she was to serve.

Rose had loved her life as a socialite, but she soon realized that she couldn't serve as she had been called and maintain such a life. She later wrote, "I remember that on the day when I realized there would be no more time for me to paint in oils or watercolors again if I attended faithfully to the work heaven seemed to be giving me to perform, it was as if a sword entered my bosom and I said, 'O God, I cannot make that one sacrifice for You.' But all the same I knew I should make it."[2] She had sacrificed much to enter the Church, suffered much in the loss of her son and then her husband; still, it's often small sacrifices that seem the most daunting.

Rose left high society behind, rented a room in the slums, and worked to earn the trust of the people so that she could come into their homes and nurse them for free. She did housework and bathed wounds. She invited the poorest to live with her. Her goal in all she did was to live in such a way that "if our Lord knocked at the door we would not be ashamed to show what we had done."[3]

A few years after Rose began this work, she received word that her estranged husband, George, was dying of cirrhosis of the liver. She rushed to his bedside but arrived just after he died. Rose knelt by his body, prayed for his soul, and then returned home and began to wonder what the future might hold.

Rose was now free to enter religious life. She and a young woman named Alice Huber eventually became Dominican tertiaries and founded the Servants of Relief for Incurable Cancer. Soon Mother Mary Alphonsa (Rose) and Sr. Mary Rose (Alice) were dressed in a Dominican habit and began to receive new vocations to their order.

From the very beginning, Mother Alphonsa was committed to serving the poorest of the poor. She accepted no payment from her patients or from their friends and relatives, instead appealing to benefactors through newspaper articles explaining her needs.

Perhaps the most remarkable element of Mother Alphonsa's approach to care was her desire that her patients enjoy themselves as much as possible, even if it meant splurging on some luxuries for them. She bought a dog for one patient and a parrot for another. Indeed, there was such joy to be found in her home that it wasn't unusual for a victim of this devastating disease to cry out with delight, "This is heaven!"[4]

When Mother Alphonsa had realized her call to serve the terminally ill, she later said, "I set my whole being to endeavor to bring hope to the cancerous poor."[5] Mother Alphonsa's mission was not so much relief as hope. Though she wanted to assuage her patients' suffering, her primary purpose was to draw their souls to the heart of Jesus. It was through her attraction to lovely things and her passion for life that Mother Alphonsa was able to lead souls to Jesus. Though earlier in life she had lamented her attachment to the things of this world, once grounded in the love of God, it became her greatest gift in the thirty years she served the incurably ill before her death at seventy-five.

Rose Hawthorne Lathrop is a testimony to the power of God to transform absolutely anybody—not only grave sinners but also socialites enmeshed in family drama and consumed by love of frivolities. Her holiness came not in a rejection of all that she had been but in its perfection; her writing talent was turned to fundraising, her charming personality to delighting the residents in her home. Rose became more herself, even as she sacrificed so much of what she loved. Through her intercession, may God purify in us what is not of him, and strengthen all that is. Servant of God Rose Hawthorne Lathrop, pray for us!

ST. MARGUERITE D'YOUVILLE

A Pioneer Woman with a Dramatic Life

———— ≈ ————

(1701–1771) ✳ Country: Canada
Feast Day: December 23

The lives of some Saints read like fairy tales. Others read more like soap operas. St. Marguerite d'Youville's was one of the latter, but melodramatic beginnings didn't prevent her from reaching a saintly end.

Born in Quebec to an aristocratic family, Marguerite's life seemed charmed at first. But her father died when she was seven, and the family found itself living in dire poverty, depending on the charity of others. At twelve, Marguerite had to leave school to work and help care for her five brothers and sisters, but she was charismatic and beautiful and had caught the eye of a wealthy young man who seemed about to propose marriage. Then Marguerite's widowed mother made an imprudent match, and the nobleman who had been courting Marguerite severed the relationship. She soon found herself married to a very different type of man.

François d'Youville was a bootlegger and a cheat, a man who thought less of his wife than of his overbearing, live-in mother. His business practices were unethical at best and illegal at worst, with the added bonus of being ineffective. He squandered the wealth he'd inherited while his unloved wife buried one child after another, losing four altogether.

After only eight years of marriage, François died, leaving nothing but debts to his wife and two surviving sons. The

Pray for Us

family's poverty worsened, and Marguerite opened a store to try to pay off her late husband's debts. Destitute, grief-stricken, and exhausted, Marguerite had every reason to despair. But even in her trials, she was possessed of a supernatural hope that caused her confessor to say to her shortly after her husband's death, "Console yourself, Madame, God has destined you for great works, and you will rebuild a crumbling house."[6]

Even in those early years, Marguerite lived a spirit of generosity that seems almost impossible given what she herself was suffering. She gave alms, visited the sick and imprisoned, and begged money to pay for the burial of criminals. Before long, she had gathered some other women to her side, and in 1737 she founded the Congregation of the Sisters of Charity of Montreal.

This community sprang from its foundress's conviction that all men and women are brothers and sisters. But despite all the good she sought to do, it took some time for Mother Marguerite to escape the shadow of her husband's reputation. In the early years, she and her sisters were called *les Soeurs Grises*, a play on words that meant, in the slang of the time, both "the Grey Nuns" and "the Drunk Nuns." Mother Marguerite embraced this name, eager to encourage the sisters to grow in humility even when false rumors about their drunkenness led priests to deny them Communion.

Her religious life was no easier than her married life had been. Sick, maligned, and poor as ever, Mother Marguerite watched the home the sisters shared with the poor and infirm burn to the ground in 1745. As she looked at the ashes, she smiled, telling her sisters that their life up to that point had been too comfortable; from then on, they would live more like those they served.

For the next two years, the sisters moved from one place to the next, with nowhere to call home. But in 1747, Mother Marguerite was asked to take over the General Hospital of Montreal, which was in a shocking state of disrepair. Though she was so weak that she had to be carried to her new home in a cart, Mother Marguerite was equal to the task and before long the hospital was running beautifully and admitting people of all races, classes, and abilities.

The government tried unsuccessfully to take the hospital from Mother Marguerite once she had repaired and reformed it. In 1765, the hospital burned to the ground; Mother Marguerite knelt in the ashes and sang praise to God, then began to rebuild. Finally, after seventy exhausting years, Mother Marguerite bade goodbye to her tragic life, a life that left her the mother of two priests, the foundress of an order that would be home to thousands of sisters over the years, an agent of social reform, and one of the greatest Catholic women yet to live in the New World.

Marguerite d'Youville could have despaired a dozen times in her life, overcome by her circumstances and unable to see anything but her own sorrow. Instead, she made her suffering a springboard to serving others in pain. Through her intercession, may God fill with hope all those for whom everything seems to go wrong, and may they be strengthened to offer their suffering for others. St. Marguerite d'Youville, pray for us!

BL. VICTOIRE RASOAMANARIVO

*The Married Woman Who Defied Her Family
to Lead the Church in Madagascar*

―――――※―――――

(1848–1894) ✳ Country: Madagascar
Feast Day: August 21

Bl. Victoire Rasoamanarivo was born to a prominent family in Madagascar, where Christianity was illegal. Along with most of the Malagasy people, Victoire practiced a sort of ancestor worship. When she was thirteen, however, the queen who had outlawed Christianity died and foreign missionaries began to preach publicly again. That same year, Victoire was enrolled in a school run by the Sisters of St. Joseph of Cluny. Their witness and instruction transformed her and she decided to be baptized at the age of fifteen.

Victoire's family had stood alongside the persecuting queen. When Victoire told them of her decision to enter the Catholic Church, they were appalled. They pulled her out of Catholic school and sent her to a Protestant one instead, but Victoire's faith remained strong. Finally, citing her baptism as a betrayal of her race, they swore that if she went through with it, they wouldn't bury her with her family—the most profound act of rejection possible in Malagasy society. But Victoire was unmoved, declaring to her unsympathetic family that the missionaries would bury her with them. She was received into the Church and not kicked out of her family home, though tensions remained high.

Victoire's heart was fixed on Christ and she wanted to become a sister. But a desire to belong completely to Christ doesn't necessarily indicate a religious vocation, and the Sisters of St. Joseph pointed out that if she were to enter, her powerful family could make life intolerable for all Catholics in the country. Victoire prayed and ultimately submitted, allowing her parents to arrange her marriage to the son of her uncle the prime minister.

Unfortunately, her husband, Radriaka, was a cruel man, a drunk and a lecher. Even his own father urged Victoire to divorce him. But whatever verbal abuse her husband hurled at her Victoire accepted as a sacrifice to offer for his conversion. Though she had the right to leave for her own safety, Victoire refused.

For a time, Victoire lived a life of quiet joy and faith, interspersed with conflicts with both her husband and her family of origin. But only a few years after her marriage, Protestantism became the official religion of Madagascar and persecutions began—subtle for most Malagasy Catholics, but overt for Victoire. Her uncle criticized and threatened her day and night. Her family had slaves throw stones at her and once set an assassin on her. Her husband demanded that she leave her faith in submission to him. But still Victoire loved well and prayed hard, spending hours a day in prayer despite her many duties at court.

In 1883, the persecution of Catholics became more severe during the Franco-Malagasy War. All foreign missionaries were expelled from Madagascar; as they left, the priests entrusted the country's Catholics to Victoire, who was just the woman for the job. When the government locked the churches, she presented herself before the queen and the prime minister to object. When they stationed soldiers outside the churches to bar entry for prayer, Victoire calmly approached the armed men, saying, "If you must have blood, begin by shedding mine. Fear will not keep us from assembling for prayer."[7] She stared them down,

Pray for Us

then led the assembled community into the church. Though the Eucharist was gone and there was no Mass, still they prayed. Victoire explained, "I place before my mind the missionaries saying the Mass, and mentally attend all the Masses being said throughout the world."[8]

Victoire encouraged Madagascar's Catholic communities, ensured that they had proper catechesis, and defended them in the face of government abuse. When the priests were readmitted three years later, they found a community of twenty-one thousand Catholics on fire for their faith. Victoire acknowledged that had she become a sister as she had hoped, none of this would have been possible.

In 1888, Victoire's husband suffered a fall; when it became clear that his injuries were fatal, he asked for Baptism. Victoire baptized him herself and saw the fruit of years of sacrifice as her husband died in a state of grace. She spent the next six years praying, serving, loving, and refusing to compromise in matters of faith. Though she had no children, she became a spiritual mother to Catholics across Madagascar. She worked with prisoners, lepers, and the abandoned poor. When the uncle who had so persecuted her fell out of favor with the court, she cared for him as well. Finally, at the age of forty-six, this strong and courageous leader went home peacefully to Christ.

Victoire Rasoamanarivo used her privilege to speak truth to those in power, fearless of the consequences she might face—even when those powerful people were her family. Through her intercession, may God give us the courage to do the same. Bl. Victoire Rasoamanarivo, pray for us!

Part 6

Saints Who Found Holiness through Suffering

I expect that if there's one thing we know about the Saints, it's that they suffered. Often we're so struck by the strength with which they endured, we forget that suffering is hard even for the holy. But while some Saints smiled as the flames licked at their toes, there were many who didn't delight in their suffering, who were heartbroken, devastated by grief, and by pain. Their stories stand before us not as a condemnation of our inclination to complain in far less trying circumstances but as a consolation: you are not alone in your suffering. You aren't alone in your anger, your fear, or even your temptation to despair. Your older brothers and sisters in the faith have been there, and they will walk with you.

It is a great mercy that we have so many Saints to look to who found holiness through suffering, through torture, chronic pain, loss, or betrayal. As we read their stories, we're reminded of the truth that our struggles are not an indication that God has abandoned us. Instead, we see the trust that grew in their hearts as their suffering united them to Christ. But we also see the anguish, the exhaustion, and the fear, and we're reminded that God can handle our honest reaction to suffering, our honest response to him.

The Saints you'll meet here are not men and women who smiled beatifically as they endured unimaginable pain. They're flesh-and-blood people who wrestled with God in their pain but never walked away from him. They teach us that holiness is found not in the supernatural removal of our difficulties but in our willingness to follow Christ, whatever path we may find ourselves on. The suffering of these Saints is an invitation, a reminder that it's possible to suffer well. It's also a consolation, a promise that you are still loved in the moments when it's too much to bear.

BL. BENEDETTA
BIANCHI PORRO

*The Medical Student Who Went Blind and
Deaf but Refused to Despair*

———— ≈ ————

(1936–1964) ✳ Country: Italy
Feast Day: January 23

Bl. Benedetta Bianchi Porro was thirteen when she began to go deaf. Though she was able to read lips quite well, it wasn't always enough, particularly once she began medical school. One day, while asking to have an oral exam question repeated, she explained to her professor that she was losing her hearing. "Who ever heard of a deaf doctor?" he demanded, as her classmates laughed. Flinging a book across the room in fury, he failed her.

Her own doctors were no more sympathetic. They ignored her concerns, calling her symptoms psychosomatic. But Benedetta refused to be put off. She researched her increasing deafness and impaired vision and soon diagnosed herself with von Recklinghausen's disease, a neurological condition that would ultimately rob her of all five of her senses before leaving her paralyzed.

Benedetta was used to doctors. Having suffered from polio as an infant she had a permanent limp and wore a back brace. And while she had endured teasing at the hands of other children, it was something else for a professor to attack her for her disability. But Benedetta had never been inclined toward bitterness, so she persevered. She continued her studies, even when the horror of her diagnosis caused her to panic and tempted her to despair.

"There are times," she wrote to a dear friend, "that I would like to throw myself out the window."[1] The raw humanity of Benedetta's writings offers such hope to those of us who struggle to embrace suffering. So many Saints throughout history, it seems, rejoiced at the opportunity to suffer. Benedetta did not. Still she found herself growing ever closer to Christ in her affliction, finding peace in him that the world had never been able to offer her. She spoke of how miraculous life seemed, of the freedom she found in her increasing paralysis, and of joy: "As to my spirit, I am completely calm, and even much more—I am happy."[2]

Benedetta was happy. Except when she wasn't. This was the tension she lived with: she was a woman who loved the Lord deeply, but the joy she found in him didn't erase her suffering and isolation.

Benedetta's blindness progressed. A surgery left her paralyzed from the waist down, and she was forced to withdraw from school just a year shy of earning her medical degree. In this suffering, she wrote to a friend: "Sometimes I find myself defeated under the weight of this heavy cross. Then, I call upon Jesus and lovingly cast myself at His feet; He kindly permits me to rest my head on His lap. Do you understand, Maria Grazia? Do you understand the ecstatic joy of those moments?"[3]

She went to Lourdes seeking a cure, but the girl in the bed next to her was cured instead. Though Benedetta felt a moment of sorrow that the good fortune hadn't been hers, she collected herself and offered herself once more to Jesus, refusing to resent the girl who had been healed. Instead, she rejoiced in the peace God had given her. After a later visit to Lourdes, she said, "I am aware more than ever of the richness of my condition and I don't desire anything but to continue in it. This has been for me the miracle of Lourdes this year."[4]

Pray for Us

Soon she was blind and deaf and could move nothing except her left hand. Her friends and family could communicate with her only by the excruciatingly slow process of spelling in sign language on her cheek, which she could still feel. But Benedetta could speak, though weakly, and she continued to tell of God's goodness, even as she lay in agony. "I do not lack hope," Benedetta said. "I know that at the end of the road, Jesus is waiting for me. . . . I have discovered that God exists, that He is love, faithfulness, joy, certitude, to the end of the ages. My days are not easy. They are hard. But sweet because Jesus is with me."[5]

Benedetta was no saccharine Saint with a smile plastered on her face whatever her suffering. She acknowledged the pain, the difficulty, the temptation to despair. But in her suffering, she found herself drawn more deeply into the heart of Jesus. And the more she knew his unceasing love, the more radiant she became, inviting others to love him too. She died at twenty-seven, having lived a life in which nothing was wasted. Everything was received with love and offered back to the God whose love gives meaning to our suffering.

Benedetta Bianchi Porro is a beautiful Saint for people with disabilities, medical students, Deaf people who experience discrimination, and people dismissed by their doctors. More than anything, she's a witness of honest suffering, of the fact that even Saints can be tempted to despair. Holiness means not that we delight in all miserable circumstances but that we choose to trust in Jesus' love, even when all around us is darkness and pain. Through her intercession, may we learn to suffer well, even when we are tempted to lose hope. Bl. Benedetta Bianchi Porro, pray for us!

VEN. RUTILIO GRANDE

A Heroic Priest Plagued by Mental Illness

———— ≈ ————

(1928–1977) ✳ Country: El Salvador

Ven. Rutilio Grande, the youngest of six children, was born into poverty in El Salvador. His parents divorced when he was four and his father moved to Honduras looking for work. Accounts of his mother's whereabouts vary, either claiming that she died or telling of another family that she began after abandoning her six children. In the absence of his parents, Rutilio was raised by his grandmother and older siblings. The children tried to eke out a living by farming their small plot of land under exploitative conditions from the landlords, but it was always a struggle.

A quiet and serious boy, Rutilio left his hometown at twelve and spent years in formation, first as a diocesan seminarian and later as a Jesuit. Throughout this time, Rutilio suffered from persistent anxiety and struggled with scrupulosity, both of which reached a crisis point when he had the first of two nervous breakdowns. He was diagnosed with catatonic schizophrenia, a condition that is often fleeting but was likely the result of years of anxiety and rooted in his childhood trauma. Rutilio was hospitalized and soon made a full recovery, but he had a similar experience the following year, again requiring some time in a mental hospital. He became physically weaker when his mental health was out of control, and his second breakdown had long-term physical effects on the young Jesuit.

Despite serious concerns that he wasn't fit for religious life, Rutilio was ultimately ordained a Jesuit priest at the age of

Pray for Us

thirty-one. But ordination wasn't the end of Fr. Rutilio's struggles with mental health. In fact, the day after his ordination he was overwhelmed by anxiety in the form of scruples that he couldn't shake for years. His anxiety was expressed in self-doubt, an obsessive conviction that he was unworthy of his vocation. But Fr. Rutilio had come to understand that anxiety was not a moral failing; it was a reality that he could embrace for love of Jesus and offer up as a sacrifice. After a few years of counseling, he emerged from this crisis as well, though he continued to live with mental illness.

When Fr. Rutilio returned to El Salvador after many years abroad, he was a respected priest entering a town where he had grown up an impoverished and abandoned child. There may have been some temptation to exult in his newfound status, but the newly ordained priest wanted nothing more than to be with and among his people. He insisted that they feed him whatever they had on hand, rather than making sacrifices to impress him. Even in later years, when diabetes restricted his diet, he was careful to ask for nothing beyond what his people could afford to offer. While working at the seminary, he helped to change the culture of priestly formation to be less formal and distant and more fatherly, immersing seminarians in the communities they were called to serve.

Fr. Rutilio's experience of poverty as a child made him a powerful advocate for the poor, speaking out on issues of social justice even when it led people to accuse him of being a Communist. The oppressive Salvadoran government wanted priests to stay out of the business of social and economic reform, and most of them, wary of anticipated consequences, were happy to comply. Even St. Oscar Romero, then auxiliary bishop of San Salvador and a close friend of Fr. Rutilio, was disinclined to oppose the injustice perpetrated by this regime.

But not Fr. Rutilio. His writings earned him quite a bit of negative attention, and his revolutionary approach to seminary formation began to be viewed with suspicion. Finally, he withdrew from his work at the seminary to focus on pastoral ministry in the region where he was raised. There, his outspoken witness and subversive preaching earned him a bloody death alongside two of his parishioners: Ven. Manuel Solórzano and Ven. Nelson Rutilio Lemus Chávez. All three were shot while driving together to the church in Fr. Rutilio's hometown.

But Fr. Rutilio's life wasn't wasted and neither was his death. It was his murder that precipitated Archbishop Romero's conversion of heart and led to his activism and ultimate martyrdom and Sainthood. When the archbishop looked upon the body of his murdered friend, there was a change in him. He later explained his sudden transformation from nervous, bookish priest to outspoken activist: "When I looked at Rutilio lying there dead I thought, 'If they have killed him for doing what he did, then I too have to walk the same path.'"[6] Pope Francis called this change in Archbishop Romero Fr. Rutilio's "great miracle."

Rutilio Grande was a broken, struggling man whose reliance on Jesus won him a martyr's crown and changed the face of the Church in El Salvador. Through his intercession, may those who struggle with mental illness come to understand that God has not abandoned them and that their illness does not disqualify them from the pursuit of holiness. Ven. Rutilio Grande, pray for us!

St. Magdalena Son So-byok

A Mother Who Buried Nine Babies

————— ≋ —————

(1801–1840) ✳ Country: South Korea
Feast Day: January 31

St. Magdalena Son So-byok was the mother of a young daughter when she lost her second child as an infant. And her third. And her fourth.

Nine children in a row. All died as infants. Finally, another little girl survived, a balm for the grieving mother's soul, though she must surely have ached for the little ones she had buried. Still, she and her husband trusted in God's goodness even in their unrelenting sorrow.

Magdalena's suffering didn't start with the loss of her children. Her mother died when she was small, and her father was exiled from Korea for his faith. Raised by her grandmother, she was very shy, a talented seamstress with a particular gift for embroidery. When she was seventeen she married St. Peter Choe Chang-hub and they began their years of alternating (and intermingling) hope and grief as they welcomed and then buried nine children in a row.

As they clung to their eleventh child, hoping that this one would live, their oldest daughter (St. Barbara Choe Yong-i) married a holy man (St. Charles Cho Shin-chol), and they delighted in their first grandson. But their joy was not to last. In 1839, when their baby was only two, Peter and Magdalena were arrested along with Barbara. When Charles heard of it, he presented himself to the authorities as well. Peter and Charles were taken to one part of the prison while Magdalena and Barbara were imprisoned with Barbara's infant son and Magdalena's young daughter.

The mothers knew this prison cell was no place for children. More than that: they knew themselves. They might be able to endure torture, but would they be able to resist the cries of their starving babies? Or would they break, apostatizing to save their children when they would never have done such a thing to save themselves? The decision was clear: their children must be entrusted to family. And so Magdalena, who had buried nine children, sent a tenth away. Then, with her firstborn, she prepared to be tortured.

Peter, Magdalena, Charles, and Barbara were tortured, but they were not cowed. Perhaps they had been strengthened by years of suffering. Perhaps they were inspired by those who had gone before, particularly Peter's brother Bl. John Choe Chang-hyeon (killed in 1801). Perhaps it was pure grace. But each one remained faithful.

Magdalena in particular had learned how to suffer. Her years of grieving and longing, of enduring childbirth only for her heart to be broken over and again, had taught her that only by grace could she survive, whether her suffering was physical or emotional. When asked yet again to deny the Lord, she said, "If God did not give me help, with my own strength I would not be able to endure even the bedbugs or fleas which burrow into my flesh and eat it. Only God can give the strength to endure pain."[7] He had sustained her through the anguish of burying one child after another, of leaving her youngest behind while watching her oldest brutalized. He would give her strength to offer her life for him as well.

Charles was killed in September, asking his executioners to tell his family to meet him in heaven. Late in December, Peter too was taken to his death, encouraging his family not to mourn but to meet him again with the crown of martyrdom. Magdalena was killed a month after her husband, Barbara the following day. Finally, the family who had spent so many years with empty arms and aching hearts was reunited with their little ones, children whose loss had drawn them into the pierced heart of Jesus and whose intercession had made it possible for them to persevere amid all their suffering.

If your grief seems unbearable, let Magdalena Son So-byok and her family carry it alongside you for a bit. They've been there. Through their intercession, may those who grieve find comfort. St. Magdalena Son So-byok, pray for us!

VEN. CORNELIA CONNELLY

*A Woman Who Didn't Hate Her
Ex-Priest Ex-Husband Even after He Took Her Children*

---≈---

(1809–1879) ✳ Country: United States, England

Ven. Cornelia Connelly is a woman who knew suffering but managed to live with joy. Born into a wealthy Philadelphia family, Cornelia Peacock married Pierce Connelly, an Episcopalian clergyman, and moved with him to frontier country. But Pierce was very unhappy in what seemed to be a dead-end position and began to question his Episcopalian faith. Before long, he renounced his priesthood and entered the Catholic Church. But Pierce, always focused on success and worldly recognition, felt convinced that he needed to become a priest, even though at that time doing so would require him to separate from his wife and small children.

Deeply in love with her husband, Cornelia was distraught, asking a trusted priest, "Is it necessary for Pierce to make this sacrifice, and sacrifice me? I love my husband; I love my darling children. Why must I give them up?"[8] But her suffering had only begun. Her infant daughter died suddenly. Not long after that, her two-year-old son was knocked into a vat of boiling sugar. Cornelia held him as he slowly died, forty-three hours of agony.

Still, Pierce was determined to become a priest. He asked his grieving wife to agree to a separation and a life of perpetual continence. Though she begged him to reconsider for the sake of their family, Pierce was adamant that he could not be happy if he wasn't ordained. Mourning the loss of her marriage, Cornelia agreed to give all to God, made a vow of continence, and moved to England, where she founded the Society of the Holy Child Jesus. In order to do so, her bishop required her two younger children, ages ten and five, to join their oldest brother in going off to boarding school. In anguish, Cornelia obeyed, and made vows as a religious sister within the year.

Mother Cornelia began to find peace amid all her troubles, but the newly ordained Pierce was becoming more and more unstable, eventually demanding to see Mother Cornelia. When she refused, he brought a lawsuit against her demanding his conjugal rights, despite having relinquished them years before. He renounced his Catholic priesthood and his faith, accused Mother Cornelia of improprieties with a bishop, and declared that he was attempting to rescue her from the Church. The English press naturally had a field day with this court case, particularly when Pierce won. Mercifully, Mother Cornelia was granted an appeal and was never made to return to the husband who had forced her to leave him and then attempted to coerce her to break her vows as a religious.

Pierce responded to this defeat by abducting their children and poisoning their minds against their mother and the Catholic Church. He ended his life an Episcopalian priest in Florence, bitter to his death against the Church that he had once served. Mercer, their oldest, died at age twenty. In her grief and worry over his soul, Mother Cornelia needed something to steady her; while she certainly turned to prayer, she also assigned herself geometry problems to work through each day as a way of focusing her mind on something other than anxiety. And while their daughter Adeline returned to the faith after Pierce's death, their son Frank died as angry and anti-Catholic as his father.

But Mother Cornelia was still a woman of joy. She didn't pretend that her suffering was delightful; indeed, she said that the Society of the Holy Child Jesus had been "founded on a broken heart."[9] Still, she saw smiling as a gift she could offer to God and to her community. Asked once why she wasn't miserable with all she had suffered, Mother Cornelia replied, "Ah, my child, the tears are always running down the back of my nose."[10] Mother Cornelia grieved deeply but chose still to live in the joy of the risen Christ. She refused to become bitter, saying, "We have all a large share of suffering, and if we had not, we should never become Christ-like as we ought."[11]

Cornelia Connelly's ability to cling to the Lord and continue to trust him, even when trusting him seemed to have destroyed her happy life, is a witness to us all. Rather than cursing, abandoning, or resenting God, she chose love. Through her intercession, may God bless all who harbor resentment against him for suffering they see as his fault. May we accept God's will (even when it's painful) and love him all the more for it. Ven. Cornelia Connelly, pray for us!

37

BL. ZDENKA SCHELINGOVÁ

The Sister Who Defied Communists and Died Abandoned by Everyone She Loved

———— ≈ ————

(1916–1955) ✳ Country: Slovakia
Feast Day: July 31

Some Saints would have seemed absolutely ordinary had they not lived in extraordinary times. Bl. Zdenka Schelingová was just such a one, a good sister who was forced to greatness by the circumstances of her life.

Born to a large Slovakian family in 1916, she studied nursing and radiology before entering the Sisters of Charity of the Holy Cross. Sr. Zdenka then began to work in the radiology department of the hospital where her community served. For fifteen years, Sr. Zdenka lived a life poured out for Christ and his people, saying, "In my hospital service, I go from the altar of God to the altar of my work."[12]

It was these years of ordinary faithfulness that prepared Sr. Zdenka for the trial that was to come. When the Communists took over from the Nazis, the situation for the Church in Slovakia went from bad to worse. Religious orders were disbanded. Priests fled the country. Those who helped them flee were convicted of treason. To protect the community, Sr. Zdenka's provincial superior asked the sisters not to resist the restrictions imposed on them by the Communist government. Always obedient, Sr. Zdenka did as she was told—until one day, when compliance would cost a man's life. At that point, her years of faithfulness bore fruit in heroism.

A condemned priest was brought to the hospital where she worked. Hearing that he was bound for Siberia and death, Sr. Zdenka slipped sleeping pills into the tea of the guard on duty and smuggled the priest to safety, guided by contacts of hers who would help him over the border into Austria. Immediately afterward, she went to the chapel, knelt before the Blessed Sacrament, and prayed, "Jesus, I offer my life for his. Save him!"[13]

It seems her sacrifice was accepted; a few days later, Sr. Zdenka attempted to smuggle three priests and three seminarians out of the country and was caught, arrested, and thrown into prison. Sentenced to twelve years, she was strangled, beaten, and thrown into solitary confinement. She was kicked repeatedly in the right breast, which was torn apart and later became cancerous, after which she was given a partial mastectomy in a prison hospital without anesthesia.

And yet with all this suffering, Sr. Zdenka clung to hope. "Do not be afraid to suffer," she said. "God always gives the necessary strength and courage."[14] As she was moved from one freezing, filthy prison to another, it soon became clear that her health was declining rapidly. Rather than allow her to die in prison and seem a martyr to the people, officials released her.

But Sr. Zdenka's suffering didn't end when she left prison. She had already learned that her fellow sisters saw her attempts to save the lives of priests as acts of disobedience; the sisters had been ordered not to resist, and Sr. Zdenka had been a renegade. Unsure what welcome she would receive, Sr. Zdenka made her way to the hospital she had worked at in Bratislava. She asked to be allowed in and was told that the superior feared what the police would say if they consorted with a convict. Her motherhouse said the same, and soon this bride of Christ who had offered her whole life to him was homeless and dying, abandoned because she had been faithful to God's laws.

Finally, Sr. Zdenka found a home with her friend Apolonia. Only a week later, she was taken to a hospital where she died at the age of thirty-eight. But just before her death, she looked to Apolonia and said, "Forgiveness is the greatest thing in life."[15]

Zdenka Schelingová was later pardoned by the authorities and declared a martyr by the Church. But this martyrdom was only possible because of her willingness to make small sacrifices, to be obedient in small things, and to suffer well. Through her intercession, may we live holy ordinary lives in preparation for the call we may one day hear to do something extraordinary. And when we feel abandoned and alone, may we cling to Christ. Bl. Zdenka Schelingová, pray for us!

38

STS. COLUMBA KIM HYO-IM AND AGNES KIM HYO-JU

Sisters Who Survived Sexual Assault but Gave Their Lives for Jesus

———— ≈ ————

(1814–1839) and (1816–1839) ✳ Country: South Korea
Feast Days: September 26 and September 3

St. Columba Kim Hyo-im was a fighter. Her sister St. Agnes Kim Hyo-ju was inclined to keep her mouth shut. As children, they both heard about Jesus from their mother. But their father had no interest in the Christian faith and insisted that his wife and six children have nothing to do with the Catholic Church. During his life, they obeyed. But when the patriarch of the family died, every one of his children joined their mother in being baptized. Columba, Agnes, and their younger sister Clara were so thoroughly converted that together they made private vows of virginity, choosing to belong only to Jesus.

Their mother was dismayed when she heard this. There was no room in Korean society for a woman who chose to remain single, much less three such women! But her daughters insisted, so she helped them to style their hair as married women and sent them to live with their brother, perhaps hoping that in a new town people would assume the sisters had husbands living elsewhere.

In their brother's home, the sisters focused on prayer, fasting, and almsgiving, until a persecution broke out and a neighbor reported the family as Christians. Soldiers raided the house, and while many of the family members escaped, Columba and Agnes were apprehended. As the soldiers dragged them from their home, Agnes meekly hung her head. But Columba, on seeing the rough way her sister was being handled, rebuked the guards. With great dignity, she insisted that they would go quietly. There was no need to abuse them.

The sisters were interrogated and tortured, but they smiled beatifically through it all. They didn't make a sound, not even to call on the name of Jesus. Their torturers took this as a challenge and redoubled their efforts, desperate to break the two young women. When they refused to deny their faith, they were dragged once more before the judge, who was baffled by their commitment and composure.

"You're adults. Why aren't you married yet?" he demanded. Columba explained that they were consecrated to the Lord. When Agnes echoed this response, the judge had an idea.

Physical torture couldn't break the will of these women, but perhaps if he could attack their virginity,* their shame would cause them to deny their faith. So the judge ordered the sisters to be stripped and their bodies burned and beaten. When that didn't convince them to apostatize, they were thrown naked into a cell filled with the worst of the male prisoners.

Mercifully, the two sisters were protected from any further assault as they huddled naked in a prison cell surrounded by criminals. One account says they were given superhuman strength to ward off their attackers; another says the men could see that the sisters were surrounded by God's power, so they left them untouched. Either way, the two days that the women remained exposed in that prison cell couldn't have been anything but traumatic. Finally, they were given their clothes and brought to a higher court to stand trial for their faith. In this interrogation, too, Columba and Agnes remained strong, though they knew that their faithfulness would cost them their lives.

After the death sentence was handed down, Columba asked permission to speak and then described the molestation the two women had endured. "Whether she is the daughter of a noble or a commoner," she said, "the chastity of a young woman has the right to be respected. If you want to kill me according to the law of the country, I will willingly accept the punishment. However, I do not think it is right to have to suffer insults that are not part of the law and I object to them."[16]

The judge was outraged to hear that such a thing had happened and ordered those responsible punished. But Columba and Agnes were still condemned criminals. They were put to death at last, wounded and bloody brides of Christ, radiant with the beauty of holiness.

---

* It's important to note that sexual assault does not render a person impure, nor can virginity be lost unwillingly. Survivors of assault are not impure because of what was done to them.

Columba Kim Hyo-im's courage in speaking out, her understanding of her own dignity, and her willingness to accuse her assailants make her a formidable intercessor for protection against sexual assault and for courage and healing for survivors. Agnes Kim Hyo-ju stands beside her as a model and intercessor for those who aren't able to speak out, showing that survivors who don't report their abuse are also deeply loved by the Father, also called to great holiness. Through their intercession, may survivors of sexual assault be comforted, healed, and wrapped in the safety of the Father's embrace. Sts. Columba Kim Hyo-im and Agnes Kim Hyo-ju, pray for us!

SERVANT OF GOD DARWIN RAMOS

A Twenty-First-Century Impoverished Teenager with Muscular Dystrophy

(1994–2012) ✳ Country: Philippines

Servant of God Darwin Ramos was a child of the slums, the son of an unemployed alcoholic. Though his mother worked as a laundress in Manila, the family was never financially stable, so from earliest childhood Darwin spent his days picking through garbage with his little sister Marimar, looking for trash that they might be able to sell. There was no time for school, nor any energy to take the children to church. Instead, Darwin and his seven younger siblings focused on trying to survive, earning money for food when they could and avoiding their father when he came home drunk and combative.

Through all this, Darwin's mother, Erlinda, spoke to her children about Jesus, about the God who had become poor for them, who had been wounded and killed for them. From infancy, Darwin knew of the love of God, and though he wasn't baptized, he resolved to have Jesus as his best friend.

When Darwin was five, his mother began to worry. He was unsteady on his feet and his muscles seemed weak. The doctor at the local clinic was little help, diagnosing Darwin with malnutrition and chiding his poor mother to feed him better. Later Darwin would be diagnosed with Duchenne muscular dystrophy. As his muscles deteriorated, Darwin was unable to dig through trash to help support his family. With no money for medical treatment, there was little hope for Darwin, but his chronically unemployed father thought that perhaps they could profit from Darwin's situation. So Darwin's father took him each morning to a train station to beg.

Darwin was ashamed to beg, to be set up as a cripple to be pitied. But his brothers and sisters were hungry, and though he knew his father would take most of the money for alcohol, at least Darwin would be able to provide something for his family. So he consented.

Over time, the daily indignity began to drive the joy from his face, but the hand of Providence was at work. Eleven-year-old Darwin was at his post one day, by this point unable to walk, when he was noticed by a social worker who asked if it might be best for him to move into their charitable foundation's home for street children. When his family agreed, Darwin left them for the Tulay ng Kabataan home for disabled children. From the moment he arrived, photos taken of him testify to his joy, always evident on a face split by an enormous grin.

Darwin had suffered grievously in the days he'd had to beg to fuel his father's addiction. Now that his natural piety was built up by Baptism, catechesis, the Eucharist, and Confirmation, he understood his disability as an opportunity. Rather than something to be lamented, pitied, or exploited, Darwin saw muscular dystrophy as his "mission for Jesus."[17] He experienced joy not *in spite of* his disability but because of it. Darwin insisted that the purpose of his condition was for him to know God better and learn to trust him more. And so with all his physical pain, Darwin was never known to complain. He became the heart of Tulay ng Kabataan, the one the other children trusted with their confidences and laments, a boy now known as "the master of joy."

Darwin's life was marked by love and gratitude. Because he wanted nothing more than to be conformed to Christ, he was happy to suffer as Christ had, once telling a teacher, "I believe that every time I hurt, Jesus is using my suffering to do good to someone on the other side of the world."[18] Darwin insisted that God had not given him a cross that was too heavy. Whatever his suffering, he continued bringing joy into the lives of the residents and staff, leading them to Jesus. The heart of his day was prayer before the Blessed Sacrament, even on days it was almost impossible for him to get out of bed. Jesus was worth it.

When he was seventeen, Darwin's breathing became labored and he was taken to the hospital. There, he suffered with his usual smile for five days. But on Thursday of that week, Darwin (who was experiencing his own holy week) begged the priest from Tulay ng Kabataan to pray for him. He was fighting the devil, he said, and his face displayed an anguish from this spiritual battle that all his physical suffering had never forced him to reveal. But the next day, the battle had been won. Darwin was smiling again. As he lay hooked up to a ventilator, he wrote his last words on a piece of notebook paper: "A huge thank you. I am very happy."[19] He spent Saturday in silence. On Sunday, he was raised up in glory, dying as he had lived: with radiant joy.

Darwin Ramos had every reason to be bitter: poverty, neglect, disease, and abuse. But he refused to see his difficulties as anything other than his path to Jesus. Through his intercession, may we learn to accept our suffering as a mission, the way we're being taught to love God. Servant of God Darwin Ramos, pray for us!

40

STS. TIMOTHY AND MAURA

A Couple Whose Marriage Only Lasted a Month

(d. 286) ✳ Country: Egypt
Feast Day: May 3

For nearly two millennia, the Church has celebrated the witness of married Saints made holy by their vocation. Some were married for decades, but Sts. Timothy and Maura show us the power of the sacrament condensed into only one month of marriage.

Timothy was the son of a priest in third-century Egypt. Raised in the Church, he became a lector, which entailed far more than simply proclaiming the readings. He read to the people of his village, preached the Gospel, and kept the holy scriptures and liturgical books safe in his home during the persecutions of the Roman emperor Diocletian. In 286, Timothy married Maura, a pious seventeen-year-old woman, and the two began a life of prayer and Christian witness together.

Timothy and Maura had only been married for twenty days when Timothy was denounced as a Christian and a keeper of the holy books. His captors, on the authority of Diocletian himself, demanded that Timothy surrender the books of scripture to them. Timothy refused, insisting that the sacred books were like his spiritual children. Arian, the governor, was baffled by such an answer. "You see, don't you, the instruments prepared for torture?" Timothy was unmoved: "But don't you see the angels of God, which are strengthening me?"[20]

So the tortures began. Timothy had white-hot irons shoved in his ears. He was blinded and his eyelids cut off. He was hung upside down with a stone around his neck. He would not budge. Then they learned about his sweet young wife. If they couldn't tempt him to deny Christ for his own sake, surely they could induce him to give in for Maura's.

Arian appealed to Maura's hopes and dreams. After all, she'd only been married for three weeks. Didn't she want to live the life she'd been promised, to raise a family with her husband, and to grow old with him? All Timothy had to do was hand over the scriptures and he'd be set free to live in peace to a happy old age. Maura listened intently and asked to speak to her husband.

When Maura was brought in to Timothy, she explained the governor's offer. Here accounts differ. Some say Maura stood firm in her faith throughout, saying, "But I, for my part, will never speak to you again if you deny Christ." Others claim Maura was overcome by grief at seeing Timothy's suffering and begged him to apostatize. Timothy was unmoved: "How is it possible, O Maura, that, being yourself a Christian, instead of animating me to die for the faith, you tempt me to abandon it; and thus, to obtain a short and miserable existence here, expose myself to the never-ending pains of hell? Is this, then, your love?"[21] With that, they say, Maura was convicted and repented of her momentary weakness.

Whether or not Maura remained faithful throughout, this much is certain: While looking on the body of her agonized husband, she confessed herself a Christian and found herself subject to torture as well. Her hair was pulled out, her fingers cut off. When immersed in a pot of boiling water, though, she was unharmed. The governor was impressed by such a miracle but soon resumed his tortures (so cruel that even the bloodthirsty crowd was scandalized) by having the young couple nailed to two crosses facing each other.

For ten days they prayed together, sang hymns, and encouraged each other as they suffered for Christ. When one was weak, the other would be strong, reminding the beloved of what Christ had suffered and of the promise of future life. Ultimately, both found themselves welcomed into the arms of Christ, glorious martyrs. The witness of their courage and joy so inspired their torturer that he soon became a Christian, was martyred himself, and is venerated in the Eastern Church as St. Arian of Alexandria.

Though they were married for only a month, Timothy and Maura understood the purpose of marriage: to challenge and encourage each other through both suffering and joy, as you follow Christ together. Because they were both believers, they were able to persist through unimaginable pain, holding each other accountable and calling each other to holiness. Through their intercession, may God bless all Christian marriages, that spouses may rejoice in suffering together and encourage each other daily to live more fully for Christ. Sts. Timothy and Maura, pray for us!

Part 7

Saints Whose Ruined Plans Opened the Way to More Beautiful Things

The lives of the Saints often seem quite linear when we read their summaries, as though every holy man or woman was given a clear call as a child and followed it directly. For many of us, though, the path to holiness is more circuitous, full of false starts and grievous mistakes that seem insurmountable.

It's easy to feel that our lives have gone irreparably wrong. We chose the wrong vocation or the wrong spouse or made one bad choice that ruined our lives. The trick of the devil is to convince us that our circumstances make holiness impossible. "Maybe I could have been a saint," we think, "if I hadn't married him or had so many children or gotten in that car accident or had an abortion or dropped out of college or become so bitter." But whatever brought them about, God uses our circumstances—the crosses we carry—to sanctify us.

None of our sins or failures is irredeemable, and Saints whose lives take twists and turns remind us that there is no limit to God's grace; he can work things for our good even when we make missteps. The Saints in this section wandered, often for years, wondering what the Lord was doing. They prayed and prayed for one outcome but were given another instead. They waited and hoped for direction, then ended up in a life that seemed all wrong. But all the while, God was working. Each one of these Saints looked back at the end of his or her life and was able to say, "Ah. *That's* what you were doing."

You may not yet have reached that moment of understanding. It's possible you never will—not in this life anyway. But God is working, whether you can see it or not. When we begin to recognize it in the lives of the Saints, it gives us hope that our lives, too, can give glory to God in all their knotted-up mess.

41

BL. LINDALVA JUSTO DE OLIVEIRA

A Life of Failure and Uncertainty Crowned with Martyrdom

———— ≈ ————

(1953–1993) ✳ Country: Brazil
Feast Day: January 7

Bl. Lindalva Justo de Oliveira is a woman whose life trajectory may feel unpleasantly familiar to many who are underemployed. Lindalva was the ninth of sixteen children born to a Brazilian peasant family. She was a lively child who loved swimming in the nearby pond, climbing trees, and making dolls out of clay that she then dressed in clothes she'd sewn from fabric scraps. But money was usually tight in the Oliveira family, and from a young age Lindalva took one job after another to contribute to the family finances. She was a nanny, then helped raise her brother's children. While caring for her three nephews, she finally (at twenty-six) obtained a diploma as an administrative assistant.

Despite this qualification, Lindalva moved from one low-paying customer service job to another. It wasn't glamorous, but it helped pay the bills. She quit working for the last few months of her father's life, staying by his bedside and nursing him through his final illness. Remembering how she'd always loved to take care of suffering people, Lindalva decided that perhaps she ought to go back to school to become a nurse.

Again, she was floundering. She was working retail, taking nursing classes, and volunteering with the Daughters of Charity in their homes for the elderly when finally she realized that she could be more than a volunteer. Here, at last, was the call she'd been waiting for: she entered the Daughters of Charity at age thirty-four.

Her long wandering in the wilderness over, Sr. Lindalva settled in to an ordinary religious life working at a home for the elderly. Usually quiet and reserved, Sr. Lindalva blossomed in her vocation . Her radiant joy was infectious, leaving her a favorite among the residents. She wasn't always happy, of course—nobody is. She chose to smile, not because she was repressing her feelings but because she saw her smile as a gift she could offer to others. "The heart is mine and can suffer," she said, "but the face belongs to others and must be smiling."[1]

Smiling became more difficult when a new resident arrived: Augusto da Silva Peixoto, a mentally unstable man who (at forty-six) was far too young to be admitted. But he had been recommended by an influential person, so nothing could be done. The unbalanced Peixoto soon fixated on Sr. Lindalva, with whom he believed himself to be in love. He was quite sure that she loved him too, despite her repeated rebuffs. When she responded to one of his many propositions by insisting that she was in love with another, Peixoto didn't realize that she was referring to Jesus; he became inflamed with jealousy.

Sr. Lindalva spoke to her sisters of her concerns. She even reported him to her superiors at the nursing home. But, as is all too often the case, little was done. Peixoto was gently chastised by various people but not removed from the home. When the other sisters urged Sr. Lindalva to leave the nursing home for her own protection, she refused to let Peixoto drive her out, insisting that she would rather die than leave the people she was serving.

Consumed by jealousy compounded by rage over these reprimands, Peixoto went out to buy a machete. If he couldn't have

Sr. Lindalva, he reasoned, nobody would. On Good Friday, Sr. Lindalva rose early to pray the Stations of the Cross and then returned to the nursing home to serve breakfast. Her stalker approached her in the dining room and stabbed her forty-four times. He then wiped her blood on his clothes and dropped the blade on the ground. "She didn't want me," he said coolly. "I did what had to be done."[2] He then sat calmly to wait for the police to arrive, his victim dead on the floor, a virgin martyr.

Lindalva Justo de Oliveira was a woman whose heart was fixed on Jesus, however uncertain the path her life was taking. Because she trusted God to lead through every twist and turn, every unfulfilled plan and discouraging failure, she is a witness to all those who find themselves in the similarly frustrating circumstances of unemployment, underemployment, or uncertain futures. She stands also as a powerful intercessor for survivors of assault, particularly those who seek the courage to report abuse. Many are unable to report for fear of suffering the same fate as Lindalva. Through her intercession, may they be protected and their abusers brought to justice, and may all who are underemployed trust in God's providence at work in their frustrating lives. Bl. Lindalva Justo de Oliveira, pray for us!

42

BL. CATALINA DE MARÍA RODRÍGUEZ

A Woman Called to the Convent but Pressured into Marriage

———— ≈ ————

(1823–1896) ✳ Country: Argentina
Feast Day: November 27

Bl. Catalina de María Rodríguez's life did not go the way she had planned. She was born to a prominent Argentinean family, the third of four children, and baptized with the name Saturnina. After losing her mother when she was three and her father when she was nine, Saturnina and her sisters moved in with an aunt.

At seventeen, Saturnina made the Spiritual Exercises (a retreat designed by St. Ignatius Loyola), where she discerned a vocation to religious life. But the only women's religious communities in Argentina were contemplative, and Saturnina felt no call to the cloister. She decided it was best to remain single and spend her time promoting the Spiritual Exercises in Argentina.

Rather than encouraging her to found a new community or to leave the country to follow her vocation, and Saturnina's spiritual director insisted that she get married. And he had a particular groom in mind: a widower and father of two, Manuel Antonio de Zavalía, who had begged Saturnina to marry him, even threatening suicide if she refused. Though her spiritual director ought to have pointed out that such behavior was appalling and abusive, instead he insisted that she was responsible for the man's soul, that she would be at fault if Manuel killed himself. Saturnina trusted her spiritual director (a childhood friend of Manuel's) and consented to the marriage, becoming Manuel's wife when she was twenty-eight.

In marrying Manuel, Saturnina became the stepmother to his son and daughter. She devoted herself to them and to her husband, supporting him in his military career and accompanying him through multiple moves. Though marriage to a man who had manipulated her by threatening to kill himself can't have been easy, Saturnina knew that she was now called to serve God by loving her husband and children. Whatever God might have been calling her to at seventeen, her vocation was now marriage. Still, she continued to volunteer with those who were running the Spiritual Exercises to which she was so devoted, and even encouraged the president of Argentina (her cousin) to invite the Jesuits back to Cordoba. Though a loving stepmother, Saturnina struggled with infertility. She and Manuel had only one child in their thirteen years of marriage, a daughter who was stillborn.

When Saturnina was forty-two, her husband died. Suddenly all her desires for religious life came flooding back. This time, though, Saturnina would not allow any obstacle to get in her way. There were no active communities in Argentina? Fine. She would start one: the Slaves of the Heart of Jesus, an order based on the rule of the Society of Jesus. Despite seven years of opposition and setbacks, she persisted and finally succeeded in establishing the community she had hoped to join more than thirty years earlier. When she made vows, she took the name Catalina de María, after her stillborn daughter, Catalina.

Mother Catalina's religious sisters supported the Spiritual Exercises by running retreat centers, cooperating with St. José Brochero and many other priests. The sisters didn't just staff retreat centers, though. In a country with no active women religious, there was great need, particularly among women who were despised by society. The Slaves served prostitutes, women of mixed race, poor women, and enslaved women, teaching and living with the most vulnerable in Argentine society. Though Mother Catalina had received only a rudimentary education, she was a strong advocate of formal education for women and saw universal public education established in Argentina before her death at seventy-two. By that time, more than two hundred women had entered the congregation, which remains active today.

Perhaps it was always God's will that Catalina de María Rodríguez get married before founding a religious order. But even if her marriage was a mistake, God didn't give up on her. He worked her choices into his plan, giving her stepchildren a mother and forming her heart to be a spiritual mother in religious life. Through her intercession, may God give peace to all who live in fear of choosing the wrong vocation or who are mired in regret at choices they've made that cannot be taken back. May all of us learn to trust that God will work all things for good. Bl. Catalina de María Rodríguez, pray for us!

43

SERVANT OF GOD LÉONIE MARTIN

The Awkward, Unruly, Unstable Older Sister of St. Thérèse

——— ≈ ———

(1863–1941) ✳ Country: France

Servant of God Léonie Martin was the sister of St. Thérèse of Lisieux and the daughter of Sts. Louis and Zélie Martin. Though born into what seems to have been a charmed family in France, Léonie struggled from the start. She contracted whooping cough as a baby, then measles, and she had eczema all her life. When her parents worried that Léonie wouldn't survive all her ailments, they prayed: "If Léonie is to become a saint one day, cure her."[3] Almost immediately her health began to improve.

But Léonie remained a difficult child. She was stubborn and volatile, intellectually slow, and rough in her play. She was awkward, both wild and shy. "As soon as she is with companions," her mother said, "she seems to lose control of herself, and you never saw anything like her unruliness."[4] In short, little Léonie was often unpleasant to be around. This was exacerbated by the death of her closest sister, Marie-Hélène, when Léonie was six and Marie-Hélène five, leaving the middle Martin girl quite alone between her two pairs of sisters.

Things became worse when she was expelled (multiple times) from the boarding school where her two older sisters had been so successful. Léonie was emotionally unstable and inclined to tantrums, even at ten years old, and the school finally determined they could do nothing more for her. Poor Léonie was close to despair, looking at her perfect sisters and wondering if she hadn't been switched at birth.

Léonie wasn't wicked. She could be quite sweet, especially to her baby sister Thérèse; her aunt (a Visitation Sister) said she had a heart of gold. But she couldn't regulate her emotions or conform to expectations. Scholars today suspect she might have been on the autism spectrum or had some mental illness; whatever the cause, Léonie's difficulties were only made worse by Louise, one of the family's maids. Louise terrorized Léonie in private, beating her and threatening her while the saintly Martin parents remained oblivious. When they learned of this abuse, Louise was forbidden any contact with Léonie, but a great deal of damage had already been done. It was a tremendous mercy that this all came to light before the death of Léonie's mother, Zélie, though; the two were able to heal their relationship in the months that remained to them before Zélie's death. Léonie's emotional health improved dramatically in that time and even more so after the death of her mother, when Zélie's intercession proved powerful.

Léonie had long been sure she had a vocation to religious life (though her despairing mother had once written, "I myself am persuaded that unless a miracle takes place, Léonie will never be able to enter a Community"[5]). In the years after Louise's dismissal and Zélie's death, Léonie found emotional healing enough that she felt she was ready for religious life. At twenty-three, she impulsively entered the Poor Clares on the day of her first visit, but left two months later because of her poor health. Seven months later, she entered the Visitation Sisters, again without much pause for reflection, but was home again in only half a year.

Back in Lisieux, Léonie agonized over her perceived failure in religious life while watching her youngest sister Thérèse leave her behind. Léonie was nearing twenty-five and had no idea

Pray for Us

where the Lord was leading her. Thérèse, to whom things came so easily, was entering Carmel at only fifteen. Léonie's pain must have been obvious to her little sister. Indeed, on the day of her profession two years later, Sr. Thérèse wrote, "Oh, Jesus! Make it Your will that Léonie become a Visitandine, and, if she does not have a vocation, I ask You to give her one. You cannot refuse me this."[6]

But it would be some time before the Lord answered the Little Flower's earnest prayer. Within a year of Thérèse's departure, their father, Louis, began to suffer from dementia. He wandered out of their home and experienced hallucinations; soon he was taken to a psychiatric hospital, where he stayed for three years.

When Louis returned home, Léonie and Céline nursed him, but Léonie's heart remained fixed on religious life. She had visited the Visitation convent often while Louis was in the hospital. Her first attempt at life there had been unsuccessful, but perhaps this time she would be able to stay?

At thirty, she tried again, leaving poor Céline feeling abandoned in the care of their father and bitter at being all alone. This time, Léonie stayed long enough to receive the habit. She remained in the convent as her father's health worsened, through his death and his funeral. But she struggled to fit in to the community, and after two years she was found unsatisfactory as a religious and sent home. She had missed the last year of her beloved father's life, missed his death, and for what? Nothing, it seemed.

Céline was gone when Léonie returned home, having entered Carmel with the other three Martin sisters soon after their father's death. Léonie, who had always felt like the ugly, awkward misfit, was alone. Though she was deeply loved by her uncle and his family, poor Léonie must have wondered what on earth was to become of her, a woman who longed for nothing but the cloister but was sent away over and again.

Into this sorrow Sr. Thérèse wrote, in her last letter to Léonie: "The only happiness on earth is to apply oneself in always finding delightful the lot Jesus is giving us."[7] Léonie sought to live this wisdom, to embrace the waiting and wondering of her life. It was during this final period of uncertainty that Thérèse died. And the little sister who had promised "After my death I will let fall a shower of roses"[8] did just that. Léonie read *The Story of a Soul* and was inspired to try joining the Visitation Sisters one more time. She was thirty-five years old.

When Léonie took vows the following year, she took the name Sr. Françoise-Thérèse, after the little sister she so admired. Sr. Françoise-Thérèse was delighted to be a nun and hopeful that this time it would last. Still, her difficulties remained. She was inclined to tears and slow to adjust to religious life, and her awkwardness made her almost obsessively meticulous.

But she was also the sister of St. Thérèse, who had said before her death, "After I die, I will make Léonie rejoin the Visitation Order, and this time she will stay."[9] With an intercessor like that, Sr. Françoise-Thérèse was finally able to adjust to religious life. She learned to be corrected. She even learned to be teased. Before long, Sr. Francoise-Thérèse was beloved by all her sisters, considered charming and courteous and referred to as "our compassionate Sister."[10]

For the next forty-two years, Sr. Françoise-Thérèse lived a hidden life in the Visitation cloister, making a daily effort to master herself. Her letters betray the fact that it continued to be a struggle, but she persisted, a model of holiness and humility until her death at seventy-eight.

Léonie was not a person to whom holiness came easily. She wasn't sweet and placid. Holiness for her was a product of fighting her own willfulness, of following the Little Way laid out by her youngest sister. But holiness was also a result of the stubbornness which, when refined, became holy determination. Léonie's health would likely have forced her to leave religious life even had she not struggled emotionally, but it was her much-maligned stubbornness that strengthened her to persevere, to return to the convent again and again until finally she was able to stay.

Those who feel out of control emotionally can find a model in Léonie Martin, who became holy not just in spite of her struggles but, in part, because of them. Léonie once said, "I belong to a family of saints and I must not blemish that heritage."[11] As members of the family of God, it's as true for us as it was for her. Through her intercession, may all who feel they don't belong, who struggle mentally and emotionally, recognize how deeply loved they are. Servant of God Léonie Martin, pray for us!

44

BL. MARÍA GUGGIARI ECHEVERRÍA

A Carmelite Nun Who Rejoiced in Her Broken Heart

———— ≈ ————

(1925–1959) ✳ Country: Paraguay
Feast Day: April 28

Bl. María Guggiari Echeverría was the oldest of seven children in a devout Paraguayan family. She was always faithful, making daily visits to the Blessed Sacrament once she reached adolescence and bringing her friends along with her. As a teenager, María became involved in the Catholic Action movement, which led her to offer herself unreservedly in service to children, the elderly, and the sick. When she was eighteen, she resolved to belong only to Jesus, making a personal vow of chastity. Her parents weren't thrilled by this choice, but María felt quite certain that the Lord was asking it of her.

María's vow was tested when, at twenty-five, she met and fell in love with a young medical student, Ángel Sauá, who was the president of the Catholic Action student group. At first, the two were only friends, but they understood each other so well that María began to have feelings for him. Soon she realized that in his company she was able to serve even more radically, visiting neighborhoods that she could never have gone to on her own. As she saw the apostolic fruitfulness of their friendship, María began to wonder if the Lord wasn't calling them to serve him together.

This was a time of painful confusion. María had made a private vow of consecration and had no intention of betraying it. But perhaps she and Ángel were being called to a Josephite marriage, living together in sexual continence for the sake of the work God was calling them to. When Ángel confessed to María that he felt called to be a priest, she finally had clarity: her love for him was not to lead to marriage but to be offered to the Lord as she prayed for him and for all priests.

Clarity isn't always pleasant, and for María it was quite painful. "I am in love with Sauá," she wrote in her diary, "but I am more in love with Jesus."[12] In sacrificing her love for Ángel, María felt she had offered Jesus something terribly beautiful. And now, she could help Ángel become a priest. His father was a Muslim and deeply opposed to his son's vocation, so María and Ángel concocted a plan: he would travel to Spain to study after finishing his medical degree. There he could have the freedom to discern.

Ángel and María wrote to each other while he was in Spain. When he decided that he would enter seminary, he asked María to inform his family and deal with his enraged father. Afterward, María turned to her own vocation. A few months earlier she had met the prioress of the Paraguayan Carmel and found in her a true spiritual mother. Since then, Carmel had begun to call her from her full life of apostolic work to the silence of the cloister. This vivacious, industrious young missionary who had so recently written "being quiet kills me"[13] now told her friends and family that she was preparing to become a contemplative nun.

At thirty, after years of uncertainty, heartbreak, and fruitful service in the Lord's vineyard, María left the world behind to enter the Discalced Carmelites. Her family was even more opposed to this than they had been to her initial vow of virginity; even the priests she knew largely opposed her vocation. They saw the success of her work with Catholic Action and thought she would be wasted in a cloister. But María was far more concerned with faithfulness than with success, and she knew that the Lord was calling her to Carmel. She wrote one last letter to Ángel: "Goodbye, until eternity!"[14] Then she entered Carmel without looking back.

Now called Sr. María Felicia of the Blessed Sacrament, she was just as lively and joyful in the convent as she had been in the city, but her time as a nun did not last long. Within four years she had contracted the hepatitis that would take her life. Sr. María Felicia felt no sorrow over the suffering and death she was preparing to experience. Her heart had always belonged to Jesus, and now she was going home to be with him.

María Guggiari Echeverría knew uncertainty, sacrifice, and heartbreak. She knew the frustration of years of discernment, the pain of a family opposed to her vocation. And through it all she persevered, rejoicing in the love of Christ. Through her intercession, may God pour healing mercies on all who are struggling with difficulties in discernment, with broken hearts, uncertainty, and confusion. Bl. María Guggiari Echeverría, pray for us!

45

St. Frances of Rome

An Introvert Who Found Holiness
in a Vocation She Never Wanted

---≈---

(1384–1440) ✳ Country: Italy
Feast Day: March 9

St. Frances of Rome, the married Saint most famous for remarking "A married woman must, when called upon, quit her devotions to God at the altar to find him in her household affairs,"[15] did not want to be married. More than anything in the world, she wanted to be a nun, and she told her father just that. Unfortunately, her father was entirely unconcerned about her desires—he insisted that she marry. In a time when fathers determined their daughters' futures, Frances's path had been decided, whether she liked it or not.

Off she went to her spiritual director, sobbing and weeping. He listened patiently to the thirteen-year-old's lamentations until she had finished and then remarked calmly, "Are you crying because you want to do God's will or because you want God to do your will?"[16]

Frances was stunned—and chastened. Much though she wanted to be a nun, God's will was clear when she truly listened. She was no St. Clare of Assisi, no Bl. Diana d'Andalo; she didn't have it in her to defy her father, to run away to a convent and refuse to return. There was nothing she could do to change her father's mind, so her choice was to accept the call put before her in peace or in misery. Frances chose to embrace her cross and soon found herself married, at thirteen, to a kind and wealthy nobleman.

But her initial consent to God's will would be sorely tried. Frances was expected to enter fully into the social life of the time, but the quiet, prayerful girl was so overwhelmed by it all that she collapsed and lay on the brink of death for months. Finally, St. Alexis, who had run away centuries before to live on the street when his family tried to force him to marry, appeared to her. He told her that God was offering her a choice as to whether she would recover. After praying in agony, Frances responded, "God's will is mine." Immediately she recovered and returned to the life she hated.

Again Frances tried to embrace her cross. Again it proved too heavy for her. It seems she was not meant to bear it alone; her sister-in-law, Vannozza, also longed for holiness. One day Vannozza found Frances crying and discovered her hidden anguish. The sisters-in-law determined that together they would live for Jesus. Always serving their families before all else, they began attending Mass together, visiting the sick and imprisoned, and even praying in a secret chapel they fashioned in an abandoned tower of their estate. With these acts of piety and charity to sustain her, Frances was finally able to fulfill her social obligations—and gladly this time.

For years, Frances and Vannozza struggled against their in-laws, determined to honor and respect them but unwilling to abandon the poor as they sometimes demanded. When their father-in-law sold all the family's extra grain and wine so that Frances could no longer give it away, the granary was miraculously filled for months (no matter how much she passed out to the poor) and the one cask of wine never ran dry. After this, her husband and father-in-law were completely converted and Frances and Vannozza were free to serve as they wished, sometimes begging to obtain alms for the poor, other times caring for the sick in their home. Frances was a Third Order Benedictine, founded an order of oblates, and for decades saw her guardian angel with her at all times. Yet despite all this, she's remembered for her simple devotion as a wife and mother.

Frances of Rome was an introvert who learned to thrive among crowds. She was a married woman who longed for a cloister. She lived in a castle but in solidarity with the poor. And every good thing in her life of contradictions came about as a result of a vocation she would never have chosen. She was disconsolate when her marriage was arranged, but it was through that very marriage that she became a Saint. Through her intercession, may God pour his grace on all those who feel trapped in their lives, particularly those who feel alone and need a Vannozza to spur them on to holiness. St. Frances of Rome, pray for us!

46

VEN. MARÍA LUISA JOSEFA

*An Infertile Wife, a Widow,
Then an Ex-Nun Twice Over*

———— ≈ ————

(1866–1937) ✳ Country: Mexico

Ven. María Luisa Josefa's life looks, on the surface, like a series of failures and frustrations. But God was working.

Luisita was the first surviving child of her parents. Frail from birth, she was taught at home by a governess. Though she eventually had ten younger siblings, she was reserved and rather withdrawn as a child. Indeed, her family's wealth seems to have made her quite haughty, until she was gently reprimanded by her father when she ignored the greetings of workers on their ranch. After that, Luisita began to learn humility and grew in a love for the poor that would drive her entire life.

The young Luisita felt sure she was called to religious life, but her parents wanted her to marry, so at fifteen she married a thirty-year-old doctor chosen by her parents. When she and her husband, Pascual, were on their honeymoon in Mexico City, she asked him to take her to see a Visitation convent. Once there, she turned to him and said, "You may go now, Pascual. I am going to stay here. I have asked for admission, and Reverend Mother has accepted me."[17] One can only imagine the reaction of her poor husband! But when Pascual explained to Mother Superior that the two had just been married, she sent young Luisita back home with her sympathetic (and long-suffering) husband.

From the outside, the whole situation seems quite unfortunate: a fifteen-year-old girl compelled to marry a powerful doctor twice her age. But Luisita and her husband were very happy together. After some years of struggling with infertility, the couple decided that the poor would be their children and they devoted their marriage to the care of those in need. For fourteen years, Pascual and Luisita lived their marriage generously—they started a chapter of the St. Vincent de Paul Society and founded a charitable hospital, which Luisita ran.

Pascual died when Luisita was twenty-nine, and though she mourned, she found hope in the fact that she would finally be able to enter religious life. She applied to the Visitation convent that she had visited on her honeymoon, but was refused entrance because of chronic health conditions. This was a blow, but Luisita soon realized that in the years since she had first applied to the Visitation Sisters, she had developed a Carmelite spirituality. Luisita entered the Carmelites in 1904, a nun at last at thirty-seven.

The hospital she and Pascual had founded immediately began to fail without her administrative wisdom. Patients were suffering as a result. On the advice of her archbishop and her superiors, Luisita left the convent to serve her children, the poor. She got things in order and even founded a girls' school and an orphanage. Before long, a community of women had gathered around her. It was impossible to found a new religious order at the time, so the archbishop asked them to unite themselves to an established community. In 1913, Luisita and the others entered the Sister Servants of the Blessed Sacrament.

Again, the hospital began to fail, and now the school with it. The archbishop asked Luisita to come back. This time, five sisters came with her: all of them elderly and illiterate. Luisita's call to religious life persisted, but it was clear that the Lord had entrusted this work to her, which required her to remain a laywoman for a while yet. Finally, at fifty-four, Luisita became Mother María Luisa Josefa of the Most Blessed Sacrament (Madre Luisita) when she and the women who served with her became an apostolic community of the Carmelite order, taking vows in 1921.

Almost immediately, Madre Luisita established other foundations, orphanages, and hospitals in Mexico, but persecution of the Church compelled her to flee to the United States in 1927. Providence was at work even in this, though, as Madre Luisita founded Carmels in the United States before returning to Mexico two years later.

Madre Luisita spent the rest of her life moving from one convent or home to another trying to avoid detection in war-torn Mexico, experiencing hunger and poverty like the people she'd mothered for so long. Her life was as unstable as in the years she was trying to enter a convent, but her heart was finally at peace, her soul at rest in the work she'd been called to do as a Carmelite sister and the mother of the poor.

María Luisa Josefa is a powerful intercessor for anyone whose life feels uncertain and out of control, especially those living with infertility or whose vocations haven't seemed to materialize. Her suffering didn't destroy her faith but led her to the essential work God was calling her to do. Through her intercession, may we trust in God even as our prayers go unanswered, knowing that he is working all things for good. Ven. María Luisa Josefa, pray for us!

Part 8

Saints Who Were Failures

A fairy tale in which the protagonist lives happily ever after is a lovely thing, as are the many stories of Saints whose circuitous paths eventually led to exactly the lives they always wanted. But while it's beautiful to find hope in stories of answered prayers and lives where everything comes right in the end, it's very easy for that hope to become certainty that God will give us all the desires of our hearts.

He did not promise that. He wouldn't be much of a God if he had.

God has promised us himself, and we who have chosen to follow him will often find that being his means prayers unanswered and wishes unfulfilled. When we fix our hearts on the things of this world, it's very easy to give in to despair. Hope becomes impossibly heavy as we cling to our plans: the job, the healing, the spouse, the child, the clarity. The stories that follow are of Saints who lived lives of failure, teaching us to hope in God instead, to let him fulfill that hope as he chooses.

For some, it was perceived failure—a life wasted in the eyes of the world. Others heard the Lord say no to their earnest prayers, again and again for decades. But all of them found that their true longing wasn't for success, esteem, comfort, or even love. It was for Jesus: the desired of all nations, the joy of every human heart. And whatever failure it took to hear him say, "Well done, good and faithful servant," it was worth it.

St. Mark Ji Tianxiang

An Opium Addict Who Never Got Clean

———— ≈ ————

(1834–1900) ✳ Country: China
Feast Day: July 7

St. Mark Ji Tianxiang was an opium addict. Not *had been* an opium addict. He *was* an opium addict at the time of his death.

For years, Tianxiang was a respectable man, raised in a Christian family in nineteenth-century China. He was a leader in the Christian community, a well-off doctor and acupuncturist who served the poor for free. But he became ill with a violent stomach ailment and treated himself with opium. It was a perfectly reasonable thing to do, but Tianxiang soon became addicted to the drug, an addiction that was considered shameful and gravely scandalous.

As his circumstances deteriorated, Tianxiang continued to fight his addiction. He went frequently to Confession, refusing to give in to this affliction that had taken control of him. Unfortunately, his confessor (along with nearly everybody in the nineteenth century) didn't understand addiction as a disease. Since Tianxiang kept confessing the same sin, the priest thought, that was evidence that he had no firm purpose of amendment, no desire to do better. Without resolve to repent and sin no more, Confession is invalid.

Today we understand that addiction impairs one's ability to choose freely and that a person can't be denied absolution if he or she earnestly desires not to sin again, however unlikely it might be. But Tianxiang's confessor didn't understand that, and eventually, he told Tianxiang not to come back until he was clean. For some, this might have been an invitation to leave the Church in anger or shame, but for all his fallenness, Tianxiang knew himself to be loved by the Father. He knew that the Lord wanted his heart, even if his life didn't match his ideals. He couldn't stay sober, but he could keep showing up.

And show up he did, for thirty years. For thirty years he was barred from receiving the sacraments. It seemed to Tianxiang that the only way he could be saved was through a martyr's crown. So for thirty years he prayed that he would die a martyr.

In 1900, when the Boxer rebels began to turn against foreigners and Christians, Tianxiang got his chance. A leader in the Christian community despite his struggles with addiction, Tianxiang was betrayed by a friend and handed over to the rebels. He was rounded up with dozens of other Christians, including his son, six grandchildren, and two daughters-in-law. Many of those imprisoned with him were likely disgusted by his presence there among them, this man who couldn't go a day without a hit. Surely he would be the first to deny the Lord.

But while Tianxiang was never able to beat his addiction, he was, in the end, flooded with the grace of final perseverance. No threat could shake him, no torture make him waver. He was determined to follow the Lord who had never abandoned him. As he and his family were dragged to prison to await their execution, his grandson looked fearfully at him. "Grandpa, where are we going?" he asked. "We're going home," the Saint replied.[1]

There in captivity, Tianxiang encouraged his family to remain strong in their faith, reminding those who were tempted, "Heaven is open. We would rather die than betray God."[2] He begged his captors to kill him last so that none of his family would have to die alone and then stood beside all nine of them as they were beheaded. In the end, he went to his death singing the Litany of the Blessed Virgin Mary. And though he had been away from the sacraments for decades, though he had failed every time he'd tried to stop using drugs, he is a canonized Saint.

Mark Ji Tianxiang is a beautiful witness to the grace of God constantly at work in the most hidden ways, to God's ability to make great Saints of the most unlikely among us, and to the grace poured out on those who remain faithful when it seems even the Church is driving them away. Through his intercession, may God grant courage and faithfulness to all living with addiction and to all those who are unable to receive the sacraments. St. Mark Ji Tianxiang, pray for us!

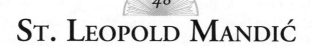

ST. LEOPOLD MANDIĆ

A Faithful Priest Whose Only Dream Never Came True

(1866–1942) ✳ Country: Montenegro, Italy
Feast Day: July 30

St. Leopold Mandić only really wanted one thing in life. Ethnically Croatian, he was raised in what's now Montenegro and longed to work for the reunion of Catholics and Orthodox. So he became a Franciscan Capuchin priest, studying several Slavic languages so that he could serve in Eastern Europe. He even made a vow to serve the Slavic people.

But Leopold had severe arthritis that had stunted his growth, leaving him only four feet five inches tall. He also had bad eyesight, chronic abdominal pain, and a severe stutter. He wasn't strong, healthy, or a good preacher. In short, he was a terrible candidate for the missions. So he was sent to Italy, far from the Eastern Orthodox he longed to serve.

For seven years after his ordination, Fr. Leopold worked in Italy. When he was finally sent to Dalmatia to serve as superior of a friary, he must have been thrilled to return to a land where Orthodox Christians lived, eager to fulfill his vow to work for the reunification of the Church. But Fr. Leopold was recalled only three years later, having accomplished nothing of note. He then taught patristics to the student friars for a few years, but he was considered too gentle by the other professors. In yet another instance of hopes dashed, Fr. Leopold was abruptly removed from the position he had come to love.

From then on, Fr. Leopold's only duty was to hear confessions. He ached to do the work for unity that the Lord had put on his heart, but he obeyed, spending fifteen hours a day in the confessional and praying four hours a night for the reunion of East and West. For years he did nothing else, consoling himself that each penitent absolved was an act of reconciliation, albeit on a small scale. "Each soul who needs my ministry will, in a way, be the Orient for me," he said.[3]

Fr. Leopold was as merciful in the confessional as he had been gentle in the classroom. When criticized for excessive compassion, he shrugged off the accusation. "If the Lord wants to accuse me of showing too much leniency toward sinners," he said, "I'll tell him that it was he who gave me this example."[4] His penitents left with light penances, not because Fr. Leopold had no hatred of sin but because he himself was overwhelmed by the generosity of God's mercy. Rather than burden his people with the feeling that they had to earn forgiveness, the good father gave them a small penance and did additional penance for them himself.

For twenty-three years, Fr. Leopold submitted to his superiors' orders that he stay in Italy, but his heart longed to return to Eastern Europe. "I'm like a bird in a cage," he wrote, "but my heart is always beyond the seas."[5] Finally, after two decades in Italy longing to work with Eastern Christians, Fr. Leopold was sent to Croatia. He rejoiced—at last, he would be able to fulfill his vow to work for unity in the Church!

He hadn't been there a week when a message arrived: he was to return to Italy. The people of Padua felt they simply could not survive without the diminutive priest who listened so compassionately to their confessions and spoke with such wisdom. Once again, Fr. Leopold resigned himself to God's will, though his heart ached. He wrote to the Blessed Mother, "You can see in what circumstances my life has developed and with what anxiety I am oppressed."[6]

Fr. Leopold never left Italy again. He never did anything notable to reunite Catholics and Orthodox and end the Great Schism. But his longing never abated. Late in life, he wrote with great confidence, "I no longer have any doubt before God that I am chosen for the salvation of the Eastern peoples."[7] He was dead a few months later, having spent his life in disappointment and failure. Still, he had rejoiced to be in God's will, trusting that God's no was a gift even when he couldn't see it. Fr. Leopold was a man of hope—not a hope that sought fulfillment in the things of this world but a hope that longed for the next. For all his aspirations to serve the cause of unity in the Church, what he really wanted most was Jesus.

Leopold Mandić was never given the desire of his heart, but he was given the heart of Jesus, the grace to absolve tens of thousands of sinners, and a halo in the end. He found joy in obedience, in accepting God's will even if his desires never changed. Through his intercession, may all who are longing for something we may never receive be given the grace to rejoice in God's will and surrender our desires, saying, "Thy will be done." St. Leopold Mandić, pray for us!

49

ST. PACIFICUS OF SAN SEVERINO

A Talented Priest Who Lost His Ability to Walk, Hear, and See

---

(1653–1721) ✳ Country: Italy
Feast Day: September 24

St. Pacificus of San Severino was born into a noble Italian family, but his parents died when he was only four or five and the cruel uncle who raised him treated him as a servant and allowed the other servants to abuse him. Unwilling to become bitter, the child clung to the faith his mother had taught him until, at age seventeen, he was finally able to leave his uncle's house to enter the Franciscans.

After his ordination, Fr. Pacificus was asked to teach philosophy, so respected was he as an intellectual. But he understood his salvation wouldn't come from learning or from the esteem of the world. His task was the salvation of souls, and for the three years that he taught, he begged to be sent out as a preacher, encountering sinners in their struggles and leading them back to the embrace of Christ. Once given permission, Fr. Pacificus wandered the countryside for five years, preaching so beautifully and giving such compassionate counsel in the confessional that the people thought him a wonder. He moved from village to village, even hiking up mountains to speak with solitary shepherds long ignored by his less assiduous confreres.

There was nobody too far for the reach of Fr. Pacificus—until his feet began to develop crippling, untreatable sores. Fr. Pacificus could no longer walk, nor stand in a pulpit for any length of time. Rather than lamenting his lost fruitfulness, he accepted this cross, giving up his successful preaching ministry to sit for hours each day in the confessional. There, too, he was useful.

But Fr. Pacificus's goodness didn't lie in his usefulness, and as his disease progressed, God was teaching him (and us) just that. Next, Fr. Pacificus lost his hearing. Sign language was very limited at the time, but he got by with crude gestures and rejoiced to carry the Cross with Christ in some small way.

Fr. Pacificus could no longer teach, preach, or hear confessions, but he could still celebrate Mass. Until his sight, too, was taken. But he could pray and fast—until his superiors ordered him to relax his penances, concerned that their severity would affect his health. To this, too, Fr. Pacificus submitted. His life was not his own, after all. He had given it over to Jesus and was content to accept any cross, any obligation.

The great orator was now blind, deaf, and unable to stand. And in this lay his great gift to the world. While he had been holy in his usefulness, he became a Saint not by accomplishing but by *being*. Fr. Pacificus embraced his suffering—even when he spent years feeling abandoned by God. His peaceful acceptance of God's will so conformed him to the heart of Christ that he experienced ecstasies, had the gift of prophecy, and worked miraculous healings on others while he continued to suffer. For nearly thirty years, Fr. Pacificus lived in joy and hope, in pain and isolation, dying at age sixty-eight.

Pacificus of San Severino became useless in the eyes of the world, but he was a great gift, less because of what he could do than because of who he was. His value didn't rest in his success, however much it may have seemed that way when he was a skillful preacher wandering the country. His value rested in the love of God, which is unchanged by disability, sin, success, or failure. Through his intercession, may those who struggle with a feeling of failure and inadequacy remember that holiness has nothing to do with success. May those who mourn the loss of gifts they once cherished trust that God is sovereign both in those abilities and in their absence. St. Pacificus of San Severino, pray for us!

50

VEN. MARIA GIUSEPPINA BENVENUTI (ZEINAB ALIF)

A Captive Ransomed from Slavery to "Waste" Her Life in the Cloister

---

(1846–1926) ✳ Country: Sudan, Italy

Like St. Josephine Bakhita, Ven. Zeinab Alif was a little girl in Sudan when she was kidnapped and sold into slavery. For a year and a half, she was passed from one cruel master to another. Finally her freedom was purchased by Servant of God Niccolò Olivieri, a priest whose mission was to help liberate enslaved Africans. Because the ten-year-old Zeinab had no way of finding her home and family, she was taken to Italy and entrusted to the nuns at a Poor Clare Monastery. At first, the spirited young Zeinab panicked, feeling imprisoned (as one can only imagine a newly freed captive might behind unscalable walls). But the nuns' love transformed her; she hadn't been there a month before they were calling her the joy of the community. After six months,

Pray for Us

she was baptized, taking the name Maria Giuseppina Benvenuti. So overjoyed was she at her baptism that she considered that day, not the day she was freed from slavery, the most wonderful day of her life.

Giuseppina learned to read and write, studied her catechism, and showed a great gift for music. Though a talented singer, her real gift was for the organ. When the town band played in the streets, young Giuseppina accompanied them on the organ, improvising duets between herself and the ensemble marching by. Throughout her life, townspeople would stand outside the convent walls to listen to her play the organ inside the cloister.

Young Giuseppina could often be found praying before the crucifix or the Blessed Sacrament. She loved the Rosary and the Saints. Before long, it was clear that Giuseppina had a religious vocation. But the mid-nineteenth century wasn't an ideal time to be discerning a contemplative vocation. The newly formed Kingdom of Italy was hostile to religious life, viewing contemplative orders as particularly useless. Religious orders that didn't provide some "useful" service to the community were dissolved by government authorities and their properties sold; new religious professions were forbidden entirely.

Rather than seeing this closed door as evidence of God's will, Giuseppina persisted. She was encouraged to embrace a missionary vocation, to return to the home of her ancestors and preach the Gospel there as only a native Sudanese could, but she knew God was calling her to the cloister. However successful she might have been as a missionary, and however much she longed to make vows as a sister, she couldn't be unfaithful to the call she had been given, no matter the obstacles.

Finally, when Giuseppina was twenty-eight, she was able to receive the habit of the Poor Clares (concealed under her lay clothes) and secretly begin her novitiate. Still, she kept hearing of the work of St. Daniel Comboni, a missionary priest who was working in Sudan. Like St. Thérèse of Lisieux, Sr. Giuseppina finally determined that she would be a missionary from the cloister, offering prayers and sacrifices for the success of the foreign missions. She made vows as a Poor Clare, though the precarious political situation kept her from making final vows for nearly thirty years. Instead, she renewed her vows annually and longed for the day when she could give herself irrevocably to her bridegroom.

There seems to have been no resistance to Sr. Giuseppina's religious vocation because of her race. In fact, she was made novice mistress and ultimately elected abbess, though she had prayed to be spared that honor. She served as her community's superior for six years. Unlike St. Josephine Bakhita, who traveled throughout Italy for six years under orders from her superiors telling the story of her captivity and redemption, Sr. Giuseppina said little to the outside world. She didn't raise money or awareness for the missions. She didn't travel as a missionary or write a memoir testifying to God's goodness in ransoming her. She embraced the hidden, silent vocation of the cloister. By worldly measures, her life was wasted. But Christians see in her someone like Mary of Bethany, anointing Jesus before his death (Mt 26:6–13): one whose sacrifice is viewed as a waste but whom the Church will always remember as pouring her life out for Christ.

Maria Giuseppina Benvenuti persevered in a thankless vocation despite the many obstacles put before her. Through her intercession, may the Lord bring joy to the hearts of those who feel useless or unwanted or who seem to encounter nothing but opposition. Ven. Maria Giuseppina Benvenuti, pray for us!

51

BL. PAUL THOJ XYOOJ

A Missionary Prodigy Who Lost Everything but His Faith

━━━━━ ≈ ━━━━━

(1941–1960) ✳ Country: Laos
Feast Day: December 16

Bl. Paul Thoj Xyooj (pronounced Tao Shiong) was first a prodigy, an evangelist to whom people flocked, throwing down their idols before him. Then he was a failure, a missionary pulled from the field under the shadow of scandal, a wonder child grown into mediocre adulthood. He was doubted, betrayed, abandoned, and ignored, and still he remained faithful unto death.

The son of a Hmong village chief in Laos, Xyooj was raised in the animist tradition of his ancestors. When he was nine, a missionary priest arrived in his village; Xyooj hung on his every word. At sixteen, Xyooj revealed that he felt called to the priesthood. Though he was unbaptized, the missionaries felt confident in his discernment. They baptized Xyooj and sent him off to school, where he studied to be a catechist with an eye to a future spot at the seminary.

But after a year, he returned home. This moment in discernment can be devastating, leaving many feeling unwanted by God. But Xyooj was confident in God's love and in his discernment, so he prepared to go out on mission, accompanying a priest who spoke no Hmong.

Wearing traditional Hmong garb, including three silver collars that had been given to him by his father, the eighteen-year-old Xyooj was a sight. When he entered the village of Na Vang, the people stared in wonder, whispering, "The king of the

Hmong!" Xyooj assured them that he was no king but had come to tell them the Good News of the King of kings, the one who vanquishes every demon.

The Hmong, who had a great dread of evil spirits, were amazed to hear of a man who conquered demons. Still, there had been Protestant missionaries who had come to their village in the past, and they were wary.

"But can we eat pork?" they asked. It seems a previous missionary had insisted that Christians could neither eat pork nor drink alcohol. When Xyooj set their minds at ease, they were enthralled by what he had to say, listening for three days and three nights. The testimonies collected years later seem almost mythical, reminiscent of medieval hagiographies, telling of one person after another asking for baptism in a village where earlier missionaries had made no headway at all. After three days, half of Na Vang had been enrolled as catechumens. Then people began to come from surrounding villages. Before long, four hundred people were taking instruction.

For seven months, Xyooj preached with the success of a St. Francis Xavier. He taught the villagers to read and write Hmong. He visited the sick and helped with farming, all while teaching several catechism classes each day. The priest who had accompanied him spoke no Hmong, so his role was mostly sacramental; it was Xyooj who evangelized.

Then, suddenly, Xyooj was recalled. The superiors in the order worried about what he was preaching while accompanied by a priest who couldn't understand. How could he possibly make the Gospel sound so appealing that people were accepting it in such numbers? Had he watered it down? Ignored the hard teachings? And wasn't he too friendly with the young women in the village? Surely he was taking advantage of them.

So Xyooj was torn from the people who had become like family to him and from the young woman he had hoped to marry because of rumors and unfounded suspicions. And, perhaps, because of clerics who had forgotten the power of the Gospel to change hearts.

The people of Na Vang wept as he left. Xyooj, too, sobbed but obeyed. He returned to his home village of Kiukatiam and tried to move on. He searched among the young women there for a wife, but none had a heart for Jesus the way his beloved had. Bl. Mario Borzaga, a young priest in Kiukatiam, entreated his superiors to allow Xyooj to return to Na Vang to marry. They refused.

After this, Xyooj floundered. The Church had failed him, refusing to allow him to do the work he was so obviously good at, refusing to allow him to marry as he pleased and live where he pleased. He knew God was calling him to marriage, and though finding a spouse was proving difficult, he still worried about how he would provide for a family on a catechist's salary. Perhaps, he thought, he would become a police officer.

Xyooj didn't lose his faith in Jesus or even in the Church, though for a time it seemed he had lost his place in the Church and his faith in the men who ran it. But Fr. Borzaga believed in him. He was going to preach to a Hmong village and asked Xyooj to join him. Xyooj was wary, but he loved the Lord desperately and he loved his people. He would go.

The men set out, thinking only of the good that could be done for souls, and not of Communist insurgents. But as they left the village of Muang Met, they were stopped by soldiers who were suspicious of Fr. Borzaga, the white man. They decided to kill only him, but Xyooj responded, "Kill me too. Where he dies, I will die, and where he lives, I will live."[8]

Paul Thoj Xyooj's last words, reminiscent of the Old Testament's Ruth, showed not only his courage but also the depth of his forgiveness. Xyooj gave his life rather than abandon a white priest, though he had been so betrayed by white priests. But he would not be defined by their betrayal any more than he was defined by his success or failure—only by the love of Jesus. He had learned firsthand that the Church is already but not yet holy, and he loved her just the same. The prodigy whose plans had come crashing down around him was, in the end, a Saint—the only title that really matters. Through his intercession may God bring hope to those who feel they haven't lived up to their potential and healing to all those who have been hurt by the Church and her ministers. Bl. Paul Thoj Xyooj, pray for us!

Bl. Charles de Foucauld

A Nobleman Who Died a Failure in Everything but Love

(1858–1916) ✳ Country: France, Algeria
Feast Day: December 1

Bl. Charles de Foucauld, the heir to a great fortune, was a French viscount descended from crusaders, statesmen, and at least one martyr. But despite the silver spoon in his mouth, his life was filled with suffering. He was five years old when he lost his mother; five months later, he was orphaned entirely. Left in the care of a loving grandfather, Charles became insufferably spoiled. His laziness and inclination to throw tantrums did not diminish as he grew, and his anger at God soon made him an avowed agnostic.

Having turned his back on God, Charles later described himself at fifteen as "all egotism, vanity, impiety, with every desire for evil."[9] With a fortune awaiting him and no moral compass to speak of, he became consumed by desire for sensual pleasure.

He was expelled from school and sent to a military academy, where he continued to live a wild life. When his grandfather died in 1878, Charles inherited a vast fortune, and from then on, nothing could stem his lascivious behavior. Indeed, he seemed to delight in scandalizing the people around him. He was even known to tell his many mistresses, "I rent by the day, not the month."[10]

Though his financial and social standing had long protected him from any real consequences for his debauchery, the French Foreign Legion, in which he was an officer, had its limits. When Charles was sent to Algeria and secretly brought along a mistress, he was given an ultimatum: send her back or lose your commission. Charles refused to leave his lover, though it seems this was more out of willfulness than love, as he tossed her aside soon after.

Charles left the military, but after that taste of Algeria, Africa was in the young nobleman's blood. He later got permission to rejoin the army. After being discharged, he spent a year exploring Morocco, disguised as a wandering Jew so that he could visit villages no European had ever entered.

But while Charles had everything the world could offer, he was empty inside. He sought to fill his hungry soul with fine food, women, even knowledge and academic accolades, but nothing was enough. Meanwhile, the Muslims he met in Africa lived with deep devotion; Charles was impressed by their dedication, but though he toyed with the idea of becoming Muslim, he ultimately found Islam unconvincing.

Returning to France, Charles began to spend time with a devout cousin, Marie de Bondy. When walking past the Church of St. Augustine in Paris, he stepped in to ask the priest a question. Finding the priest in the confessional, Charles was quickly persuaded—quite unexpectedly—to make his confession. There, in that moment, the Holy Spirit brought about a miracle of conversion. "The moment I realized that God existed," Charles later wrote, "I knew I could not do otherwise than to live for him alone."[11]

Though his soul had finally come home, his life would continue to be one of wandering. He made a pilgrimage to the Holy Land, then entered a Trappist monastery. But the Lord had made short work of his wickedness, and he was too holy for the Trappists, if that's possible. His superior remarked, "Too much perfection and that worries me." Even the abbot said, "The only thing he's missing is wings!"[12]

He moved from one Trappist monastery to another, leaving for good only a month before his final vows. He spent several years as a gardener for the Poor Clares in Nazareth, then Jerusalem. All this time, the Lord was refining in him a desire to be simple and poor, to come to others with no agenda other than friendship.

In 1901, at forty-two, Charles was ordained a priest and returned to the desert that had captured his heart so many years before. There in Algeria, miles and miles from the nearest Christian, Fr. Charles hoped to found a religious order with an apostolate of friendship. Nobody joined him. He sought to love the Algerian people so well that they would come to know Jesus. Nobody converted. For long stretches of time, until he obtained a papal dispensation to celebrate Mass alone, he was without even the Eucharist.

Fr. Charles had one goal for his life in the desert, "'I would like to be so good that people say, 'If such is the servant, what must the Master be?'"[13] There he succeeded. His life won the hearts of the Tuareg people. Still, not one entered the Church. But since Fr. Charles was there in the desert, Jesus was there too, present above all in the Eucharist Fr. Charles spent so many hours adoring.

That was what he was doing when the raiders rode up. They seized him and demanded that he recite the *Shahada*, the Muslim profession of faith. Fr. Charles must have felt a thrill at the prospect of a glorious martyrdom, but even this was denied him. When he refused to apostatize, he was tossed aside. Later, one of the guards was startled and accidentally discharged his weapon, killing Fr. Charles.

Three weeks later, a detachment of French soldiers came to see to the priest's proper burial. There in the sand, they saw a glint of gold: the monstrance, with the Body of Christ within. The commander mounted his horse and held the monstrance before him, riding at the head of the company: a twenty-five-mile long eucharistic procession through the Algerian desert.

In death, Fr. Charles began to achieve the success that was never his in life. In the twenty years after he died, three different religious orders were founded on his spirituality, with many more since. Today, thousands of people have been converted and thousands more strengthened in their faith through the witness and intercession of a wandering hermit with a checkered past.

Charles de Foucauld was given meaning and joy after a life of emptiness, all because he came to know Jesus. Though in life he was a failure, in death he was successful beyond his wildest imaginings. Through his intercession, may all who seek fulfillment without Christ come to know him in a way that fills their hearts with deep, abiding joy. Bl. Charles de Foucauld, pray for us!

Part 9

Saints Who Lived with Great Humility

When asked what three virtues were most necessary for the Christian life, St. Augustine famously replied, "Humility, humility, humility." True humility is not, of course, self-loathing veiled in piety. It's a conviction that we are everything the Father sees in us and only what the Father sees in us. It's a certainty that there's no use in comparing ourselves to others—all that matters is that we are who we were made to be.

Saints who model humility are important witnesses both for those who struggle with pride and for those who err on the side of insecurity. Humility frees us from the need to posture, allowing us to receive the love of God and pass it on to those around us, with no need to grovel for human respect.

In this section, you'll find Saints for whom humility meant leaving behind position and fortune, and another whose humility led him to persevere despite racism from peers and subordinates. You'll find one who worked for years to see himself as God did and another who gladly gave up his reputation for love of souls. For some, this virtue manifests itself as magnanimity, a generosity in pouring oneself out even for one's enemies. For others, humility means fading out of the spotlight and eschewing all attention. For each of us, humility is always rooted in the truth that we are made good by a good God and that all our goodness comes only from him.

53

St. Vitalis of Gaza

The Hermit Who Spent Every Night with a Different Prostitute

(d. 625) ✳ Country: Egypt
Feast Day: January 11

St. Vitalis of Gaza was a seventh-century Egyptian hermit, fasting and praying as all the Desert Fathers had before him. But when Vitalis was about sixty years old, after many years in the wilderness, he left behind his eremitical life and moved to Alexandria. There he became a day laborer, working all day at backbreaking tasks to earn a wage, then proceeding to the local brothel to spend it.

Every night, this former hermit paid to spend the night with a different prostitute. The Christians of Alexandria were (not unreasonably) appalled by this behavior and denounced him to the patriarch of Alexandria. However often they complained, though, the patriarch insisted that they mind their own business.† Unable to stop Vitalis themselves, they could do nothing but treat him with disgust. Vitalis was ridiculed and harassed, his life made miserable, until one day he was attacked in the street and killed.

---

† It's to be hoped that the patriarch knew what Vitalis was doing and didn't just think all religious above reproach. Allegations of abuse and impropriety should always be taken seriously.

When he was found, he was clutching a paper with 1 Corinthians 4:5 written on it: "Therefore, do not make any judgment before the appointed time, until the Lord comes, for he will bring to light what is hidden in darkness and will manifest the motives of our hearts." But the Christians of Alexandria had already judged. "Good riddance," they thought.

Until his funeral.

After he was killed in the street, dozens (if not hundreds) of former prostitutes wept at his funeral. Each testified that she owed her soul to Vitalis, who had come to her room, handed her all the money he had, and said, "Here's your money. I want to buy you one night without sin." She was free to sleep. He, meanwhile, would hold vigil and pray over her.

"Why are you doing this?" the women would ask, and Vitalis would tell them that they were loved, worth more than what they'd done or what had been done to them. He would tell them that Jesus had died to save them and set them free from sin, that the Father delighted in them—no matter what.

He prayed with them and read scripture to them. And when they were ready to accept all this, he found them a way out. He worked to arrange marriages, provide dowries, and even find monasteries willing to accept them. The only thing he asked was that they keep quiet about what he had done. If his good deeds had been known, after all, he would have been kept far from the women he wanted to serve.

Every night. For years. All at the cost of his reputation and ultimately his life.

Long before people understood that victims of human trafficking are just that—victims—Vitalis looked at them and saw not fallen women but chosen daughters of the King. He wasn't just trying to stop them from sinning; he was trying, whatever the cost, to show them what they were worth and how deeply they were loved.

The world needs preachers, but it also needs people like Vitalis: subtle, gentle missionaries preaching first by love, then by murmured words to one aching soul. Vitalis went without sleep or food for the sake of telling broken, suffering women that they were loved; for his troubles he got a rock to the head and a heavenly crown.

May the witness of Vitalis of Gaza remind you what you're worth. May he inspire you to fight for the dignity of the used and abused, the sinner, the traumatized, the hardened, and the fragile. May he give you the courage to preach the Gospel, whatever the circumstances, whatever the cost. And through his intercession, may we all learn to love Jesus more than our reputations, more than our very lives. St. Vitalis of Gaza, pray for us!

54

St. Maria Bertilla Boscardin

The Village Simpleton Who Became a Brilliant Nurse

———≈———

(1888–1922) ✳ Country: Italy
Feast Day: October 20

St. Maria Bertilla Boscardin never bothered thinking much about herself, no matter how people ridiculed her. She knew what she was—clumsy, awkward, and rather unintelligent—but far more important, she knew *who* she was: the beloved of God.

Born to an Italian peasant family, she was called Annetta as a child. Her father was a violent drunk whose rages frequently forced his wife and daughter to flee their home. A childhood hemmed in by fear left Annetta shy and clumsy, always afraid of setting her father off.

Nor could she escape to the village school. Annetta was often kept home from school, which so slowed her progress that she was made to repeat the first grade. Her academic difficulties combined with her awkwardness made her a target for the other children. They ridiculed Annetta for her slow-wittedness, nicknaming her Goose.

The poor child accepted their treatment as no more than she was due. It does seem to have been true humility, though, a genuine assessment of her failings rather than a self-loathing brought on by abuse. Because while Annetta agreed that she was slow and clumsy, she wasn't bothered by it. She knew that whatever the other children thought, whatever her father thought, there was a God in heaven who delighted in her.

Every morning, Annetta would sneak out of her house and run down to the village church to contemplate the Holy Family and imagine what it would be like to live in a home filled with love and peace. Sensing the depth of her love for the Lord and ignoring her academic difficulties, Annetta's pastor allowed her to receive her first Communion early. But when, at fifteen, she told him that she wanted to be a nun, he responded with incredulity: "But you aren't able to do anything! What would the nuns do with you?"[1] Poor Annetta agreed, so aware of her own flaws and certain of God's love that she wasn't hurt by his callous reply.

That night the priest wondered if he had been too hasty. Certainly, the child was no intellectual shining light, but she was pious and obedient. When he next saw Annetta, he asked, "Do you know how to peel potatoes at least?" She replied eagerly that she could. Father nodded. "That will be enough."

Annetta was thrilled! The sisters were less thrilled. What could they do with a girl who could manage nothing more intelligent than "I am ignorant, but I believe in everything that the

Pray for Us

Church believes in"?[2] But at the prompting of the Spirit, they relented. Annetta entered the Sisters of St. Dorothy, taking the name Sr. Maria Bertilla and making no pretenses. "I'm not good at anything," she told the mother superior. "I'm a poor goose. Will you teach me what I must do? I want to become a saint."[3] Sr. Bertilla wanted holiness so badly that she held nothing back. Her prayer (recorded in her journal) was that she would die a thousand times rather than do a single thing to be noticed.

Willing as she was, Sr. Bertilla was utterly incompetent. Her superior tried to convince her to return home, certain she would be a burden on the community. When that failed, she sent Sr. Bertilla to the kitchens or the laundry—anywhere but the hospital. Sr. Bertilla would be a disaster there.

But one day the superior found that she had no other options: either Sr. Bertilla went to work as a nurse or the sickest children would have nobody to care for them. Grimacing, she sent the clumsy, awkward sister into a ward filled with critically ill children, where a moment's delay could cost a life. To everyone's amazement, Sr. Bertilla was a brilliant nurse! Children who were wild with fear calmed almost instantly before her. Parents took the worst possible news with grace when they heard it from Sr. Bertilla. Nervous young doctors drew strength from her. She was kind, calm, and (shockingly) competent. When air raids threatened the hospital in World War I, Sr. Bertilla proved to be courageous as well, insisting on staying with the patients who could not be moved.

At one point, a jealous superior moved Sr. Bertilla to the laundry. But Sr. Bertilla was still humble, in spite of her new-found success. She submitted—until four months later, when she was returned to the hospital and made ward supervisor. Sr. Bertilla served tirelessly through war and epidemic. During the outbreak of Spanish flu, she was hardly ever known to leave the ward. One night, when the boiler blew, Sr. Bertilla stayed up most of the night tending a fire she had built in the yard, boiling small pots of water and bringing each hot-water bottle up a hundred steps to provide some comfort to the sick in the frigid ward.

Unconcerned with esteem, success, or reward, the "useless sister" served as a nurse until five days before she died of cancer at thirty-four. Even then, some of the sisters sneered at the "good-for-nothing" Sr. Bertilla, wondering what all the fuss was about. In her last days, Sr. Bertilla, too, wondered why anyone would care that she was dying. Her whole life, she had been too busy focusing on Jesus to notice herself, so she hadn't realized that she had become a Saint.

Maria Bertilla Boscardin's childhood is all too familiar to many of us, but her peace of heart and genuine humility seem almost miraculous for one who was ridiculed for so long. Through her intercession, may all who are objects of derision and abuse be convinced of the love of the Father, whatever their flaws or deficiencies may be. St. Maria Bertilla Boscardin, pray for us!

55

BL. FRANCISCO DE PAULA VICTOR

The Man Freed from Slavery
Who Fought Using Gentleness and Humility

≋

(1827–1905) ✳ Country: Brazil
Feast Day: September 23

Bl. Francisco de Paula Victor didn't consider himself a revolutionary. He didn't take up arms, and usually didn't even raise his voice. But he fought against racism every day of his life simply by being whom God made him to be.

Victor was born into slavery in Brazil, his father unknown.[‡] He was baptized a week after his birth, with his mother's enslaver standing as godmother. His godmother saw to it that Victor was educated, so he learned to read and write, to play the piano, even to speak French, though he was apprenticed to a tailor and wasn't expected to do anything beyond the work of a craftsman.

But Victor, who had been freed at some point in his youth, had dreams. Though he had never met a Black priest, he longed to become a priest of Jesus Christ. When he confessed this aspiration to the tailor he worked for, the man was furious that Victor would think he had a right to a white man's position. He dragged Victor into the street and beat him.

---

‡ Though nearly all biographies speak of Victor as being born into slavery, recent scholarship suggests that Victor may have been born free and that his godmother, Mariana Barbara Ferreira, may have been a mixed-race woman who used her status to support Victor in his pursuit of the priesthood.

Thus began Victor's quiet resistance. He didn't fight back, knowing it would be suicide. But he didn't give up either. He spoke about his vocation to his mother, godmother, and parish priest. At the time, canon law forbade the ordination of a child born out of wedlock, but the bishop, Ven. Antônio Ferreira Viçoso, a staunch abolitionist, was convinced that Victor had a vocation. So his godmother paid his tuition, and Victor set off for the seminary.

When Victor arrived at the seminary, the other students assumed he was a servant and sent him around back to the servants' entrance. Even when they realized he was one of them, they didn't accept him. Victor endured all kinds of taunts and discrimination, but he refused to fight back through blows or even words. He knew that would only lead to disaster; his battle must be one of silent holiness. Before long, the gentle young man's patience and radiant love for Christ had changed even the hardest hearts at the seminary. "Victor always had hope," one of his classmates remarked in wonder.

It was that hope that kept him going, even when he had no way of knowing if priesthood was even possible for him. Much of Victor's seminary education was conducted under the shadow of uncertainty. He had persuaded the bishop to ordain him, but there was still the matter of canon law. Eventually his bishop obtained an indult for his ordination and Victor was ordained, having fought through all those obstacles to become a priest at only twenty-four. He was sent to the town of Três Pontas to be a parochial vicar and soon a pastor.

The white, slave-owning parishioners who made up a third of Fr. Victor's parish were enraged to find they'd been sent a Black priest. Many refused to receive Communion from him. Again, Fr. Victor had a battle to fight; again, he took a strategic tack. While today we would be rightly horrified at a priest who chose not to rebuke overt racism, Fr. Victor knew that most of his people weren't ready for such correction. What they needed was the witness of his holiness. So he ignored their protests and fury and set about being a holy priest.

Fr. Victor welcomed the poor into his rectory, allowing them to live there when necessary. One man with leprosy had nowhere to go, so Fr. Victor gave him a room and nursed the man himself. When he was given money, he generally gave it away to the next needy person he met, without even counting it first. Soon, Fr. Victor decided to fight the root causes of poverty as well. He founded Três Pontas's first school, which was free and racially integrated; he taught French and Latin there himself when he wasn't riding into the hills to bring the sacraments to those who couldn't come to town. Gradually his people came to respect him, even to love him.

But Fr. Victor's preference for a quiet, humble response to racism wasn't absolute. When he was slighted, he was happy to turn the other cheek; when others were in danger, he would stand up and shout. Once, when a mob of armed men came to town intent on burning down the home of an abolitionist who was housing escaped slaves, Fr. Victor stood at the town's entrance holding up a crucifix to show these men the bloodied face of their Savior who had become a slave for them. "Come in!" he shouted. "Come in! But come over the corpse of your priest." They retreated, and many lives were saved that night.

Fr. Victor's legendary generosity wasn't without cost, and soon it became known that he had accumulated tremendous debts. Ashamed, Fr. Victor decided to resign in disgrace. But his years of humble service had made him so beloved that his people collected enough money to pay off the debts and presented it to him, making him promise not to leave them. These same men and women who had despised and ridiculed him all those years earlier now couldn't imagine life without him. Fr. Victor served in Três Pontas for fifty-three years before dying at age seventy-eight.

Fr. Victor stands as a witness of the power of perseverance, particularly in dismantling racism. He fought against prejudice primarily by serving in quiet humility, but his refusal to surrender in the face of such opposition proves that he was a warrior, even in his gentleness. Fr. Victor discerned that raging against this particular evil wasn't going to work. He could stand and shout and lose, or he could be the Saint God made him to be and win hundreds of souls.

Some of us are called to stand up and shout against injustice, as Fr. Victor did on occasion; others are called to be meek and gentle. Most will find that we're called to both at different times. It takes wisdom and grace to discern how God is calling us to give voice to the truth: with what passion or gentleness or eloquence or simplicity, through which media, and with which acts of service. In some relationships we will have to speak boldly, and in others we will have to bide our time.

Through the intercession of Francisco de Paula Victor, may we be strengthened to fight for justice, whatever it might cost and however long it might take. May we be given clarity to know when to be silent and when to speak up. Bl. Francisco de Paula Victor, pray for us!

56

ST. HUGH OF GRENOBLE

A Bishop Convinced He Wasn't Good Enough
(Despite His Success)

―――――≈―――――

(1053–1132) ✳ Country: France
Feast Day: April 1

Whatever our gifts, it's easy to feel inadequate to the task the Lord has put before us. Each time we fail, our temptation is to give up, certain that we can never be enough.

St. Hugh of Grenoble knew something about this.

Born to a pious family in France and praised for his intelligence from a very young age, the twenty-seven-year-old layman protested loudly when he was chosen bishop. "But I repeat to you that I am not worthy of it!" he exclaimed.

"What fairy tale is this that you're telling me?" asked the bishop of Die. "Who is asking you to act on your own strength? Count first on God, who will give you help."[4] For the first time, Hugh of Grenoble was taught the lesson that would form the chorus of his life: "The LORD will fight for you; you have only to keep still" (Ex 14:14).

Bishop Hugh was overwhelmed by the tasks that lay before him when he inherited a diocese filled with corruption and disinterest. But he took up his bishop's staff and began fighting simony, ignorance, and clerical unchastity throughout the diocese. For two years he persevered, but to little effect. Discouraged by his slow progress, he declared himself unfit for the episcopacy and retreated to a monastery to live out his life as a Benedictine monk. For a year, letters went back and forth between the monastery and the Vatican, with the pope reminding him firmly that the Lord asked not for talent but for faithfulness.

When Bishop Hugh insisted yet again that he was utterly incapable of fulfilling his office, Pope Gregory didn't contradict him. No, Hugh couldn't do much, but he was bishop, the Holy Father continued, and the sacrament could do everything. Chastened, Bishop Hugh returned to Grenoble to continue what he was certain would be a fruitless battle. Often it's only we who can't see the good effect of our work, and Bishop Hugh spent the next fifty years attempting again and again to resign his post, unable to see the reform his leadership and example were accomplishing.

Probably best known for his assistance to St. Bruno in the formation of the Carthusians, Bishop Hugh often retreated to their monastery. Each time there was a new pope, he would tender his resignation, pleading with the Holy Father to find someone better suited to the task. Each time, Rome and St. Bruno would remind him of his duty, both to his diocese and to the God who was working through him.

In the end his labor proved fruitful. After Bishop Hugh's fifty-two-year episcopate, the Diocese of Grenoble was an entirely different place, transformed by his natural gifts and the power of God making use of a humble servant. He had spent half a century reforming the clergy, giving to the poor, and inspiring the faithful to follow in his humble footsteps. Despite suffering debilitating headaches for years, he neither complained nor slowed in his work, and at the end of his life he was worthy of the Father's words: "Well done, good and faithful servant" (Mt 25:23).

Self-confidence didn't come easily to Hugh of Grenoble, but the Lord kept working in and through him just the same. Through his intercession, may God bless all who feel inadequate for the life the Lord has put before them, that in humility they might recognize that God himself will fight for them. St. Hugh of Grenoble, pray for us!

Part 10

Saints Whose Generosity Changed the World

We live in a miserly age, our fists clenched tightly around what surplus we have, with less and less squeezed out for the widow, the orphan, and the alien. This meanness doesn't stop at our checkbooks; our unwillingness to give so often extends to our time, our energy, and our goodwill. We're overworked and exhausted, pumped full of stories of atrocities all around the world that almost seem designed to induce compassion fatigue. It's so much easier to binge TV and ignore the starving and oppressed.

You and I probably don't count ourselves among those who are selfish. Particularly when compared with most of our peers, we measure up pretty well. We don't murder people; we pay our taxes. Even more: we tithe, volunteer, and write our representatives. Still, thinking about the billions who live in poverty can leave us overwhelmed, immobilized by guilt and powerlessness. What can we do in the face of such suffering? It's all too much.

But the extraordinarily generous Saints who changed the world weren't generally men and women with billions of dollars and folders full of well-researched plans. The Saints in this section are ordinary people who saw a need and chose not to look away. More often than not, they were relatively uninterested in helping humanity but intent on helping just one human being. In looking to them, may we recognize what heights of holiness are possible when we simply love the person in front of us.

57

St. Dulce Pontes

*The Sister Who Played Soccer with Orphans,
Pulled a Dozen People out of a Burning Bus,
and Nearly Won a Nobel Prize*

———— ≈ ————

(1914–1992) ✳ Country: Brazil
Feast Day: August 13

St. Dulce Pontes entered religious life hoping to find holiness through small acts of faithfulness. Instead, she changed the face of her nation and was nominated for a Nobel Prize.

Baptized with the name Maria Rita, she was a joyful child of a well-to-do professor of dentistry. She loved watching soccer and was an enormous fan of the Ypiranga soccer team. But a visit to the slums when she was thirteen left her with a longing to serve the poor. She brought suffering people into her own home and offered basic medical care to the homeless, giving them haircuts, too. Her sister, laughing, complained that the beggars at the door scared away all her suitors.

On graduating from high school, Maria Rita asked her father for only one graduation present: that he let her become a sister. She entered the Missionary Sisters of the Immaculate Conception of the Mother of God, taking the name Sr. Dulce in memory of her mother, who had died when Maria Rita was seven. Sr. Dulce was first assigned to teach geography, but her heart was always given over to the poor. She taught literacy in the slums, to children during the day and their parents at night. Then she sought out people on their lunch breaks to catechize them and teach them to read. At only twenty-two, Sr. Dulce founded the first Catholic workers' organization in the state to support the working poor and help them to organize and fight for just treatment. A few years later, she started a school for workers and their children.

Soon people were seeking Sr. Dulce's help. Determined to leave no one unaided, Sr. Dulce went begging for necessary food and medicine for the needy. She even provided homes for the homeless, often in abandoned buildings whose doors sometimes had to be broken down. When they were evicted from the homes where Sr. Dulce had them squatting, she took them to an old fish market. Made to leave that property as well, she approached her Mother Superior for help.

Before long, Sr. Dulce had formed a hostel in the convent's chicken yard. The only stipulation was that she take care of the chickens—which she did by feeding them to her guests. From that makeshift beginning grew a hospital that today cares for thousands of patients each day. And in the midst of all this, Sr. Dulce (who had already trained as a teacher and a nurse) finished a pharmacy course so that she could be of more use to her beloved poor.

Sr. Dulce also founded the Charitable Works Foundation of Sister Dulce, which is today one of the largest charitable organizations in Brazil. Through that foundation she established nursing homes for the elderly and the disabled, an orphanage, and a free clinic, all while continuing to serve the poor with her own hands. She played soccer with orphans, played the accordion to entertain workers—she was all things to all people. Once when a bus crashed outside the convent, Sr. Dulce ran outside, climbed on a crate, broke the window of the burning bus, and pulled a dozen passengers out to safety. Nothing could stop her when lives and souls were at stake.

Sr. Dulce was not physically strong; for the last thirty years of her life, her lungs only worked at 30 percent capacity and her body was noticeably frail. Still, when she found people in need, she would pick them up herself and carry them to the hospital she had built from the ground up. She was always out seeking the lost, even when exhausted by her efforts.

By the end of her life, Sr. Dulce was one of the most famous women in Brazil. She had two private audiences with Pope John Paul II. She was nominated for a Nobel Prize. The president of Brazil *kissed her feet*. But what really mattered to Sr. Dulce was the love of God and the love of his people, especially the poor who are so dear to his heart. When she died at seventy-seven, the whole nation mourned—but Sr. Dulce rejoiced.

Dulce Pontes is a beautiful reminder to live one step at a time. When she was shuttling people from one abandoned building to the next, she probably felt frustrated and overwhelmed, but because she did what needed to be done each day, thousands were saved and Brazil was forever changed. The Mother Teresa of Brazil, Sr. Dulce was a woman whose efforts to do small things saved the lives and honored the dignity of thousands of people. Through her intercession, may we live with the same focus and the same abandon. St. Dulce Pontes, pray for us!

VEN. PIERRE TOUSSAINT

*The New York City Philanthropist
Who Was Born into Slavery*

———— ≋ ————

(1766–1853) ✳ Country: Haiti, United States

Ven. Pierre Toussaint had no time for bitterness—he was too busy changing lives. Born into slavery in Haiti, Pierre was brought to New York City when his enslavers fled the impending unrest in Haiti in 1787. There he was trained as a hairdresser, a particularly complicated and lucrative profession in an era of elaborate updos.

Skilled at his work, Pierre was also peaceful, joyful, and discreet. He gave good advice and refused to gossip, insisting that he was a hairdresser, not a news journal. So virtuous was he that many of his clients referred to him as "our St. Pierre." All this combined to make Pierre very much in demand among New York's elite. While most of his wages went to his owners, Pierre used his free time to work and collect money to purchase the freedom of his beloved sister Rosalie.

Not long after their move to New York, though, the family discovered that they had lost their fortune; Pierre's master returned to Haiti in an attempt to recover it, but died there, leaving his young widow destitute in New York. Rather than purchasing his own freedom, Pierre spent his savings to protect and provide for Marie, the woman whose lifestyle had been built on the backs of his people. He continued in slavery for sixteen more years because he was concerned that she wouldn't allow him to serve her if he were free. Nor did he content himself with

Pray for Us

paying her bills. Pierre saw Marie's sorrow and took it upon himself to lighten her load however he could. She had no claim to such kindness, except inasmuch as she was a human being. But the man who would become one of New York City's great philanthropists didn't think twice about helping her.

When the meager amount he allowed himself to retain from his wages finally added up, Pierre purchased his sister's freedom instead of his own. And after Marie finally freed him on her deathbed, the forty-one-year-old Pierre earned enough to buy the freedom of Juliette Noel, a woman twenty-two years his junior with whom he had fallen in love. The couple married four years later. Pierre continued to work sixteen hours a day to earn money for his charitable ventures while also investing in real estate, banks, and insurance companies. Through it all, he never missed daily Mass. For sixty-six years, Pierre could be seen kneeling each morning at 6 a.m. in St. Peter's Church, eagerly receiving the graces that would make it possible for him to pour himself out in service all day.

Though Pierre and Juliette were unable to have children, they adopted his sister's daughter, Euphemia, when the child was only six months old. Pierre loved Euphemia so deeply, she scarcely thought herself unfortunate to have lost both parents. One day, on learning that orphans had neither father nor mother, young Euphemia looked downcast on their behalf. Then, suddenly, she brightened. "But have they no uncle?"[1] she asked, convinced that an uncle such as hers was worth all the mothers and fathers in the world.

When Euphemia died at fourteen, Pierre was disconsolate. He withdrew from society and began to look thin and drawn. But as he grieved, he continued to go to Mass each morning and eventually the hope of heaven succeeded in pulling him through to the other side of grief. Once more, he took up his work with the poor and the suffering.

Over the course of his long life, Pierre provided significant funding to the orphanage run by St. Elizabeth Ann Seton and to the Oblate Sisters of Providence (an order for Black sisters founded by Servant of God Mary Elizabeth Lange[2]). With his wife, Pierre founded New York's first Catholic school for Black children, as well as a credit bureau and employment agency for Black people. He gave so much to the building fund of Old St. Patrick's Cathedral that on the day of its dedication a seat was reserved for him at the front of the church—though when he first arrived, the usher didn't realize who Pierre was and turned him away entirely because of the color of his skin.

His generosity wasn't limited only to financial gifts. Pierre also had a heart for being present to the sick and the sorrowing. He cared for victims of yellow fever, occasionally taking those who had been abandoned into his own home. When he visited the grieving, he wasn't one to offer platitudes or advice; more often than not, he just sat with the one who was suffering. After one visit, a friend asked him, "What did you say to her?" "Nothing," he responded. "I could only take her hand and weep with her and then I went away; there was nothing to be said."[3]

The Toussaints ransomed enslaved people and fostered orphan boys, opening their homes to Black children who would otherwise have found themselves on the street. So eager was Pierre to be of service that he furtively offered help to those who were disinclined to accept a Black man's generosity. And he felt no bitterness toward those who avoided him from shame after their fortunes changed. Instead, he was glad that they no longer needed him.

Pierre continued his grueling work schedule long after it was necessary. Urged to retire, Pierre responded, "I have enough for myself, but if I stop working I have not enough for others."[4]

Pierre described himself as having a quick temper, but if he did he seems to have mastered it young. Friends said of him that they never knew him to speak a harsh or uncharitable word, even

Pray for Us

in the face of racism and ingratitude. Indeed, even those most inclined to find fault could find none with Pierre; accounts that are dripping with racism still describe him as elegant, dignified, gentle, and so virtuous as to make one wonder if he was truly a man of flesh and blood. At his funeral, the priest declared, "There were few left among the clergy superior to him in devotion and zeal for the Church and for the glory of God; among laymen, none."[5] Another white man put it quite simply: "The most perfect gentleman I have ever known is Pierre Toussaint."[6]

Pierre Toussaint was one of the great philanthropists of nineteenth-century New York, above all because he refused to allow other people's prejudices and sins to dictate his charity. He poured his whole life out in service to anybody who needed it, whatever their race, and whether or not they deserved it. Through his intercession, may we be given hearts as generous as his, extravagant in offering mercy as well as charity. Ven. Pierre Toussaint, pray for us!

59

BL. AUGUSTINE THEVARPARAMBIL KUNJACHAN

*An Unremarkable Priest Who Became
the Apostle to the "Untouchables"*

———— ≈ ————

(1891–1973) ✳ Country: India
Feast Day: October 16

Bl. Augustine Thevarparambil Kunjachan was rather unremarkable. He was a short man with no particular talents to speak of—he wasn't a theologian or a great orator. But by virtue of his priesthood, he was a father. And as a father, he changed the lives of thousands of outcasts, simply because he loved them.

Born to a Syro-Malabar family in the Kerala region of India, an area with many Catholics, Augustine was the youngest child in his family and always the shortest in his class, never reaching even five feet. He was ordained a priest at age thirty and given the nickname Kunjachan (Little Father) because of his diminutive stature. For a few years, Kunjachan lived the ordinary life of a parochial vicar, but he was compelled to move back home to recuperate from a serious illness.

It was there that Kunjachan began to notice the plight of the people he (and most of India) had always overlooked: the Dalits (often called "untouchables"). These were people who were considered unclean by the caste system, who were treated as subhuman and used for what amounted to slave labor. Though

St. Kuriakose Elias Chavara had devoted his life to their service, most Indians, Catholic and non-Catholic alike, had avoided contact with these abandoned children of God. For the first time, Kunjachan began to question this. He started visiting the Dalits in his home parish, speaking to them about Jesus and inviting them to be baptized.

Kunjachan wasn't a compelling speaker, nor a brilliant administrator capable of mobilizing missionaries into the slums. He was simply a father, and as a father he went searching for his Dalit children. Each day he rose at 4 a.m. to celebrate Mass and then set off with a catechist to visit his people. That he bothered to learn their names, let alone enter their homes, was a tremendous testimony to their dignity. He helped children obtain an education, starting schools in sheds to fight the universal illiteracy among the Dalits, who were barred from entering the public schools. He assisted women in obtaining fair pay and helped change the narrative surrounding this people despised by their compatriots. But more than anything, he spoke the name of Jesus to people who were longing (perhaps more than most) for the love of Christ.

For nearly fifty years, Kunjachan lived with the Dalits, baptized them, and used any money that came his way in their service. Rather than accept the lie that the Dalits were subhuman, he fought to honor their innate human dignity, whatever the cost. He ignored opposition from Christians and non-Christians, many of whom felt that his work was unbecoming a man of his status. Having encountered a God who gave his life for outcasts, Kunjachan disagreed.

Kunjachan had no interest in other people's good opinion. He worked for love of his people, not for any accolades that might come. And outside the parishes whose Dalit population he served (crossing parish boundaries to be with his people), he was almost entirely unknown. This humility gave him the freedom to be a true father to his people. At his funeral, the priest who buried him announced, "We are participating in the funeral of a saint."[7] Unlike most graveside canonizations, this one wasn't hasty. It was the culmination of a life of humble service lived by an ordinary man with nothing to offer but the heart of the Father.

Many Saints have left behind organizations and foundations to continue their work long after their death, but not Kunjachan. In all his years of service, Kunjachan accomplished no systemic change, founded no hospitals or universities. His work wasn't about changing the world but rather about speaking hope into one heart at a time. He was never even made a pastor, preferring the freedom of a lowlier position that allowed him to spend his days eating with the Dalits, sitting by their bedsides, praying, weeping, and hoping with them. Instead of leaving behind a legacy of foundations and structures, he left behind five thousand Catholic Dalits, men and women transformed by the love of Christ.

Augustine Thevarparambil Kunjachan is a Saint for the ordinary Christian, for all of us who find holiness not by headlines but by loving the person right in front of us. Through his intercession, may we leave behind all desire for human respect and focus on doing small things with great love. Bl. Augustine Thevarparambil Kunjachan, pray for us!

60

VEN. FELIX VARELA Y MORALES

A Condemned Criminal Who Spent His Life Serving Immigrants

———— ≈ ————

(1788–1853) ✳ Country: Cuba, United States

Ven. Felix Varela y Morales was a Renaissance man of unparalleled intelligence who gave up his country for love of enslaved people and spent his life for love of immigrants. He died in poverty and obscurity and is celebrated as one of the great intellectuals of Cuban history, though he spent most of his life in exile.

Born in Cuba, Felix Varela was orphaned by the age of six and sent to St. Augustine, Florida, to be raised by his grandfather. The old general wanted to send Felix to a military academy to follow in his footsteps, but Felix was sure that he had a priestly vocation. He returned to Havana to study and was ordained at twenty-three.

After his ordination, Fr. Varela was made a seminary professor, teaching philosophy, chemistry, physics, constitutional law, and economics. A talented violinist, he helped form the first philharmonic society in Cuba. He wrote several Spanish-language philosophy textbooks, unusual for a discipline typically taught in Latin. His work as an educator was so formative that José de la Luz y Caballero, one of the great intellectuals of nineteenth-century Cuba, said, "Whenever you think about Cuba, you will think with respect and veneration of him, the first who taught us how to think."[8] Indeed, that phrase, "the one who taught us how to think," is nearly synonymous with the name Varela among many Cubans even today.

After a decade of teaching, Fr. Varela was sent to Spain to represent Cuba at the Spanish Parliament, where he advocated for independence for the colonies and an abolition of slavery. It came as no surprise when he met with resistance. Knowing that he was facing imprisonment (at best), Fr. Varela fled the country, stopping in New York City on his way home. Once there, word reached him that he had been condemned to death for his advocacy for the rights of Black and Latino people; returning to Cuba would cost him his life. Fr. Varela had given up his homeland in a failed attempt to save his people. It would be nearly sixty-five more years before slavery was abolished in Cuba and seventy-five years before the Cuban people won their independence.

Though New York wasn't under Spanish rule, Fr. Varela wasn't entirely outside the reach of his enemies. The Spanish crown was writing letters warning against "the dangerous Cuban reformer," which made the bishop of New York reluctant to accept Fr. Varela. Worse, the Spanish governor of Cuba sent an assassin after him. But Fr. Varela was already well loved by his Irish parishioners who, on seeing a one-eyed, Spanish-speaking thug skulking about the neighborhood, took matters into their own hands. Thoroughly intimidated by the threats he received, the would-be assassin returned to Cuba, leaving Fr. Varela free to serve.

Most of Fr. Varela's work in New York was with the much-despised Irish, a group of recent immigrants who were the objects of systemic discrimination. For love of them, Fr. Varela built orphanages and parishes, established schools that taught girls as well as boys, nursed the sick during a cholera epidemic, and helped parishioners find work and fight alcoholism. He learned to speak Irish as well as English, a fact that offers a challenge to any descendants of those Irishmen who may be disinclined to return the favor in serving Spanish-speaking immigrant communities.

Fr. Varela helped parishioners find work and fight alcoholism. He spent hours in the confessional and more hours visiting the sick, despite his chronic asthma. He spoke of mercy to everyone, once even accompanying Spanish pirates to the gallows. And he continued his intellectual pursuits as a theologian, a writer, and an inventor. He edited and wrote for several publications, including a Spanish-language revolutionary newspaper that was secretly distributed in Cuba. He developed a system of air circulation to be used in hospitals and held a patent for "easy motion, pavement-saving wheels," designed to reduce noise from carriage wheels.

When Fr. Varela was made vicar general of the Archdiocese of New York, he didn't stop being a pastor. He continued his work in the trenches, even while serving as theological advisor to the Baltimore Catechism. He was a model of restraint and respect in his disputes with Protestants at a time when anti-Catholic sentiment often turned violent. More than anything, Fr. Varela's work in serving immigrants and integrating them into the American Catholic Church set the tone for the immigrant Church thriving in the United States today.

Toward the end of his life, Fr. Varela was offered a pardon by the Spanish government; accepting it would mean the end of his long exile but also acknowledging that he had committed a crime in advocating the abolition of slavery and the independence of Spanish colonies. Fr. Varela would never compromise on the universality of human dignity, even to return home. Instead, his health worn out by decades of service, he moved from New York to St. Augustine, where he spent the last few years of his life before his death at sixty-four.

Felix Varela y Morales was an intellectual, a revolutionary, a warrior for human dignity, and above all a humble priest who loved his people. Through his intercession, may we be given the wisdom to see how our particular gifts are needed in the fight to defend human dignity, and the courage to serve. Ven. Felix Varela y Morales, pray for us!

BL. JOSÉ GREGORIO HERNÁNDEZ

The Medical Genius Who Served the Poor for Free

———— ≋ ————

(1864–1919) ✳ Country: Venezuela
Feast Day: October 26

Bl. José Gregorio Hernández is among the best-loved figures of Venezuelan history: a medical pioneer whose life was marked by genius and quiet piety. He was born to a working-class family, the second of seven children. His father owned the store in their small town, supplying the locals with dry goods, medications, and herbal remedies. José Gregorio's mother died when he was only seven; his father soon remarried and had six more children.

From a young age, José Gregorio's intelligence was evident. His family sent him to Caracas to study at thirteen. Soon, José Gregorio was fluent in Spanish, English, German, French, Italian, Portuguese, and Latin; he studied music, philosophy, and theology in addition to science, history, and math. But José Gregorio's path had already been chosen for him by a father who was fascinated by medicine, so seventeen-year-old José Gregorio entered medical school.

On completing school, José Gregorio returned home to practice rural medicine with hopes of moving into remote areas in

Pray for Us

the Andes to serve. But after a year he learned that he had won a scholarship to the University of Paris, so off he went to study bacteriology, histology, and experimental physiology with some of the greatest minds in Europe. Upon his return three years later, José Gregorio was awarded a position as a medical professor at the University of Caracas—a position that had been created just for him since he was the only man in the country qualified for it.

José Gregorio spent seventeen years transforming the study of medicine in Venezuela. He brought the first microscope to Venezuela, built the first experimental physiology lab in Latin America, isolated the bacterium causing the plague, and advocated for laboratory analysis as an instrumental component of the diagnostic process. He's called the "founder of bacteriology in Venezuela" and the "Venezuelan Pasteur."

But for all his worldly success, José Gregorio longed for more. At forty-three, when he finally felt that he had done his duty in supporting his many siblings, he sailed to Italy to enter the Carthusians, but he was forced to leave after nine months because of poor health. Immediately upon returning to Venezuela, he applied to the diocesan seminary, but colleagues and students begged him to return to the university, and he felt he had no choice. Not long after, he went to Rome to study; once again his health forced him to abandon any hope of entering religious life, this time for good.

After this last disappointment, José Gregorio resigned himself to a life of lay service to the poor and to the medical community of Venezuela. He returned to Caracas and took up his work again, teaching medical students and continuing to write. Over the years, he published books and articles on bacteriology and embryology as well as literary works and a philosophy textbook. He was a vocal opponent of the theory of evolution as divorced from the creative power of God, but by 1912 he was voicing a nuanced understanding of evolution as God's creative hand at work in the world.

José Gregorio was the driving force behind the modernization of Venezuelan medicine, but he was first and foremost a Christian, a man of prayer who rose before 5 a.m. each day to attend Mass. He saw Christ in the poor and spent hours each day making house calls to people who could not pay. When patients came to his home, they left what they could pay in a tray by the door. If they couldn't pay, they were welcome to take what they needed from that same tray.

On the last day of his life, José Gregorio was called away from a rare moment of rest to the bed of a sick woman. After examining her, he went to a nearby pharmacy to purchase her medication. As he was crossing the street, one of the few cars in Caracas struck and killed him. So beloved was the simple, diminutive professor that thousands attended the funeral of this man who had changed Venezuela forever by educating its people and caring for her poor.

José Gregorio Hernández is a role model for geniuses and for ordinary working people. He didn't allow his brilliance to make him arrogant or his busyness to make him selfish. Nor did he allow his thwarted dream of priesthood to make him bitter. Whatever he did, he did for love of God and man, undistracted by the opinions of others. Through his intercession, may we live with such humility, industry, and openness to God's will. Bl. José Gregorio Hernández, pray for us!

62

VEN. SATOKO KITAHARA

An Aristocratic Convert Who Moved to the Slums and Became Holy by Smiling

(1929–1958) ✳ Country: Japan

The daughter of an aristocratic university professor, Ven. Satoko Kitahara was raised Shinto. She had a privileged upbringing and enjoyed many luxuries and cultural opportunities, becoming a skilled pianist and studying to be a pharmacist. But World War II, particularly the surrender of Japan, left her deeply disillusioned. Like many Japanese young people in the wake of the war, she wondered if life was truly worth living.

Satoko sought to drown out the questions that kept her up at night by spending every possible hour at the cinema. Without realizing it, she had embarked on the course that so many people follow: existence as a desperate series of distractions from the agonizing emptiness of life without Christ.

It's likely that her life would have continued that way but for a chance encounter with a poorly made statue of the Blessed Mother in a church Satoko had entered at random. In Mary's face Satoko saw the peace she longed for. She began to ask questions, to seek out Christians. Again and again she saw that Christians had a hope that nobody else had. Satoko realized that this was what she'd been searching for and, at twenty, she became a Catholic.

On the day of her baptism, a sister approached Satoko, telling her what a beautiful smile she had. Then she asked Satoko to promise God that she would try to smile whenever she could.

Satoko made that promise and her smile brought light to count-less lives.

After her Baptism, Satoko asked one religious community after another to accept her as a postulant. Always the reply came that she was too ill; she had contracted tuberculosis years earlier and been seriously weakened by it. But God had something beautiful in mind for Satoko, and it began when a companion of St. Maximilian Kolbe, Br. Zeno, met her at random and invited her into the world of the desperately poor.

In the years after the war, Japan's streets were filled with the destitute. Ashamed to beg, most Japanese sought work—any work. A few hundred had gathered in a shantytown called Ants Town (in reference to how industrious ants are). These people were ragpickers: men, women, and children who go through other people's trash to find things to sell. They were dirty, smelly, and covered with lice. Satoko smiled at them and invited them to her home for piano lessons.

For some time, the children came by for piano lessons and tutoring. Satoko began to experience the beauty of spiritual motherhood as she learned to love these bedraggled children. The more she loved them, the harder it was to feel that she was doing enough. Satoko had a realization: "I had thought I was a great Christian because I condescended to dole out some free time, helping Ants children with their homework! . . . It hit me now. There was only one way to help those ragpicker children: become a ragpicker like them!"[9] So the refined aristocrat joined them in the streets, picking through dumpsters alongside them, always with a smile on her face.

Even this wasn't enough for Satoko, though. Souls were being lost because these people couldn't believe that they truly mattered to God. If they saw how much they mattered to her, perhaps they would believe. She packed a few meager possessions and, smiling, moved to Ants Town. There she taught the children, took them on excursions to the country, improved their manners, and, above all, preached the Gospel. Many of the children came to know Christ, as did their parents. Even the bitter alcoholic who ran Ants Town was eventually baptized.

All the while, Satoko was getting sicker. Her tuberculosis had returned, and she was no longer strong enough to get out of bed, though people still flocked to her for a kind word or a smile of encouragement. But Satoko, gentle as she was, had an iron will when it came to protecting her people. When word came that the authorities were planning to evict the residents of Ants Town, she calmly appended a note to the letter the community sent in response. She informed them that if they drove the people from their homes, she would sit in front of the city office, fasting and praying, until officials offered the people a new site to build on. Or until she died.

The authorities worried at the reaction her public starvation would warrant and so left Ants Town alone, in the capable hands of a fragile young woman. Satoko died there at only twenty-eight, having smiled through so much pain and darkness and thus brought so many to Christ.

Satoko Kitahara changed the fate of hundreds of souls by walking alongside them with a smile. Through her intercession, may we too be able to love so well that others come to Christ because of the peace and joy they see in us. Ven. Satoko Kitahara, pray for us!

Part 11
Saints with Sinful Pasts

If there's one thing that keeps people from accepting the love of God, it's a conviction that their sins disqualify them, that the shame that binds them somehow makes them unlovable. Or if they understand enough about the Cross to realize that the Blood of Christ is poured out for even the most wicked, they see themselves as second-tier Christians: not beyond salvation but certainly not in the running for a halo.

Mercifully, there's a Saint for that. The canon of Saints is filled with mass murderers, adulterers, Satanists, rapists, persecutors of Christians, or blasphemers. Because there is *nothing* that puts us beyond the power of grace: no sin that God can't redeem, no addiction that God can't turn to glory. To prove this, the Church offers us Saints with hideous backstories, but she also offers us Christians who fell and had to be converted anew. She offers us decent men and women who struggled against certain vices all their lives, real people with real brokenness and real shame, and then shows us how God was glorified in them.

When we read these stories, we're reminded of the truth that every one of us is called to holiness. Because you are not your sin. You are not your shame. You aren't your abortion, your addiction, your bank account, or your résumé. You are loved beyond imagining by a God who died to save you. May the Saints in this section give you hope: it's not too late.

63

BL. BARTOLO LONGO

A Satanic High Priest Turned Preacher of the Rosary

———— ≈ ————

(1841–1926) ✳ Country: Italy
Feast Day: October 5

Sometimes reading the lives of the Saints is discouraging. They may have been imperfect, as we all are, but it can seem that none of them ever sinned the way people today do. Even proverbial bad boy St. Augustine was a decent guy by today's standards. It's easy for those of us who have made terrible choices to feel discouraged.

And then there's Bl. Bartolo Longo.

Like many Saints, Bartolo was raised in a faithful Catholic family that prayed the Rosary daily. Unlike most Saints, Bartolo spent his twenties as a satanic priest.

As a young man, Bartolo had many hobbies: learning to play the flute, the violin, and the piano; directing a school band; and studying literature, fencing, and dancing. But when he began university studies in Naples, he was eager to enter fully into the experience of a secular university. In mid-nineteenth-century Italy, that meant anticlericalism, atheism, and ultimately the occult.

Bartolo began attending séances and experimenting with drugs. He even got involved in orgies. He lured people away from the Catholic faith, publicly ridiculing the Church of his childhood. Before long, the newly minted lawyer was "ordained" a priest of Satan. As a Satanic bishop intoned blasphemous words, the walls of the room shook and disembodied screams terrified those in attendance.

Bartolo soon found himself paranoid and miserable, on the brink of a nervous breakdown. But his family prayed, and their faithful prayers finally broke down the wall of anger and sin that Bartolo had built around himself. One night, he heard the voice of his long-dead father crying out to him, "Return to God!"

Horrified, Bartolo visited a friend who lived nearby, Professor Vincenzo Pepe. When Pepe realized what had become of Bartolo, the way his depravity was endangering his soul and his sanity as well, he cried, "Do you want to die in an insane asylum and be damned forever?"[1] Pepe's courage in pointing out the danger his friend was in cut through Bartolo's defenses, and he agreed to meet with a Dominican priest, Fr. Alberto Radente.

Fr. Alberto encouraged Bartolo to make a thorough confession. After a month of direction, Bartolo was finally absolved and began his work of drawing people back to Christ. He stood up in the middle of cafés and student parties and denounced occult practices. He served the poor and instructed the ignorant. Eventually he pronounced vows as a lay Dominican on the Feast of Our Lady of the Rosary. Cleansed and consecrated, Bartolo visited one last séance. He walked in, held up a rosary, and called out, "I renounce spiritualism because it is nothing but a maze of error and falsehood."[2]

But Bartolo continued to struggle with memories of his past. He felt unworthy of God's forgiveness, certain that he was permanently marred by his sin. One day, Bartolo began to consider his past way of life. "Despite my repentance, I thought: I am still consecrated to Satan, and I am still his slave and property as he awaits me in hell. As I pondered over my condition, I experienced a deep sense of despair and almost committed suicide."[3]

In that moment, Bartolo remembered the Rosary of his childhood and the love of the Blessed Mother. He felt our Lady tell him that his path to heaven was through teaching others to pray the Rosary—not that he could earn salvation but that this work could remind him that he had been won by the Blood of Christ and consecrated to the Blessed Mother. Satan had no power over him.

Bartolo moved to Pompeii, where he began Rosary groups, organized Marian processions, and began work on a shrine to Our Lady of the Rosary. His work was funded by the Countess di Fusco, with whom he worked so closely that rumors began to spread about the nature of their relationship. Though Bartolo had taken a private vow of chastity, he was encouraged by Pope Leo XIII to marry the countess for the sake of the work; the two entered into a Josephite marriage and continued to serve the poor.

For more than fifty years, Bartolo preached the Rosary, founded schools for the poor, established orphanages for the children of criminals, and transformed a ruined city of death into a renewed city dedicated to the living Mother of God. At his beatification, Pope John Paul II proclaimed Bl. Bartolo Longo "the man of Our Lady" (*l'uomo della Madonna*).[4]

Bartolo Longo was a vile, degenerate, blasphemous satanic priest. But this is his legacy: the transformative power of grace. Through his intercession, may God pour healing mercy on all who are caught up in the occult, on all who think that they're beyond hope, that their purity can never be restored and their lives never made whole, that they've lost their chance at holiness. May they join the ranks of murderers, addicts, and Satanists whose halos shine undimmed around the throne of the unblemished Lamb of God. Bl. Bartolo Longo, pray for us.

St. Mary of Egypt

A Life of Depravity Handed Over to Jesus

―――――≈―――――

(344–421) ✳ Country: Egypt, Palestine
Feast Day: April 1

St. Mary of Egypt is often referred to as a prostitute, but she wasn't. She didn't charge money.

Mary had run away from home at twelve. Was she running from abuse? Suffering from mental illness? We can't know for certain, though in the earliest account of her life she does speak of her parents' love. Regardless of her motivations (and of who might have taken advantage of her once she reached Alexandria), Mary began a life of "insatiable desire and an irrepressible passion,"[5] as she later told St. Zosima of Palestine, begging on the street and spinning flax to fund her hedonism.

The object of Mary's life was pleasure, and whether she took this pleasure from a willing partner, seduced a less-than-willing one, or even forced a man to it was of no matter to her. Indeed, we have proof of this last in her earliest biography. While explaining the depravity of her life, she said, "To all this I frequently forced those miserable youths even against their own will."[6]

Forced them. Against their will. That's the kind of person Mary was.

But God's mercy was bigger than even her sin.

Curiosity led the young woman to join a pilgrimage to the Holy Land. On her way, she amused herself with the passengers on board, including innocent youths traveling to venerate the Holy

Pray for Us

Cross. Mary's depravity continued when she got to Jerusalem, until she followed the crowds on the Feast of the Exaltation of the Holy Cross. When she reached the Church of the Holy Sepulchre, she attempted to enter but was unable. Even after the crowds dissipated, she found herself stopped at the threshold of the church; no amount of strength could force her across.

Initially baffled, she gradually became aware that it was her sin that barred her entry. Marvelously, this was a tender moment, not a cruel one. She later said, "The word of salvation gently touched the eyes of my heart and revealed to me that it was my unclean life which barred the entrance to me."[7] Mary began to weep over her sin—not the sorrow of self-loathing but a compunction rooted in the love of God, a guilt that leads to true repentance.

At that moment, Mary's eyes fell on an image of the Mother of God. She pleaded with the Virgin Mary to intercede for her, that she might enter the church and see the Cross of Christ. Then she entered unhindered, looked upon the Cross and the Eucharist, and begged God's mercy. She received Communion (presumably after confessing her sins) and then followed the promptings of the Blessed Mother into the desert.

We would expect, given how Saint stories often go, for Mary then to have been pure and joyful all the days of her life. But conversion is often gradual and usually takes hard work, even for Saints. Mary had spent seventeen years in sin, and she spent seventeen years fighting against passions, memories, and desires. She longed for wine, was tempted to sing satanic songs, and was tormented by lust. But with every moment of temptation and shame, Mary cried out to her heavenly protectress, the Mother of God.

Finally Mary was freed of her temptations. She lived another thirty years of prayer and penance, her clothes fallen away in tatters and her only food what she could scavenge from the barren desert. That she survived so long was clearly miraculous, as St. Zosimas of Palestine insisted when he discovered her forty-seven years after her conversion: a grievous sinner who had been transformed by grace.

Mary's life is clearly not one to be imitated, either before her conversion or after. She was sent into the desert where she had no access to the sacraments nor even a Bible. But God's grace was at work even there. Mary became a Saint so remarkable, so revered, that in the Byzantine Church she's one of the few whose feast is celebrated on a Sunday. By God's abundant mercy, the very sin that ought to have kept her from him drew her to him.

"Her many sins have been forgiven; hence, she has shown great love" (Lk 7:47), Jesus said of the sinful woman who anointed him. He may well have said it of Mary of Egypt. Perhaps you, too, will hear those words if you allow him to transform your past. There is no past sin that disqualifies you from sainthood. God's mercy is always bigger. Through her intercession, may all who are far from Christ be transformed and made witnesses to his mercy. St. Mary of Egypt, pray for us!

STS. MARY OF EDESSA AND ABRAHAM OF KIDUNAIA

A Hermitess Who Became a Prostitute and the Father Who Brought Her Home

———≈———

(d. 371) and (d. 366) ✳ Country: Turkey
Feast Day: October 29

Some Saints are sweet and sinless their whole lives; others live for years as wild sinners before experiencing great conversions. Then there are those who try a little of both, like St. Mary of Edessa.

Mary was born to a noble family in fourth-century Turkey. Her parents died when she was only seven, but she was adopted by her uncle, St. Abraham Kidunaia, and began to live a remarkably holy life.

For twenty years, Mary lived as an anchoress, following the advice of her hermit-uncle as she sought a deep life of prayer and sacrifice. But one day a monk with evil intentions caught sight of Mary when he was visiting Abraham. Determined to seduce her, he spent a year insinuating himself into her life and then grooming her, becoming more and more intimate until he manipulated her into sleeping with him.

Though Mary was truly a victim of clerical sexual abuse, she blamed herself (as many do). She tore her tunic and wished for death, convinced that she was irredeemably sinful and unworthy of mercy. Like Adam and Eve, she was so ashamed she hid from the one who loved her. "How shall I even try to speak with my holy uncle?" she asked in anguish. "Seeing that I am already dead and have no hope of gaining salvation, I had better leave here and go to some foreign land where nobody knows me."[8]

Even if she had been at fault, Mary should have remembered the mercy of God and cast herself upon it. To be a Christian, after all, is to be deeply loved by a God who sees us in all our sin and loves us anyway. She had only to turn to the Lord and beg for healing, letting him sign his name over her past once again and claim her as his own. Instead she succumbed to a despair that convinced her that she could never again be holy. She fled her sacred home in the desert for a brothel, there to live as the sinner she was convinced she was destined to be.

Abraham, meanwhile, was oblivious to all that had happened. But that night he had a vision of a dragon consuming a dove; two days later, he saw the same dragon with its belly torn open. He reached in to pull out the dove, miraculously unharmed. He called out to Mary to tell her about it, but when he received no answer Abraham realized that she was the subject of the vision. The devil had carried off the daughter of his soul, and all he could do in her absence was to pray for her.

Pray he did, for two years. Finally a report reached him that his sweet, pure Mary was living the harlot's life. Had she known that he would learn of her lifestyle, Mary likely would have expected him to be disgusted. But Abraham was a Christian, a priest, and a father. Like the Good Shepherd, he was off without a moment's hesitation, eager to bring his lost lamb home.

Abraham hadn't left his hermitage in decades, but he disguised himself as a soldier and began his journey. He made an appointment with Mary the prostitute, who didn't recognize him until he began to weep, begging her to come home. While he spoke to Mary in her brothel, Abraham reminded her, "There is nothing new in falling down in the contest; the wicked thing is to keep on lying there."[9]

And so, like Jesus under his Cross, she got back up again. Moved by her father's powerful love, Mary returned to her hermitage and began a life of penance for her years as a prostitute. But she had no need to earn God's mercy, and he wouldn't allow her to continue in her shame. Within three years, God gave her the gift of miracles, particularly the miraculous conversion of sinners; Mary hadn't just returned to her original state of holiness but had been brought through trauma and sin to greater prayer, greater virtue, and greater power in Christ.

Mary of Edessa is a powerful witness to what God is capable of when we offer him our sin and our shame—and what we're capable of when we don't. Abraham of Kidunaia, meanwhile, is an image of true fatherhood, modeled on God the Father and his unchanging love. Through their intercession, may survivors of abuse (particularly clerical abuse) experience the unceasing love of the Father and find healing and peace. May those who have loved Jesus but have fallen away be given the courage to be reborn. St. Mary of Edessa and St. Abraham Kidunaia, pray for us!

66

St. Michael Hồ Đình Hy

A Scrupulous Former Adulterer
Who Finally Realized He Couldn't Earn Mercy

(1808–1857) ✳ Country: Vietnam
Feast Day: May 22

St. Michael Hồ Đình Hy was a pillar of the Christian community and an adulterer, a man of great charity and a traitor. Born to a high-ranking Christian family, Michael married a Christian woman and became a mandarin, a bureaucrat in the Vietnamese government who ultimately rose so high in the ranks that he oversaw all the country's silk manufacturing. He was trusted by the king and envied by his colleagues, whose attempt to have him fired ended with Michael being given a raise instead—by the king himself.

But for all Michael's wealth and fame, his time at court wreaked havoc on his soul. Though a practicing Catholic, Michael felt compelled to attend pagan rituals. And while he may not have directly participated in those ceremonies, he was certainly affected by other elements of court life. Michael took a mistress and fathered three illegitimate children. Still he considered himself a Catholic, though rather a tortured one. He had each of his children baptized, but for several years was unable to live according to his convictions.

Finally Michael realized the peril his soul was in. He repented of his sin and embarked on a life of impressive service. He ransomed two girls from slavery and adopted them. He brought an opium addict into his home and cared for the man until his death. He smuggled missionaries throughout Vietnam, and eventually became a leader in the local Church.

Michael was thrilled when his oldest son wanted to enter seminary. But when his only other son died, the cultural expectation was that Michael's seminarian son would return home to serve his parents and carry on the family name. Persecution of Christians was ramping up, though. Michael, concerned that his son would be unable to practice the faith if he returned to Vietnam, insisted that his son stay at his seminary in Malaysia and be ordained when the time came.

Michael's generosity was motivated, at some level, by love of God and neighbor. But he was also driven by a fear that his sacramental absolution wasn't enough. Michael couldn't grasp the enormity of God's mercy that had truly made him a new man. "We have to do as many good deeds as possible to atone for our sins," he told a friend, not understanding that only the Blood of Christ can do that. And despite all his charitable work, Michael worried that only martyrdom could save him, saying, "I think even all the water on this earth could not wash away my sins. It is probable that only my own blood could cleanse myself."

This feeling that he needed to earn the forgiveness that God had already given him must have been exhausting. More so when he failed again. Michael was arrested on suspicion of being a Christian and broke under torture. Though he didn't deny his faith, he gave the names of priests and lay Christians, resulting in the arrest of twenty-nine people; eight apostatized while the rest were sent into exile.

Michael was devastated. For all his years of trying to be good enough, to do all the right things and earn God's love, he had failed. Perhaps it was this, though, that finally convinced him of the power of grace. Because even there, broken and bruised, a traitor condemned to death, God was still offering him mercy. A priest managed to visit Michael in prison to hear his confession. After all he'd done, after the damage his weakness had caused the Church, still this father was willing to risk his life to bring him the Father's mercy.

Michael no longer had a frantic spirit, a desperate need to earn forgiveness. Instead, he resigned himself to death and even rejoiced at being able to shed his blood for Jesus. After weeks of public torture, Michael was taken out to be beheaded. When he arrived at the place of his execution, he calmly washed his feet, smoked one last cigarette, arranged his hair and clothes, then knelt to pray. As he prayed, two priests hidden in the crowd absolved him one last time before the mercurial, fearful man died in confidence and peace, transformed by the power of grace.

Michael Hồ Đình Hy is a beautiful witness to those who have fallen, especially those who've betrayed their marriage vows. But his story is most powerful for the scrupulous, those who see their sin as too big for God's mercy, who worry they haven't repented well enough or done enough good deeds to atone for their sins. If you struggle with scrupulosity, you are not alone. The path to peace lies not through countless acts of charity or perfectly recited Rosaries, but through grace, through the certainty that you are loved by the Father. This is what Michael Hồ Đình Hy finally learned, and what he wants to show you. Through his intercession, may all who fear that they're unworthy of the love of God come to know that his love and mercy are given freely for the asking. St. Michael Hồ Đình Hy, pray for us!

67

ST. BRICE OF TOURS

A Bishop So Arrogant Only a Saint Could Put Up with Him

---≈---

(370–444) ✳ Country: France
Feast Day: November 13

Only a Saint could have loved St. Brice of Tours. Mercifully, that's just who the Lord sent him. Abandoned as a child, Brice was raised by St. Martin of Tours in the monastery of Marmoutier. From childhood, he was difficult but in rather ordinary ways. So when he sought ordination, the bishop who loved him like a father was happy to oblige.

Unfortunately, Brice was more than a little arrogant and had become quite enamored of the power and wealth he had some-how managed to accrue. As an eighteen-year-old deacon, he had slaves and stables and was much in need of fatherly advice. But when Martin attempted to remind him of the Gospel call to poverty and humility, Brice sneered at him. He ridiculed the good bishop as a barbarian, mocking him for being born in what is today Hungary and demanding to know how a man who had been raised in a military camp could possibly correct one raised in a monastery. He treated Martin with contempt, calling him "the old fool" to monk and stranger alike. His attitude was so vile that some even believed him to be possessed. They insisted that Martin expel him from the community and remove him from the clerical state, but Martin was patient. "If Jesus could come to terms with Judas," he said, "then I can certainly come to terms with Brice."

Somehow Martin loved him, and even shared with him a prophecy: the ambitious, unruly young priest would be made bishop after Martin's death, though his tenure would not be smooth. The clerics of Tours were irate at this. Surely Martin could do something to prevent such an arrogant, self-serving man from being named a bishop. Again, Martin reassured them. He had no illusions about Brice's worthiness, but he knew grace well and was sure that God would provide.

Brice was indeed elected bishop after Martin's death. At that point, mediocrity seemed the best anyone could hope for. For thirty years, his governance was unremarkable—Brice was rather lax, quite ambitious, and repeatedly investigated by the Church to determine if he had done anything that was worthy of censure.

Perhaps that's why people were so inclined to believe his accuser when she insisted that he was the father of her child. Brice maintained his innocence; legend has it that he demanded that the infant tell the assembled crowds whether Brice was his father and the month-old child spoke up in his defense. When this only convinced the assembled crowds that Brice was practicing sorcery, he carried burning coals in his cloak, proving his innocence when they didn't scorch his cloak. But the people of Tours were not disposed to believe anything good of him. Finally, their suspicions had been vindicated! Brice was just as wicked as they had always known, and if he wanted forgiveness, he would have to go to Rome and beg it of the pope.

They were ready to drive their bishop from the city, using physical force if necessary, but Brice was more than willing to go. This was the dreaded adversity Martin had warned him of, and he was all too glad to get past it at last.

But exile was good for Brice. The man who was unconverted by the love of St. Martin of Tours, by the grace of Holy Orders, or by decades as a bishop finally began to realize just what danger his immortal soul had been in all those years. The seed Martin had planted began to sprout, and then to bloom. After seven years of exile, Brice returned to his see a changed man, humbled by all the Lord had done through the animosity of his people. Word of his conversion preceded him, and the people (reluctantly) received him back as bishop.

Mercifully, the change was lasting. Brice had finally realized how despicable he had been in his youth and how very little he had done to make up for it. He lived his last seven years in such holiness and humility that upon his death he was immediately revered as a Saint, because only a Saint could have been so radically transformed by grace.

You may be a Brice of Tours. Or you may love a Brice of Tours. Or you may just be stuck putting up with a Brice of Tours. But whether you're asking his intercession for yourself or for a relationship with somebody else, his story offers great hope: a man detested even by Saints who went on to become a Saint himself. Through his intercession, may we who are proud be humbled and given loving, selfless hearts like his. St. Brice of Tours, pray for us!

68

SERVANT OF GOD
BARTOLOMÉ DE LAS CASAS

*A Slaveholding Priest Who Fought Prejudice in Himself
and Became a Champion of the Marginalized*

---～---

(1484–1566) ✳ Country: Spain, Dominican Republic

Servant of God Bartolomé de las Casas was a slaveholding priest who went on raids into Indigenous villages to capture and enslave people. And though he eventually revised his stance on the enslavement of Indigenous peoples, he continued to support Black slavery.

He's on the path to Sainthood.

How?

Because his racial violence and continued racism weren't the end of his story. Bartolomé de Las Casas was, above all, a man capable of confronting his own sinfulness and being converted. It happened gradually, it happened at great cost, but it happened. And someday soon he may be raised to the altar, not because he was always a good man but because he wasn't afraid of recognizing what was evil in him and doing the work (with God's grace) to root it out.

Born in Spain, Bartolomé de Las Casas sailed for Hispaniola when he was eighteen, where he became a slaveholder and participated in violent raids to kidnap and enslave Native people. In 1510, he became the first priest to be ordained in the New World. Still, he saw no problem in continuing to exploit enslaved peoples on his *encomienda* (a sort of feudal plantation).

But when Dominican friars arrived on the island, they denied absolution to all slaveholders. Fr. de Las Casas was enraged by what seemed an appalling overreach, but the Dominicans refused to bow to political pressure. On Christmas Eve, Fray Antonio de Montesinos preached passionately against slavery and racism, shouting, "You are in mortal sin, and live and die therein by reason of the cruelty and tyranny that you practice on these innocent people."[10]

Fr. de Las Casas fought back, appealing to the crown. The Dominicans were recalled from Hispaniola, and the colonizers, including Las Casas, continued to enslave Native people. Fr. de Las Casas managed to compartmentalize his life as a colonizer (including witnessing horrific violence in the conquest of Cuba) all while continuing to serve as a priest. Some years later, he wrote, "I saw here cruelty on a scale no living being has ever seen or expects to see."[11]

But the seed had been planted. By 1514, Fr. de Las Casas's conscience was speaking louder than his culture. While preparing for a Pentecost sermon, Fr. de Las Casas read Sirach 34:27: "To deny a laborer wages sheds blood." He became thoroughly convinced of the humanity of Native people, renounced his claim to the Indigenous serfs on his encomienda, and sailed for Spain to advocate against the enslavement of Indigenous people.

Fr. de Las Casas was named "Protector of the Indians" and sent back across the Atlantic to attempt reforms, but he was resisted by slaveholders and by clergy who thought him too idealistic. Hated by all, he sought refuge with the Dominican order, which he entered. As a Dominican friar, he continued to advocate for the rights of Indigenous people, particularly their right not to be forcibly converted to Christianity. He wrote extensive histories detailing the abuses wrought by Spaniards in the New World; one volume was so shocking that it convinced the king of Spain to enact the New Laws, which ended Indigenous slavery in the New World and limited the encomienda system to one generation.

Slave-owning Spaniards were enraged, but worse was still to come for them. When appointed bishop of Chiapas, Mexico, de Las Casas enacted a policy in his diocese that denied sacramental absolution to slave owners and encomenderos even on their deathbeds, unless they freed all their captives. When political pressure led to the repeal of the New Laws, colonists celebrated with riots, during which Bishop de Las Casas was shot at by his people. After eighteen months as bishop, he left Chiapas for Mexico City in early 1546. Within another year he abandoned all hope of returning to his see and made his way back to Spain.

But all this time, Bishop de Las Casas continued to support Black slavery and even owned four enslaved Africans himself; he was convinced that Africans were hardier than Indigenous people (when in fact they were just immune to the European diseases that devastated the Native Americans). He was also misinformed about the provenance of these enslaved people, having been told that they had been captured in just wars, not kidnapped and sold. More than anything, he wasn't yet convinced that slavery was a crime against humanity.

But Bishop de Las Casas had learned to listen to the cry of the oppressed, and after his return to Spain he finally realized the dignity of Black people as well. He wrote, "I soon repented and judged myself guilty of ignorance. I came to realize that Black slavery was as unjust as Indian slavery . . . and I was not sure that my ignorance and good faith would secure me in the eyes of God."[12]

Bishop de Las Casas spent the rest of his life in Europe, fighting against all racism and exploitation. He wrote scathing histories of the Spanish conquest and was repeatedly accused of exaggeration, treason, and even heresy. But he was so convinced of the injustice of the Spanish position that such opposition didn't silence him. He wrote a book describing the many atrocities committed by the Spaniards and left instructions for it to be published after his death, "so that, if God determines to destroy Spain, it may be seen that it is because of the destruction that we have wrought in the Indies and his just reason for it may be clearly evident."[13] He later chose to publish the work, deciding that the truth must be known, whatever the consequences might be.

Bishop de Las Casas argued not only against slavery but also against conquest, insisting that Indigenous Americans weren't the uncivilized savages they were made out to be. When others argued that Spanish rule was necessary to protect weaker communities from stronger ones, he asserted that it was better for the weaker Indigenous to suffer at the hands of the stronger, rather than all Indigenous people suffering at the hands of Spain. Though Bishop de Las Casas longed for the conversion of the Americas, he knew that it could only truly happen through genuine evangelization, not conquest and forced conversion.

These were dangerous ideas. Bishop de Las Casas was denounced to the Inquisition. His writings were occasionally burned. He was hated in life and maligned for centuries after his death, considered a traitor because he challenged the racism of his country.

Bishop de Las Casas is an incredible witness not because he was a savior to Black and Brown people but because he did the hard work of reflecting on his own prejudice and privilege and changing his behavior, even when it caused great shame, cost him dearly, or required a lifetime of work.

Bartolomé de Las Casas stands as a powerful intercessor for those who are actively racist, who enact or advocate for oppressive laws and systems. But he is also a convicting witness to those of us who would never utter a racial slur or refuse to hire a person of color but still might harbor prejudices or hesitate to stand on behalf of marginalized people. Through his intercession, may we engage in honest self-reflection, examining our prejudices and refusing to justify them. May we do the hard work of fighting for justice, even if it puts us at odds with those we love. Servant of God Bartolomé de Las Casas, pray for us!

BL. ANTHONY NEYROT

An Arrogant Priest Who Was Kidnapped, Sold into Slavery, and Committed Apostasy before Finally Becoming Holy

———— ≈ ————

(c. 1423–1460) ✳ Country: Italy, Tunisia
Feast Day: April 10

Everyone loves a good conversion story, a Saint who was a mass murderer or a Satanist before coming to Christ. But for those of us who are years past our own conversion and are still somehow plagued by habitual sin, the stories of the Saints can leave us feeling that we're neither holy enough nor wicked enough to become Saints. For us, there's something comforting about the life of a Saint who was converted but not fully, a mediocre monk or petulant daily communicant who somehow still found his way to sanctity.

Bl. Anthony Neyrot is a perfect example of an unconverted Christian, a man who checked all the right boxes without even trying to give the Lord his heart. Received into the Dominican order by St. Antoninus, he was obedient enough. He went through the motions (though he resented the long, slow years of study that he felt he had no need for) and was eventually ordained a priest.

But early success at preaching had given Fr. Anthony a big head. With no desire to be conformed to Christ, he allowed his arrogance to become his dominant feature, demanding the adulation of his parishioners and becoming irritable when he felt unappreciated. Inadequately flattered at his first assignment in Florence, the impatient and willful Fr. Anthony insisted on being moved. His mentor St. Antoninus warned him of grave dangers to his soul if he persisted in demanding this change, but to no avail. When Fr. Antoninus refused to send him to Sicily, the self-willed Fr. Anthony petitioned Rome and got his orders. Unsurprisingly, he was unhappy in Sicily as well—they weren't half clever enough, he thought, to see what a wonder he was. Again, he informed his superiors that he required a transfer and found himself on a ship to Naples.

If he had continued in this vein, Fr. Anthony might well have whined and demanded his way to damnation, but God loved him too much to leave him a selfish priest. In his mercy, he sent Moorish pirates to intercept the ship. It's an odd thing to imagine pirates as instruments of salvation, but in God's providence there's nothing that can't work for our good.

Unfortunately for Fr. Anthony, he didn't need a quick spiritual healing but a full-on resurrection, which meant he was going to have to hit rock bottom. Even being kidnapped and sold into slavery to Muslim captors wasn't enough to break him of his pride. Despite being well treated in the caliph's household and allowed to move about Tunis with few restrictions, Fr. Anthony's petulance and arrogance continued, and eventually his exasperated master locked him up, allowing him only bread and water.

In lockup he didn't succumb to torture, nor was he even threatened. He simply couldn't handle the discomfort of his cell. Rather than live for a few weeks on bread and water, he denied Christ, accepted Islam, and was immediately set free. Given what a prize an ex-priest was, the caliph showered Fr. Anthony with honors, adopting him as his son and marrying the Dominican friar to a Turkish noblewoman.

His worldly comfort secured, Fr. Anthony was unstinting in his apostasy. He gave up faith in Christ completely and even began translating the Qur'an (into either Latin or Italian) to spread Islam to the West. But much as Fr. Anthony studied the Qur'an, he struggled to see it as true. For four months he persisted, enjoying his status as the caliph's son, until word came of the death of his mentor, St. Antoninus. That night, the deceased bishop appeared to him in a dream and called him to conversion. He warned of the threat to Fr. Anthony's soul if he persisted in his apostasy.

Fr. Anthony was shocked to realize what he had become. Chastened, he sent his wife back to her family and began the life of a penitent. He spent his days praying the Rosary, humbly begging the Lord for the courage to do what he must. Fr. Anthony knew that a public apostate must be a public penitent, and in order to repair some of the damage he had done to the Body of Christ, he arranged to announce his reversion to the world. Having confessed his sins, he begged the forgiveness of the Christian community on Palm Sunday, and presented himself, dressed in his Dominican habit, to the caliph during a public procession the ruler was holding.

There on the steps of the palace, Fr. Anthony proclaimed his faith in Jesus Christ as Lord and lamented his previous weakness in denying him. Stunned, the caliph tried to persuade him to continue in his apostasy, since renouncing Islam was a capital crime. But Fr. Anthony only preached the name of Jesus more loudly. Before long, he was dragged off to prison and stoned to death four days later, on Holy Thursday.

The life of Anthony Neyrot is a perfect illustration of St. Paul's maxim: "Where sin increased, grace overflowed all the more" (Rom 5:20). When he was a "faithful" priest, he had a hardened heart. It took great suffering and ultimately great sin for him to see his need for God's mercy. Like many of us, Anthony had to hit rock bottom before he could allow God's grace to work in his life. He is a powerful witness to the fact that God is never finished, that he never gives up on even the most impossibly fallen of us. Through his intercession, may God pour the grace of conversion on those of us who live in the grace of Christ but not wholeheartedly. Bl. Anthony Neyrot, pray for us!

St. Jerome

*An Angry Man Who Became
a Saint through His Temper*

———≈———

(347–420) ✳ Country: Slovenia, Palestine
Feast Day: September 30

You probably know a few things about St. Jerome. He was a Church Father, the one who translated the Bible into Latin directly from the Hebrew texts of the Old Testament instead of relying on the Greek translation known as the Septuagint.

You also probably know about his temper.

Generally speaking, those are the things we mention when we talk about St. Jerome. We don't say he once had a temper and then he conquered it. No, we share scathing (but eloquent) insults from a man some have dubbed "the great name-caller," perhaps remarking that if Jerome won a halo, there's hope for us.

Indeed—Jerome is a marvelous witness of God's mercy poured out on the most persistent of sinners. But we don't canonize people simply for being recipients of mercy; we canonize them for being models of how that mercy can transform us, and that's exactly what Jerome is.

Though born to Christian parents, Jerome wasn't baptized until he was nearly twenty. Gradually he became more and more devoted to his faith, but while his academic work was theological, his free time was spent with great pagan literature. Until one night, when Jerome dreamed that he stood before the judgment seat of God. "Who are you?" the Lord asked. "I am a Christian," Jerome responded. "No, you are no Christian. You are a Ciceronian. For where your treasure is, there will your heart be also," came the reply. Convicted, Jerome stepped away from the worldly things that had consumed him and began in earnest the pursuit of holiness.

Jerome became a monk and a great ascetic. When tempted by sins of the flesh, he turned to the arduous study of Hebrew as a distraction. He was a spiritual director for many women, a few of whom themselves became Saints (including St. Fabiola[14]), and took great care to educate them in Greek, Hebrew, Latin, and theology. He wrote prolifically, his eyes fixed on the Word of God, always seeking to bring it to God's people.

Nor were his good works merely intellectual. Jerome moved to Bethlehem and opened both a school and a home for pilgrims so that "should Mary and Joseph visit Bethlehem again, they would have a place to stay."[15] When Rome was sacked, Jerome lamented the steady stream of refugees pouring into the Holy Land and stepped up to help. "I have put aside my commentary on Ezekiel and almost all study," he wrote. "For today we must translate the precepts of the Scriptures into deeds; instead of speaking saintly words, we must act them."[16]

But for all this, Jerome was an angry man. He wrote insult after insult about heretics and Saints alike. He loathed St. Ambrose and attacked St. Augustine, who, being more naturally charitable, said of Jerome, "What Jerome is ignorant of, no mortal has ever known."[17] He hated the heresies of Arius and Origen, and he hated anyone who seemed to embrace them.

More than anything, though, Jerome hated his anger. He was harder on his own faults than he was on anyone else's. In one letter attempting to reconcile with an estranged aunt, Jerome cried, "Woe to me, wretch that I am!"[18] He went to great lengths to defeat his temper, even carrying a stone around with him with which to beat himself when his anger threatened to overcome him. Pope Sixtus V, passing by a painting of St. Jerome holding this rock, is said to have commented, "You do well to carry that stone, for without it the Church would never have canonized you."[19]

More than just intellectual ability, Jerome offers us a witness of mundane penitence. He was just an ordinary man—an ordinary genius, rather—with a temper. All his life he prayed to be released from the vice of anger, which he called "the door by which all vices enter the soul,"[20] but to no avail.

Still, Jerome never gave up. Again and again he sought forgiveness. Again and again he tried to hold his tongue, to calm his nerves. Occasionally he triumphed over his anger and pride, as when he deferred to Pope Damasus I on the question of which books belong in the Bible. More often, he failed and repented again. By God's grace, Jerome continued to seek peace, patience, and humility, despite being singularly agitated, impatient, and proud.

This is what makes Jerome a great Saint—not his translations or commentaries, his letters or controversies, but the fact that he never stopped trying to be a Christian in deed and in name. When we become discouraged by our repeated failures, may we remember Jerome, his failures and his ultimate triumph. Through his intercession, may we all be granted the strength to persevere in our pursuit of holiness, regardless of our faults and failures. St. Jerome, pray for us!

St. Fabiola of Rome

A Divorcée Who Spent Decades without the Sacraments

———≈———

(d. 399) ✳ Country: Italy
Feast Day: December 27

St. Jerome[21] was not a man known for his effusive praise, much less lavished on a woman who had spent much of her life in open defiance of Church teaching. But St. Fabiola of Rome was no ordinary woman, and her conversion was so complete that it led the irascible Jerome to describe her as "the praise of the Christians, the marvel of the gentiles, the sorrow of the poor, and the consolation of the monks."[22]

Born to a storied Roman family, Fabiola was bound for an advantageous marriage. But while her first husband was rich, he was also vile and lecherous, treating Fabiola so poorly that Jerome later said of his faults that "not even a prostitute or a common slave could have put up with them."[23] Significantly, Jerome, not known for his progressive views on women's rights, praised her for leaving him. Indeed, he considered their divorce heroic, as Fabiola took on the shame of leaving her husband rather than making manifest his sins.

Up to this point, Fabiola had done nothing blameworthy. Then as now, there was no sin in leaving an unfaithful or abusive spouse (though the wagging tongues of the ill-informed might indicate otherwise).[24] But then she did what countless others have done: though still married in the eyes of the Church, she married another man. Even here, Jerome wrote with sympathy, acknowledging how difficult it can be to persist in the single state

Pray for Us

for decades. Fabiola, it seems, knew that celibacy was held in high esteem by the Church but didn't realize that a second marriage after a divorce was forbidden by the Church she loved. She soon came to realize that her civil marriage with a second man barred her from receiving Communion as long as her first husband was living, though. She was encouraged to leave her second husband, to do penance and be readmitted to Communion. But no matter how she may have hungered for the Eucharist, Fabiola chose her second husband instead.

We don't know her heart, whether she wrestled with her conscience or rolled her eyes at what seemed like the legalism of it all. But it appears that Fabiola's desire for the Eucharist grew over the years. After the death of her second husband, she presented herself before the pope (her bishop) and begged forgiveness. She dressed herself in sackcloth and approached the Basilica of St. John Lateran weeping, her face pale and her hair disheveled. So moving were her repentant tears that the assembled crowd began to weep as well. With unimaginable humility, Fabiola had laid her sins bare before the Church. She was made to do penance, as was the custom of the day.

But Fabiola became far more than a fallen woman grudgingly readmitted to Communion. She ran after holiness so fervently that even St. Jerome was nearly speechless with wonder at the good things God did in her soul. Worried that the company she had kept might become a near occasion of sin, Fabiola removed herself from their ranks, selling all she could of her estate so that she would be in no danger of attracting a man with her fortune. With this money she founded a hospital, likely the first in the Roman Empire, and served the poor with her own hands, nursing people with the most unpleasant of conditions. She traveled from island to island in the Mediterranean Sea seeking the lost and abandoned, offering comfort, healing, and financial support to all.

So complete was Fabiola's transformation that she decided to leave the secular world and enter a religious community in Bethlehem. There she spent time poring over the scriptures with Jerome, asking questions so astute that even that great biblical scholar couldn't answer. But for all her love of contemplation, Fabiola was still called to action. Eventually she left behind the silence of Bethlehem and returned to her work as nurse and philanthropist, building a pilgrim's hostel and providing housing for the homeless as well as medical care. When she died, she was mourned by all of Rome, not as a noblewoman or even as a penitent but as a Saint, a Christian of such generosity and selflessness that the world still remembers her name.

Fabiola of Rome is a case study in God's providence at work in and through the brokenness of our lives. Perhaps it was her years in exile from the sacraments that stirred up in her that longing for holiness. We can condemn the sins of her youth without discounting the good God brought out of them. Through her intercession, may God give us the grace to trust that he's working through our errors just as powerfully as he did through hers. St. Fabiola of Rome, pray for us!

Part 12

Saints Who Were Merciful

We who have been saved by mercy ought to be better practiced in extending mercy to others. Instead, many of us collect grievances to be used in future disputes. Or perhaps we simply enjoy remembering the faults of others. The frightening thing about forgiveness isn't just that it requires healing and generosity; it also requires us to recognize that we, too, are broken and sinful and in need of mercy.

The lives of the Saints are filled with stories of forgiveness, often baffling to those among us who are inclined to hold grudges. But when we truly understand what it means that we are made new by the Blood of Christ, we begin to realize that everyone deserves mercy just as much as we do—both not at all and entirely.

The stories below range from offering strangers God's mercy to forgiving a cruel and abusive spouse, from absolving prisoners to teaching a nation to forgive an atrocity. There's Elisabeth Leseur,[1] whose husband was wonderful in most ways, and Daphrose Rugamba,[2] whose husband was a scoundrel. And then there's an order of ex-con nuns, to remind us all of the transformative power of mercy. As you read these stories, ask yourself:

Where am I holding back? To whom is God asking me to offer mercy? And what's stopping me?

SERVANTS OF GOD
CYPRIEN AND
DAPHROSE RUGAMBA

A Broken Marriage Made Whole by Grace

(1935–1994) and (1944–1994) ✳ Country: Rwanda

Servant of God Cyprien Rugamba was a composer, a choreographer, a poet, and an author. He was a hero in Rwanda, a man who had devoted his life to promoting traditional Rwandan arts after colonialism had threatened to erase them.

He was also a cad, an adulterer whose treatment of his wife was inexcusable.

And he's on track—with his wife, Daphrose—to become Rwanda's first Saint.

Cyprien had once hoped to become a priest. He entered seminary as a young man but was scandalized by the bad theology that was taught and the bad example that was given. Disillusioned, Cyprien left seminary and began a career in the arts, both as an artist and as a civil servant working to promote traditional Rwandan culture. He fell in love with a young woman named Xaverina, and the two were soon engaged. But before they could marry, Xaverina was killed; her death destroyed what was left of Cyprien's faith.

Though heartbroken, Cyprien still felt that he needed to honor his commitment to Xaverina's family, so he married her cousin Daphrose. Daphrose was a faithful Catholic whose life was centered on prayer. Cyprien had become an avowed atheist, though he dabbled in traditional animist practices as well. It's no great surprise that their marriage was less than peaceful. Cyprien was more than just disdainful; he was cruel. The couple lost their first child to miscarriage. Their next baby was born healthy, but not long after his birth Cyprien's family convinced him that Daphrose was involved in the occult. He accused her of witchcraft and repudiated her, sending her to her family home and keeping the baby with him. After eight months, Cyprien realized the untruth of the rumors of black magic and brought his wife home. The two went on to have nine more children, but their marriage was plagued by Cyprien's repeated infidelities and the birth of his illegitimate child (whom Daphrose eventually welcomed into their home to raise as her own).

For nearly twenty years, Daphrose and the children prayed unceasingly for Cyprien's conversion. He hated the faith; even the sight of a crucifix could send him into a fit of rage. Once, in the hospital room where Daphrose had just given birth to a child, Cyprien grabbed a crucifix from the wall and broke it in two. But Daphrose knew the power of offering up her suffering, and all her pain became a sacrifice offered for the conversion of her husband.

Though his home life was miserable, Cyprien was doing remarkable work in his career. He was a nationally recognized poet, composer, and choreographer whose Rwandan ballet was widely respected. And he never stopped working for ethnic harmony in the deeply divided nation.

In 1982, Cyprien became sick and gradually lost his singing voice, his ability to dance, and even his hearing and sight. Daphrose remained by his side. Seeing this, Cyprien began to wonder at a God who could make a woman so loving to her husband despite all she had suffered at his hands. Then, while flying to Belgium to seek further treatment, he felt suddenly better. His voice, hearing, and sight all returned. Overcome with gratitude,

Pray for Us

Cyprien began composing a song and suddenly felt inspired, singing to the Lord for the first time in decades.

Though astonishing, Cyprien's healing seemed like nothing compared to the miracle of his conversion and the resurrection of his marriage. Truly, their marriage had been raised from the dead; pictures of the couple almost invariably show Daphrose gazing at her husband, clearly a woman in love. This might be the most incredible component of the Rugambas' story: not Cyprien's conversion but Daphrose's forgiveness. The mercy she offered her husband left no room for hidden resentment. He had been made new, and she loved him as though he hadn't hurt her for all those years. The couple became inseparable, their tenderness and intimacy visible to all who encountered them.

Cyprien and Daphrose founded a branch of the Emmanuel Community in Rwanda, reminding those who joined that they weren't Hutu, Tutsi, or Twa but brothers and sisters in Jesus. As the family struggled financially, Daphrose sold potatoes at a roadside stand, where she encountered street children in need of love and began to help them. Their son Olivier described his parents as "the champions of the marginalized." Cyprien fought to have ethnic designations removed from Rwandan identity cards. This, along with his open disdain for ethnic prejudices, proved his undoing.

On April 6, 1994, the Rwandan president was killed, and a genocide began. When they heard the news, Cyprien and Daphrose gathered the seven of their children who were at home to pray before the Blessed Sacrament in their family chapel. The next morning, armed men broke in. They shot the tabernacle first and then turned to Cyprien.

"Are you a Christian?" they asked.

"Yes, very Christian!" Cyprien replied, then quoted one of his songs. "And I will enter heaven dancing!"[3]

He did. Cyprien and Daphrose Rugamba were murdered that morning along with six of their children. In life they offered a witness of mercy to the Rwandan people, and after death they pray without ceasing for healing of a country torn apart by hatred. Through their intercession, may all who need mercy find it, and may all who have been wronged extend it. Servants of God Cyprien and Daphrose Rugamba, pray for us!

SERVANT OF GOD TAKASHI NAGAI

A Physician, Convert, Poet— and Victim of the Atom Bomb

(1908–1951) ✳ Country: Japan

A Japanese saying describes the difference between the two cities devastated by atomic bombs in 1945: "Hiroshima rages, Nagasaki prays." One reason for this dramatic difference between the two cities? A Catholic radiologist and poet who died of radiation poisoning.

Servant of God Takashi Nagai was raised in the Confucian and Shinto traditions of his ancestors. While adolescence found him doubting the existence of anything beyond what could be empirically observed, his mother's death left Takashi in no doubt as to the reality of the human soul and its existence even after death. Reading Blaise Pascal's *Pensées* convinced him that he ought to try prayer, simply as an experiment.

The young medical student decided to look for a Catholic family to board with while he continued his studies in Nagasaki, where he also played for his college basketball team. In the heart of Catholic Japan, where "Hidden Christians" had survived unnoticed for 250 years, Takashi found the Moriyamas, a family descended from generations of Japanese Christians. From the moment they met him, the couple and their daughter Midori began to pray for Takashi's conversion. After some time, they invited him to join them for midnight Mass. Surrounded by five thousand Japanese Christians singing joyfully and praying in absolute silence, Takashi was struck by a profound sense of divine presence. He later said of that evening, "There was a living Someone present in the Urakami Cathedral."[4]

But that flash of insight wasn't enough for the young scientist. He continued to search, even when sent to serve as an army medic in Manchuria. During that year, he read the little catechism Midori had sent him and then returned to Nagasaki to study scripture and liturgy, all the while contemplating the contrast between the misery he'd seen in the field and the joy and grace he saw in sweet Midori. But none of it convinced him fully until he returned to Pascal and read, "There is sufficient light for those who want to see, and sufficient darkness for those who don't."[5] This brought him enough clarity to accept the Gospel (and his own limitations). He was baptized and then married Midori two months later.

Despite the known risks of exposure to radiation, the young radiologist threw himself into his work. Both he and Midori saw his efforts as an act of charity, even of worship. Takashi understood that only God could truly heal his patients and that medicine was inseparable from prayer. "In the end," he said, "it is not the doctor who cures the patient, but God's good will. Once that is understood, medical diagnosis gives rise to prayer."[6] For Takashi, medicine was inseparable from prayer, even when his work was less diagnostic. Takashi was at the leading edge of radiology research, and he labored to give glory to God.

When the Nagais' oldest son was two and their daughter a newborn, Takashi was shipped out to serve as a doctor in the Sino-Japanese War. During his three-year absence, his father and daughter both died. After Takashi's return, the couple had two more daughters, but lost one shortly after birth. Takashi split his time between his young family and the hospital, though life was often interrupted by air raids during World War II, which began six months after his return. And then came Takashi's diagnosis: chronic leukemia, brought on by his work in radiology. He was given three years to live.

When Takashi told his wife of his illness, she took some time to weep before the crucifix in their home, then composed herself and said to her husband, "We said before we were married . . . that if our lives are spent for the glory of God, then life and death are beautiful."[7] Her peaceful resignation strengthened him to accept the death that awaited him with her by his side.

But there are no certainties in life, especially not during war. On August 9, 1945, the atomic bomb that was dropped on Nagasaki hit only a few hundred yards from the hospital where Takashi was working. Many of his students were killed, and all his research destroyed. Takashi rushed into the street, leading the effort to pull people from the rubble and nurse the wounded. When those helping him began succumbing to despair and to the lethargy brought on by their exposure to radiation, Takashi rallied them by making a Japanese flag using a bedsheet painted with his own blood.

It was two days before Takashi could go looking for his wife. When he arrived at their home, he found it destroyed. All that remained of the beautiful Midori were a few charred bones. But Takashi could tell that his wife had been holding the Rosary she had prayed so fervently for his conversion. He was grateful that she had died praying. Their two living children had, mercifully, been evacuated to the country and were unharmed, but Takashi's condition deteriorated rapidly. When his pastor urged him to take better care of his health, Takashi responded, "Thank you, Father, but if it's for the glory of God, living and dying are just the same."[8] He had learned this detachment from his beloved Midori. Still, he hoped to delay the day his children were orphaned. So when he found himself close to death a few months after the bombing, Takashi prayed to St. Maximilian Kolbe, whom he had known when Kolbe lived in Nagasaki, though he hadn't yet heard of Kolbe's heroic death. Soon, Takashi's cancer was in remission.

In the months after the bombing, Takashi spoke to a devastated nation about peace, about the need to forgive. He called upon Nagasaki's Christians in particular to offer their suffering to the Lord as sacrificial victims. When his illness made it impossible for him to leave his bed, he continued his research on radiation poisoning while spending as much time as possible with his children. He also began to write masterful works of poetry, essays, and novels that were devoured by the Japanese people. This man, who had found his wife's charred remains, spoke of mercy to a people devastated by war. Takashi's fame brought him visits from the emperor, a cardinal sent by the pope, and even Helen Keller, all of whom visited him in the tiny hermitage where he lived with his children, built on the wreckage of his bombed-out home.

Those who suffer will find in Takashi Nagai a witness to the power of suffering to sanctify. Those who struggle to forgive will similarly find an intercessor who taught his people to offer mercy in the face of an unspeakable horror. Through his intercession, may we suffer with such peace and forgive with such grace. Servant of God Takashi Nagai, pray for us!

74

BL. JEAN-JOSEPH LATASTE

A Dominican Who Founded an Order of Convict Nuns

———— ≋ ————

(1832–1869) ✳ Country: France
Feast Day: September 5

There's little that's more compelling as a witness of God's mercy than Christians who love those the world has deemed unlovable. Bl. Jean-Joseph Lataste had a ministry to women the world had written off. His work and witness continue to affect the life of the Church—and the lives of those far from the Church—to this day.

Born Alcide Lataste, he was raised by a Catholic mother and an atheist father in France. Alcide felt called to the priesthood from a young age, but he fell in with rather a frivolous set in high school and stopped praying or seeking God's will; for a time he wasn't even sure if he could remain a Christian. But ultimately he overcame his doubts, largely through the experience of serving the poor through the St. Vincent de Paul Society.

Still, priesthood seemed to be no longer an option, and the beautiful Cécile very much was. Lataste fell wildly in love and soon proposed, but his family blocked the marriage. Distraught, Lataste asked the Blessed Mother to make God's will clear to him. His answer came two years later—the sudden death of his beloved. Lataste mourned for two years and then entered the Dominican order, developing a strong devotion to St. Mary Magdalene and taking the name Jean-Joseph.

Soon after being ordained, Fr. Jean-Joseph was asked to preach a retreat at a women's prison. He went, but with strong reservations. After all, what hope could there be for these inveterate criminals? But the Holy Spirit was more powerful than his prejudice, and as he was preaching the retreat, he found himself struck by how similar the inmates were to his beloved Mary Magdalene. He spoke tenderly to these women, pointing out how dearly God must love them. After all, he could have left them in their sin, but instead he had them sent to prison that they might be saved.

Imagine seeing incarceration as a sign of God's merciful love! But Fr. Jean-Joseph did, and he convinced the women that God's love wasn't diminished by their sin. He told them that their lives had meaning, that even in prison they could serve the Lord. Just as nuns lock themselves up as a gift to the Lord, these prisoners could offer their monotonous lives to God, consecrating their very punishment. The eyes that had been glassy only an hour before were now filled with new hope!

As the retreat continued, Fr. Jean-Joseph began to worry. These women had been transformed by God's mercy, but what would become of them when they reentered a world that despised them? What, especially, could be done for any who felt that God was calling them now to religious life? No religious community would overlook the stigma of prison and accept a convict, yet to leave them to fend for themselves was unthinkable.

So Fr. Jean-Joseph began a new community that would welcome women with unsavory pasts—indeed, that existed for the sake of those women. He called them the Dominican Sisters of Bethany, "because the Gospel tells us that at Bethany lived Martha, of inviolable virtue, and Magdalene, the sinner. And Jesus loved to come and rest in their home."[**]

The Dominican Sisters of Bethany offered a home to modern Magdalenes, a contemplative house of prayer that sent sisters to

---

[**] There is significant disagreement as to whether Mary Magdalene and Mary of Bethany were two women or one; in the nineteenth century, most Catholics in the West believed them to be the same woman, and Fr. Jean-Joseph operated under that assumption.

women's prisons to console and encourage the inmates. Though Fr. Jean-Joseph lived only long enough to see the order established, his community has lasted one hundred and fifty years; today it has houses in France, Switzerland, Italy, Germany, Latvia, Belgium, and the Netherlands, and draws women of all backgrounds. In its choir stalls, class presidents stand beside prostitutes, girls-next-door beside murderers; what a perfect foreshadowing of heaven, where the greatest sinners may wear the most beautiful crowns while petty sinners rejoice to call them friends. Mercy, indeed. To both.

Jean-Joseph Lataste is a powerful witness of overcoming prejudices and seeing with eyes of mercy, reminding us that God's love isn't just for the immaculate but for all. Through his intercession, may we learn to look at each soul and see not what she's done or how she's fallen but who she can be in the love of Christ. Bl. Jean-Joseph Lataste, pray for us!

75

SERVANT OF GOD ELISABETH LESEUR

A Gentle Woman Whose Prayers for Her Atheist Husband Led to His Conversion— after Her Death

———— ≈ ————

(1866–1914) ✳ Country: France

Servant of God Elisabeth Leseur didn't plan on marrying an atheist. Raised in a loving Christian home in France, Elisabeth wanted the same for her future children. When she met Felix Leseur and fell in love, she assumed that their life among the intellectual elite of Paris would be a Christian life, that they'd have children and raise them Catholic. Elisabeth got the high society, the salons held in their elegant Paris home, the trips all over Europe and North Africa, but faith had no part in their life as a couple. Felix was an atheist, but he promised Elisabeth that he wouldn't try to prevent her from practicing her faith, and Elisabeth was certain that he would come around.

He didn't, and was quite open about his convictions: publishing anticlerical articles, criticizing the Church, and encouraging his friends to join him in mocking Elisabeth's faith. In all other ways he was an excellent husband; the two loved each other deeply, and Felix was generally kind and thoughtful. In this area, though, he was obdurate.

For a time, his constant picking at Elisabeth's faith worked. Overwhelmed, she fell away from the Church and abandoned her relationship with God. But when Felix pressed Elisabeth, an intelligent polyglot who devoured the classics, to read various atheistic works, she began to find holes in the arguments. This resulted in a profound conversion of heart when Elisabeth was thirty-two. Felix had unintentionally pushed her back toward the faith, and she would not be drawn away again.

A journaler from her youth, Elisabeth began recording her spiritual insights. She resolved to pray assiduously for Felix—indeed, to make prayer for his conversion the primary focus of her life. It was clear to her that argument would be of no avail. Felix wasn't the type to be convinced, not once his mind was made up. So Elisabeth wouldn't fight him. She would live for Jesus, as a sacrifice offered for Felix, and trust God to handle the rest.

Even Felix's attacks on her faith were ammunition in the long war Elisabeth was waging for his soul. When he laughed at her "superstitions" or rolled his eyes at Elisabeth's pious practices, she had one more thing to offer up for his salvation. It pained her to imagine heaven without him, this man whose antagonism toward her faith couldn't destroy the deep love she had for him. But she trusted that God would answer so sincere a prayer. She never lost hope, not through decades of infertility, chronic illness, spiritual loneliness in a marriage to a man she loved so much, or even her final battle with cancer. She had offered her life in sacrifice for Felix's soul, and she trusted that if God was taking her home to himself, Felix would be saved. At the time of her death, she had no fear—she believed with absolute certainty that Felix would become a Christian.

But Elisabeth's death only made Felix more hostile to the God who had stolen her from him. He was unmoved by the crowds that attended her funeral, people Elisabeth had loved and served when she had been relatively healthy and in the years she had been homebound. Even reading her diaries didn't immediately penetrate the hardness of his heart. Instead, Felix pored over her words of love for the Lord (and intercession for her husband) and determined to prove his late wife wrong once and for all. He would go to Lourdes, he decided, and expose it as a fraud.

Felix hadn't counted on grace. When he arrived in Lourdes, Elisabeth's diaries in tow, he found himself overwhelmed by a sense of God's presence and Elisabeth's too. Elisabeth's lifelong prayer had at last been answered. So converted was her husband that he decided to become a Dominican priest. Once ordained, he spent most of his priesthood working to spread the message of his wife's life: her heart poured out in merciful love for him, a hostile unbeliever.

It is essential that we preach the name of Jesus, that we invite people to know him not just by our lives but also by our words. For those closest to us, though, it's often the case that our words won't be effective. The ones we love can fight all day against our claims, standing on the far side of bridges we've burned by incessant arguments. But they can't argue with lives of Christlike love, and they can't fight the grace that pours out because of our intercession.

Elisabeth Leseur spoke the truth and then closed her mouth, loved hard, prayed harder, and trusted. Through her intercession, may we imitate her charity toward our loved ones who are hostile to the faith, offering them mercy, however hurtful they might be. Servant of God Elisabeth Leseur, pray for us!

Notes

Part 1: Saints Who Defied Expectations

1. Jean-Baptiste Serres, *La Catinon-Menette* (Clermont-Ferrand, France: Impr. de Mont-Louis, 1864), 21, my translation.

2. Serres, *La Catinon-Menette*, 65.

3. Serres, *La Catinon-Menette*, 38.

4. Serres, *La Catinon-Menette*, 47–48.

5. Michael Scott, "Nicolaus Steno (1638–1686)," *Earth Observatory*, July, 20, 2004, https://earthobservatory.nasa.gov/features/Steno.

6. Alan Cutler, *The Seashell on the Mountaintop: A Story of Science, Sainthood, and the Humble Genius Who Discovered a New History of the Earth* (London, England: Arrow, 2004), 27.

7. R. Shane Tubbs et al., *History of Anatomy: An International Perspective* (Hoboken, NJ: Wiley Blackwell, 2019), 154.

8. The Society of the Sisters of Social Service, "Beatification—Sára Salkaházi," accessed March 28, 2021, https://www.salkahazisara.com/en/beatification.

Part 2: Saints Who Never Gave Up

1. Luke O'Hara, "Samurai Martyrs: Father Peter Kibe," Kirishtan.com, September 17, 2013, https://kirishtan.com/samurai-martyrs-father-peter-kibe/, accessed March 30, 2021.

2. Mary Purcell, *Matt Talbot and His Times* (Chicago, IL: Franciscan Herald Press, 1977), 43.

3. Sue E. Houchins and Fra Baltasar Molinero, *Black Bride of Christ: Chicaba, an African Nun in Eighteenth-Century Spain* (Nashville, TN: Vanderbilt University Press, 2018), 145.

4. Lorenzo Fazzini, "Bearing Witness to Christ at the Peril of One's Life, Says Father Ragheed in Mosul," Fondazione PIME Onlus, September 12, 2004, http://www.asianews.it/news-en/Bearing-witness-to-Christ-at-the-peril-of-one's-life,-says-Father-Ragheed-in-Mosul-2084.html.

5. Sandro Magister, "The Last Mass of Father Ragheed, a Martyr of the Chaldean Church," Gruppo Editoriale L'Espresso Spa, June 5, 2007, http://chiesa.espresso.repubblica.it/articolo/145921%26eng%3Dy.html.

6. "Rome: In the Basilica of San Bartolomeo, the Delivery of the Stole of Ragheed Aziz Ganni, Chaldean Priest Killed in Mosul in Iraq," Comunità di Sant'Egidio, June 2, 2011, https://archive.santegidio.org/pageID/2346/langID/en/Rome-In-the-Basilica-of-San-Bartolomeo-the-delivery-of-the-stole-of-Ragheed-Aziz-Ganni-Chaldean-priest-killed-in-Mosul-in-Iraq.html.

7. Magister, "The Last Mass of Father Ragheed."

8. "Terrorism Seeks to Take Away Life, the Eucharist Gives It Back, Says Iraqi Priest," Fondazione PIME Onlus, May 30, 2005, http://www.asianews.it/news-en/Terrorism-seeks-to-take-away-life,-the-Eucharist-gives-it-back,-says-Iraqi-priest-3403.html.

9. J. F. Faupel, *African Holocaust: Story of the Ugandan Martyrs* (Nairobi, Kenya: St. Paul Publications, Africa, 1984), 133.

10. Diane Batts Morrow, *Persons of Color and Religious at the Same Time: The Oblate Sisters of Providence, 1828–1860* (Chapel Hill, NC: University of North Carolina Press, 2002), 27.

11. Francis Xavier Nguyễn Văn Thuận, "How Faith Survived in a Communist Prison" (Cardinal Francis Xavier Nguyễn Văn Thuận Foundation, May 2003), http://www.card-fxthuan.org/his-works/faith-survived-in-prison.php.

12. Benedict XVI, *Spes Salvi* (Vatican City: Vatican Press, 2008), sec. 32.

13. Francis Xavier Nguyễn Văn Thuận, "How Faith Survived."

14. Hubertus Blaumeiser, "Rev Hubertus Blaumeiser's Experience with Cardinal Thuan," Cardinal Francis Xavier Nguyễn Văn Thuận Foundation, accessed March 28, 2021, http://www.card-fxthuan.org/writings/blaumeiser.php.

Part 3: Saints Who Had Great Adventures

1. John Paul II, "Apostolic Journey to the Czech Republic: Homily at Mass for the Youth," vatican.va, April 26, 1997, http://www.vatican.va/content/john-paul-ii/en/homilies/1997/documents/hf_jp-ii_hom_19970426.html.

2. Pascual Chavez, "Venerable Maria Troncatti," *Salesian Bulletin*, 2011.

3. Francis Van Ortroy, "St. John Francis Regis," *The Catholic Encyclopedia*, vol. 8 (New York, NY: Encyclopedia Press, 1913).

4. See page 179.

5. M. J. Maher, "St. John Francis Regis," *St. John Francis Regis* (Melbourne, Australia: Australian Catholic Truth Society, 1950).

6. Ann Ball, "Bishop Luigi Versiglia and Father Callisto Caravario," in *Modern Saints: Their Lives and Faces*, book 1 (Rockford, IL: TAN Books and Publishers, 1991), ebook.

7. Ball, "Bishop Luigi Versiglia."

8. Ball, "Bishop Luigi Versiglia."

Part 4: Saints Who Lived Ordinary Lives

1. Dom Antoine Marie, "Blessed Luigi and Maria Beltrame Quattrocchi," Saint Joseph de Clairval Abbey, April 8, 2008, https://www.clairval.com/index.php/en/letter/?id=2090408.

2. Claire Schaeffer-Duffy, "Models of Holiness and Married Life," *National Catholic Reporter*, December 28, 2001, http://natcath.org/NCR_Online/archives2/2001d/122801/122801a.htm.

3. Marie, "Blessed Luigi and Maria."

4. Marie, "Blessed Luigi and Maria."

5. Beckett Ghioto, tran., *Lamp and Lily: The Letters and Writings of Venerable Antonietta Meo* (Steubenville, OH: Becket, 2018), letter 1.

6. Ghioto, *Lamp and Lily*, letter 35.

7. Ghioto, *Lamp and Lily*, letter 70.

8. Stefania Falasca, "Le Lettere Di 'Nennolina,'" 30Giorni, 2010, accessed March 29, 2021, http://www.30giorni.it/articoli_id_22547_l1.htm, my translation.

9. Ghioto, *Lamp and Lily*, letter 9.

10. Falasca, "Le Lettere."

11. See page 68.

12. See page 245.

13. "Bl. Lucien Botovasoa," April 14, 2015, https://saintscatholic.blogspot.com/2018/08/blessed-lucien-botovasoa.html.

14. "Bl. Lucien Botovasoa."

15. Fra Gabriel M. Mesina, "Mary Was Her Life: Venerable Teresita Quevedo," *Missio Immaculatae Magazine*, January 20, 2017, https://missiomagazine.com/mary-was-her-life-ven-teresita.

16. Mesina, "Mary Was Her Life."

17. Ann Ball, "Venerable María Teresa of Jesus Quevedo," in *Modern Saints: Their Lives and Faces*, book 1 (Rockford, IL: TAN Books and Publishers, 1991), ebook.

18. Mesina, "Mary Was Her Life."

19. Mesina, "Mary Was Her Life."

20. Mesina, "Mary Was Her Life."

21. Blake Britton, "Antonio Cuipa and Companions," Word on Fire, May 14, 2019, https://www.wordonfire.org/resources/blog/antonio-cuipa-and-companions/24149.

22. Peggy Dekeyser, "Cause Opens for Florida Martyrs," *St. Augustine Catholic*, 2015.

23. A Poor Clare Colettine Nun, "Take the High Road: The Life of Sister Mary Francis of the Five Wounds," *Boston Catholic Journal*, accessed March 30, 2021, http://www.boston-catholic-journal.com/take-the-high-road-the-life-of-sister-mary-francis-of-the-five-wounds-margaret-sinclair.htm.

24. A Poor Clare, "Take the High Road."

25. Josemaría Escrivá, *The Way: The Essential Classic of Opus Dei's Founder* (New York: Image/Doubleday, 2006), paragraph 817.

26. *United States Catholic Catechism for Adults* (Washington, DC: United States Conference of Catholic Bishops, 2019), 214.

27. "Biographies of Blesseds—1997," EWTN Global Catholic Television Network, accessed March 30, 2021, https://www.ewtn.com/catholicism/library/biographies-of-blesseds--1997-5265.

28. Ary Waldir Ramos Diaz, "The Mother of Venerable Carlo Acutis Says He Was Her Little Savior," Aleteia, May 12, 2019, https://aleteia.org/2019/05/12/the-mother-of-venerable-carlo-acutis-says-he-was-her-little-savior.

29. "Sayings," Blessed Carlo Acutis, February 19, 2021, https://blessedcarloacutis.com/sayings.

30. Ramos Diaz, "The Mother of Venerable Carlo Acutis."

31. "Sayings."

32. Carole Breslin, "Catholic Heroes . . . Venerable Carlo Acutis," The Wanderer Newspaper, March 5, 2020, https://thewandererpress.com/saints/catholic-heroes-venerable-carlo-acutis/, accessed March 30, 2021.

33. Breslin, "Catholic Heroes."

34. Carlo Acutis, "Scopri Quanti Amici Ho in Cielo," accessed March 30, 2021, http://www.carloacutis.net/pages/amis.html, my translation.

Part 5: Saints with Difficult Families

1. See page 99.

2. Patrick Allitt, "Rose Hawthorne Lathrop," in *Women in World History: A Biographical Encyclopedia* (Waterford, CT: Yorkin Publications, 1999).

3. "Rose Hawthorne Brief Biography," Dominican Sisters of Hawthorne, https://hawthorne-dominicans.org/biography.html, accessed March 29, 2021.

4. Ann Ball, "Rose Hawthorne Lathrop," in *Modern Saints: Their Lives and Faces*, book 1 (Rockford, IL: TAN Books and Publishers, 1991), ebook.

5. "Rose Hawthorne Brief Biography."

6. Dom Antoine Marie, "St. Marguerite D'Youville," Saint Joseph de Clairval Abbey, September 30, 2001, https://www.clairval.com/index.php/en/letter/?id=2031001, accessed March 29, 2021.

7. Paul Camboué, "Madagascar," *The Catholic Encyclopedia*, vol. 9 (New York: Robert Appleton Company, 1910).

8. Dom Antoine Marie, "Blessed Victoire Rasoamanarivo," Saint Joseph de Clairval Abbey, June 8, 2014, https://www.clairval.com/index.php/pt/carta-2/?id=2060814.

Pray for Us

Part 6: Saints Who Found Holiness through Suffering

1. Dom Antoine Marie, "Blessed Benedetta Bianchi Porro," Saint Joseph de Clairval Abbey, January 21, 2011, https://www.clairval.com/index.php/en/letter/?id=2190111, accessed March 29, 2021.

2. Marie, "Blessed Benedetta."

3. "Blessed Benedetta Bianchi Porro," CatholicSaints.info, September 29, 2020, https://catholicsaints.info/blessed-benedetta-bianchi-porro.

4. "Blessed Benedetta Bianchi Porro," Catholicsaints.info.

5. Marie, "Blessed Benedetta."

6. Ruth Tucker, *Parade of Faith: A Biographical History of the Christian Church* (Grand Rapids, MI: Zondervan, 2011), 474.

7. Alex Jensen, "Korea's Martyred Mothers," Knights of Columbus, June 1, 2017, http://www.kofc.org/en/columbia/detail/korea-martyred-mothers.html.

8. Member of the Society of the Holy Child of Jesus, *The Life of Cornelia Connelly, 1809–1879, Foundress of the Society of the Holy Child Jesus* (New York: Longmans, Green, and Company, 1924), 24.

9. Francis P. Le Buffe, "Review: The Life of Cornelia Connelly," *America: A Catholic Review of the Week*, October 14, 1922.

10. Ann Ball, "Cornelia Connelly," in *Modern Saints: Their Lives and Faces*, book 1 (Rockford, IL: TAN Books and Publishers, 1991), ebook.

11. Member of the Society, *The Life of Cornelia Connelly*, 232.

12. Dom Antoine Marie, "Zdenka Schelingová," Saint Joseph de Clairval Abbey, July 16, 2006, https://www.clairval.com/index.php/en/letter/?id=2190706.

13. "Zdenka Cecilia Schelingová," Vatican.va, accessed March 29, 2021, https://www.vatican.va/news_services/liturgy/saints/ns_lit_doc_20030914_schelingova_en.html.

14. Marie, "Zdenka Schelingová."

15. Mary Frances McCarthy, "Local Relative of Slovakian Martyr Attends Beatification," *Arlington Catholic Herald*, September 19, 2016, https://www.catholicherald.com/news/b_local_relative_of_slovakian_martyr_attends_beatification_-b.

16. "Agnes Kim Hyo-Ju," Catholic Bishops' Conference of Korea, accessed March 29, 2021, https://cbck.or.kr/en/CatholicChurchInKorea/103-Korean-Martyr-Saints/30?page=3.

17. "Darwin Ramos' Biography," February 8, 2021, https://darwin-ramos.org/darwin-ramos-biography.

18. "La Mission De Darwin Ramos: 'Plus Fort Que Les Ténèbres,'" ZENIT, March 20, 2015, https://fr.zenit.org/2015/03/20/la-mission-de-darwin-ramos-plus-fort-que-les-tenebres, my translation.

19. "Darwin Ramos' Biography."

20. Nikolaj Velimirović, "The Holy Martyrs Timothy and Maura," *The Prologue from Ohrid: Lives of the Saints and Homilies for Every Day in the Year* (Birmingham, AL: Lazarica Press, 1985).

21. Alphonsus Liguori, *Victories of the Martyrs* (London, England: Benziger Brothers, 1888), 264.

Part 7: Saints Whose Ruined Plans Opened the Way to More Beautiful Things

1. "Beatificação Da Serva De Deus Lindalva Justo De Oliveira," Vatican.va, accessed March 29, 2021, https://www.vatican.va/roman_curia/congregations/csaints/documents/rc_con_csaints_doc_20071202_beatif-lindalva_po.html, my translation.

2. "Bl. Lindalva Justo De Oliveira (1953–1993): Biography," Vatican.va, accessed March 30, 2021, https://www.vatican.va/news_services/liturgy/saints/ns_lit_doc_20071202_suor-lindalva_en.html.

3. Albert H. Dolan, *God Made the Violet Too: Life of Leonie, Sister of St. Therese* (Chicago, IL: Carmelite Press, 1948), 26.

4. Dolan, *God Made the Violet Too*, 30.

5. Juan Marrero, tran., "A Life of Léonie Written by Her Visitation Sisters, 1941," *Léonie Martin, Disciple and Sister of St. Thérèse of Lisieux*, accessed March 29, 2021, http://leoniemartin.org/life-of-leonie-from-the-visita.

6. Marrero, "A Life of Léonie."

7. Maureen O'Riordan, "Léonie Martin, Disciple and Sister of St. Thérèse of Lisieux," *Léonie Martin, Disciple and Sister of St. Thérèse of Lisieux*, accessed March 30, 2021, http://leoniemartin.org.

8. Thérèse Martin, *The Story of a Soul: The Autobiography of Saint Thérèse of Lisieux* (Rockford, IL: Tan Books, 1997), 213.

9. Marie Baudouin-Croix, *Léonie Martin: A Difficult Life* (San Francisco, CA: Ignatius Press, 2017), 75.

10. Dolan, *God Made the Violet Too*, 94.

11. Dolan, *God Made the Violet Too*, 68.

12. "Primera Carmelita Guió En Su Vocación En 'Chiquitunga,'" *La Nacion De Paraguay*, September 5, 2017, 8.097 edition, p. 37.

13. Emilia Flocchini, "Beata María Felicia Di Gesù Sacramentato," Santiebeati.it, June 25, 2018, http://www.santiebeati.it/dettaglio/95831, my translation.

14. Julio Felix del Barco, "El Apostolado . . . ésa Es Mi Vocación," *La Obra Maxima*, May 2010, p. 17, my translation.

15. Alban Butler, "March 9: St. Frances, Widow," *Butler's Lives of the Saints* (London, England: John Murphy, 1815).

16. "St. Frances of Rome—Saints and Angels," *Catholic Online*, accessed March 30, 2021, https://www.catholic.org/saints/saint.php?saint_id=49.

17. Anne Tschanz, "Ven. María Luisa Josefa of the Most Blessed Sacrament," Carmelite Sisters of the Most Sacred Heart of Los Angeles, accessed March 30, 2021, https://carmelitesistersocd.com/2016/religious-life-article.

Part 8: Saints Who Were Failures

1. Emilia Flocchini, "San Marco Ji Tianxiang," Santiebeati.it, November 17, 2014, http://www.santiebeati.it/dettaglio/61110, my translation.

2. "庚子年幽燕殉道诸圣," 幽燕西亞, September 13, 2017, automatic translation, https://yuyencia.org/2017/09/13/%E5%BA%9A%E5%AD%90%E5%B9%B4%E5%B9%BD%E7%87%95%E6%AE%89%E9%81%93%E8%AF%B8%E5%9C%A3.

3. Michael H. Crosby, "Leopold Mandić: Jubilee Year Saint of Mercy and Reconciliation, Personal and Ecclesiastical," accessed March 30, 2021, http://www.sjpcommunications.org/images/uploads/documents/LEOPOL-3.pdf.

4. Crosby, "Leopold Mandić."

5. Crosby, "Leopold Mandić."

6. Crosby, "Leopold Mandić."

7. Dom Antoine Marie, "St. Léopold Mandic," Saint Joseph de Clairval Abbey, July 1, 1998, https://www.clairval.com/index.php/en/letter/?id=57, accessed March 29, 2021.

8. Roland Jacques, "The First Witnesses of the Church in Laos: The Missionary Oblates of Mary Immaculate and their Laotian Companions," http://archive.omiworld.org/upload/biblioteca/martyrs-of-laos.pdf, accessed January 2021.

9. Bazin René, *Charles De Foucauld, Hermit and Explorer* (New York: Benziger Brothers, 1923), https://archive.org/stream/charlesdefoucaul00bazi/charlesdefoucaul00bazi_djvu.txt.

10. Woodeene Koenig-Bricker, *Praying with the Saints: Making Their Prayers Your Own* (Chicago, IL: Loyola Press, 2001), 52.

11. Ann Ball, "Ven. Charles de Foucauld," in *Modern Saints: Their Lives and Faces*, book 1 (Rockford, IL: TAN Books and Publishers, 1991), ebook.

12. "Charles De Foucauld, a Witness to Jesus and His Gospel," Jesus Caritas, accessed March 30, 2021, http://www.jesuscaritas.info/jcd/fr/4753/news-general-chapter-little-sisters-jesus.

13. Six Jean-François François, *Itinéraire Spirituel De Charles De Foucauld* (Paris, France: Editions du Seuil, 1958), 352, my translation.

Part 9: Saints Who Lived with Great Humility

1. Antonio Sicari, "St. Maria Bertilla Boscardin," Vita dei Santi, accessed March 30, 2021, http://users.libero.it/luigi.scrosoppi/santi/bertillaing.htm.

2. Sicari, "St. Maria Bertilla Boscardin."

3. Sicari, "St. Maria Bertilla Boscardin."

4. Katherine I. Rabenstein, "Saints of the Day—Hugh of Grenoble," CatholicSaints.info, May 28, 2020, https://catholicsaints.info/saints-of-the-day-hugh-of-grenoble.

Part 10: Saints Whose Generosity Changed the World

1. Hannah F. Lee, *Memoir of Pierre Toussaint, Born a Slave in St. Domingo* (Boston, MA: Crosby, Nichols, and Company, 1854), 52.

2. See page 42.

3. Lee, *Memoir of Pierre Toussaint*, 70.

4. Lee, *Memoir of Pierre Toussaint*, 87.

5. Lee, *Memoir of Pierre Toussaint*, 114.

6. Lee, *Memoir of Pierre Toussaint*, 120.

7. "Blessed Kunjachan," accessed March 29, 2021, http://blessedkunjachan.com/lifehistory.php?id=Death.

8. Vidal Morales y Morales, *Nociones De Historia De Cuba* (Havana, Cuba: La Moderna Poesía, 1906), 180, my translation.

9. Sherry A. Weddell, *Saints Who Transformed Their World* (Frederick, MD: The Word Among Us Press, 2019), 33.

Part 11: Saints with Sinful Pasts

1. "A Former Satanist Priest Who Became a Saint," Dominican Friars Foundation, November 26, 2014, https://dominicanfriars.org/former-satanist-priest-became-saint.

2. Ann Ball, "Blessed Bartolo Longo," in *Modern Saints: Their Lives and Faces*, book 2 (Rockford, IL: TAN Books and Publishers, 1991), ebook.

3. "A Former Satanist Priest."

4. John Paul II, "Beatificazione Di 3 Servi Di Dio: Omelia Di Giovanni Paolo II," vatican.va, October 26, 1980, http://www.vatican.va/content/john-paul-ii/it/homilies/1980/documents/hf_jp-ii_hom_19801026_beatificazioni.html.

5. Sophronius of Jerusalem, "The Life of Our Venerable Mother Mary of Egypt," accessed March 30, 2021, https://stmaryofegypt.org/files/library/life.htm.

6. Sophronius, "The Life of Our Venerable Mother."

7. Sophronius, "The Life of Our Venerable Mother."

8. Ephraem the Archdeacon, "The Life of St. Mary the Harlot, the Niece of Abraham the Hermit," vitae-patrum.org.uk, accessed March 30, 2021, http://www.vitae-patrum.org.uk/page44.html.

9. Ephraem the Archdeacon, "The Life of St. Mary the Harlot, the Niece of Abraham the Hermit."

10. Richard H. Powers, *Readings in European Civilization since 1500* (Boston, MA: Houghton Mifflin, 1961), 98.

11. Ruth Tucker, *Parade of Faith: A Biographical History of the Christian Church* (Grand Rapids, MI: Zondervan, 2011), 285.

12. Brian Pierce, "Bartolomé De Las Casas and Truth: Toward a Spirituality of Solidarity," *Spirituality Today*, 1992.

13. Enrique Dussel, "Bartolomé de Las Casas," *Encyclopedia Britannica*, January 4, 2021, https://www.britannica.com/biography/Bartolome-de-Las-Casas.

14. See page 240.

15. Joseph Vann, *Lives of Saints: With Excerpts from Their Writings* (New York: John J. Crawley, 1954), 86.

16. Vann, *Lives of Saints*, 90.

17. Leonard Foley, *Saint of the Day: Lives and Lessons for Saints and Feasts of the New Missal* (Cincinnati, OH: St. Anthony Messenger Press, 1990), 254.

18. Jerome, "Letter 13," NewAdvent.org, accessed March 30, 2021, https://www.newadvent.org/fathers/3001013.htm.

19. Alban Butler, "September 30: St. Jerome, Priest," *Butler's Lives of the Saints* (London, England: John Murphy, 1956).

20. Alphonsus Liguori, *Sermoni Compendiati. Sermons for All the Sundays of the Year*, 5th ed. (Dublin, Ireland: James Duffy, 1860), 254.

21. See page 237.

22. Jerome, "Letter 77," NewAdvent.org, accessed March 30, 2021, https://www.newadvent.org/fathers/3001077.htm.

23. Jerome, "Letter 77."

24. *Code of Canon Law* 1152.

Part 12: Saints Who Were Merciful

1. See page 255.

2. See page 245.

3. "Rwanda: The Christian Couple, among the First Victims of the Genocide in 1994," ACN International, May 6, 2019, https://acninternational.org/rwanda-the-christian-couple-among-the-first-victims-of-the-genocide-in-1994.

4. Paul Glynn, *A Song for Nagasaki: The Story of Takashi Nagai. Scientist, Convert and Survivor of the Atomic Bomb* (San Francisco, CA: Ignatius Press, 2009), ebook.

5. Frank Weathers, "The Conversion of Takashi Nagai, and His Vocation of Love," *Why I Am Catholic*, June 8, 2015, https://www.patheos.com/blogs/yimcatholic/2013/04/the-conversion-of-takashi-nagai-and-his-vocation-of-love.html.

6. Weathers, "The Conversion of Takashi Nagai."

7. Glynn, *A Song for Nagasaki*, 148.

8. Takahashi Shinji, "Listening to the Wishes of the Dead: In the Case of Dr. Nagai Takashi," accessed March 30, 2021, http://www.uwosh.edu/faculty_staff/earns/takahash.html.

9. Ann Ball, "Father John Joseph Lataste," in *Modern Saints: Their Lives and Faces*, book 2 (Rockford, IL: TAN Books and Publishers, 1991), ebook.

Alphabetical Index of Saints

Chronological Index

Feast Day Index

Geographical Index

Topical Index

Meg Hunter-Kilmer is a Catholic speaker, author, retreat leader, and itinerant missionary whose work appears regularly on *Aleteia* and on her blog, *Held by His Pierced Hands*.

Hunter-Kilmer is the author of *Saints Around the World*. She has written for *Magnificat*, *Our Sunday Visitor*, *The Catechetical Review*, and *Take Up and Read*. She has appeared on a variety of Catholic media, including CatholicTV, SiriusXM's *The Catholic Channel*, Relevant Radio, and Ave Maria Radio.

Hunter-Kilmer earned bachelor's and master's degrees at the University of Notre Dame. She previously served as a teacher, youth minister, and campus minister.

www.piercedhands.com
Facebook: mhunterkilmer
Twitter: @meghunterkilmer
Instagram: @mhunterkilmer
Pinterest: ndmeg
YouTube: https://www.youtube.com/user/ndmeg

AVE

AVE MARIA PRESS

Founded in 1865, Ave Maria Press,
a ministry of the Congregation of
Holy Cross, is a Catholic publishing
company that serves the spiritual and
formative needs of the Church and its
schools, institutions, and ministers;
Christian individuals and families; and
others seeking spiritual nourishment.

For a complete listing of titles from

Ave Maria Press

Sorin Books

Forest of Peace

Christian Classics

visit www.avemariapress.com

AVE MARIA PRESS
Notre Dame, IN
A Ministry of the United States Province of Holy Cross